T0041635

Upside-Down Zen

Upside-Down Zen

Finding the Marvelous in the Ordinary

Susan Murphy

Foreword by
John Tarrant

 WISDOM PUBLICATIONS • BOSTON

Wisdom Publications, Inc.
199 Elm Street
Somerville, MA 02144 USA
www.wisdompubs.org

© Susan Murphy 2006
All rights reserved.

No part of this book may be reproduced in any form or by any means, electronic or mechanical, including photography, recording, or by any information storage and retrieval system or technologies now known or later developed, without permission in writing from the publisher.

Library of Congress Cataloging-in-Publication Data
Murphy, Susan, 1950–
  Upside-down Zen : finding the marvelous in the ordinary / Susan Murphy ; foreword by John Tarrant.
      p. cm.
  Includes bibliographical references and index.
  ISBN 0-86171-279-X (pbk. : alk. paper)
  1. Zen Buddhism—Doctrines. 2. Religious life—Zen Buddhism. I. Tarrant, John, 1949–
II. Title.
  BQ9268.3.M874 2007
  294.3'927—dc22
                                    2006031688

First Wisdom Edition
First Printing
10 09 08 07 06
5 4 3 2 1

Cover design by Rick Snizik. Interior by DCDesign. Set in Electra LH 11/16 pt.
Cover photo, "Reflections of Fall," (c) 2006 Joel D. Lusk; flickr.com/photos/casaverdesol/
    Courtesy of the photographer.

Wisdom Publications' books are printed on acid-free paper and meet the guidelines for permanence and durability of the Production Guidelines for Book Longevity set by the Council on Library Resources.

Printed in the United States of America.

♻ This book was produced with environmental mindfulness. We have elected to print this title on 50% PCW recycled paper. As a result, we have saved the following resources: 32 trees, 22 million BTUs of energy, 2,770 lbs. of greenhouse gases, 11,498 gallons of water, and 1,476 lbs. of solid waste. For more information, please visit our web site, www.wisdompubs.org

For John Tarrant and Ross Bolleter

Contents

Foreword

SUSAN MURPHY IS A GIFTED LEADER in the new generation of Zen masters. The task she has taken on is to open the ancient, beautiful tradition of koan Zen so that it is useful to people in the twenty-first century. This is not such an easy labor; first she had to learn the version that was designed for East Asian culture, and then reimagine the profound discoveries of that tradition in an entirely new context. It is the interchange between these great tasks that makes this book so enticing.

One of the most satisfying things about Zen is that it is based on discovery rather than belief. There is nothing you need to believe before you embark. For this reason, you set off in all sincerity and yet do not quite know how it will turn out. Indeed, where most people seek certainty and confirmation of the world they already know, in Zen you depend on uncertainty, on going beyond what you have learned and are sure of (which is the part that isn't really interesting) and into what you have not previously imagined. Strangely enough, this reliance on uncertainty is the source of freedom and happiness.

At the same time, if you go on the inner journey there are recognizable way stations where you will spend a night or a year, and certain angels and demons from your own mind who will arise. In this, the spiritual journey is similar to the creative journey. You do not know the next line of the poem, or the next moment of your life, yet it will come and cannot be forced. Although this path is open and free there are also useful methods: this is where a guide comes in handy.

Connecting with a guide is itself a lucky, uncertain thing. Many guides of course are useful just for the stage where you set off. They may not be sensitive to the direction you need to take, or not have gone very far themselves. Also, credentials might be nice in a guide, yet they aren't really the thing either since, by definition, on any journey worth taking you will be in new territory a lot of the time. And so being knowledgeable about old territory isn't enough either. Yet there are good guides.

With a good guide, it's not about the guide. The question in Zen is not how to be someone different but how to be more richly and entirely who you already are. So it comes down to you. You have to look inside and ask yourself if, when you are with a certain guide, you are more enlightened, or kinder, or more generous, or can face your fears; whether life is more beautiful and forgiving. If a guide has that sort of effect on you, then she's a good guide. That's what a guide is for.

And in those terms, Susan and her book are terrific guides for the real work of transformation. Susan is anchored in the old Asian tradition but she is also helpful if you have the courage to want more than that—a spirituality that is a creative force and useful each moment of your life. She brings her knowledge of myths and cultures to bear. She shows how Zen and the Western, along with the older, native traditions, illuminate each other.

This book locates spiritual work where it has always really belonged— bang in the middle of whatever is happening. As well as being an excellent writer, Susan is a filmmaker by trade and here she shows a feeling for the value of the moment and the way a moment opens beyond itself into whatever is most loved in life. She is a poet as well as a storyteller, offering compelling images and subtle shifts of language.

Zen ought to be an inclusive path. It's not about being right or perfect or unattached. It is about allowing the whole of your life into the spiritual practice. The very thing you might have thought was unacceptable might be the thing that offers the most possibilities for transformation. The areas with no-trespassing signs might be where you want to go. Susan has a good feel for the dark gifts of difficult and hidden things.

In the end, Zen is only true if it is has a good heart. This book shows how empathy and intimacy with life and with nature are at the bottom of things, not just an add-on. Empathy is the mark of enlightenment, I think—the criterion by which we know that we are seeing clearly and not caught in small motives. This book enlarges the reader's sense of fellow-feeling, with people and animals and with trees and rivers and with all the transitory textures that dream life up out of nothing. It increases my sense of gratitude for life, which is a gift worth having.

JOHN TARRANT
Late winter 2004
Santa Rosa, California

Preface

ZEN IS A DIRECT PATH INTO REALITY, a direct path into the hard and exhilarating questions of being alive. The path of Zen is a mountain path. Walking it is like choosing to walk deeper, ever deeper into mountains. When you climb a mountain it has the curious effect of disappearing under you and closing around you. It no longer stands, a discernible shape against the sky. There is just the next rise of rocks and trees. It can be hard to judge where the summit has gone. Yet gradually you feel the mountain in every fiber of your being, aching muscles, pounding heart, amazed eyes. There can be sudden vistas and the summit itself is worth every step of a hard journey, but when you stand there at last with the wind cooling your hot blood and every muscle singing its song, the quietest joy is not that you have climbed so far but that you have begun to *become* mountain. You haven't conquered the mountain. Indeed, in some cultures it is thought disrespectful even to point at mountains; mountains so clearly point to your self-nature, which is felt to be enough. Rather, you and the mountain have exchanged selves in some measure and you begin to know yourself more as mountains know you. Gradually you might become more and more like this.

The chapters in Part One, "The Path of Zen," offer a walk into the foothills. They explore the fundamentals of meditation and breath-awareness; examine mindfulness; see what it is to have a "practice"; look at the kind of commitment that underpins such a practice; engage with the serious playfulness of the Zen Way; meet the unique koan dimension of Zen; and see a little way into the nature of the face-to-face teaching and teacher-student relationship that is particular to Zen.

Zen is also characterized as a path of crooked wisdom. You already possess the jewel of your own self-nature even though you live for much of the time somewhat remote from such awareness. You cannot be given what you already have and you cannot be taught what is earlier than knowing: the "crookedness" of the Way, its resort to energetic and sometimes surprising means to awaken realization that there is nowhere to go even while it is hard to truly arrive where you already are, stems from this strange fact. A monk once said to the tenth-century Zen master Yunmen, "This is not the function of mind. This is not the matter before me. What is it?" Yunmen immediately cried, "One teaching upside-down!" The monk, whether he knew it or not, was plainly demonstrating in his very question the invariable nature of what is. Yunmen struck like lightning to meet him in this place before knowing could presume to have a foothold. "Exactly so!" he says. Your very question can only be the one teaching. Upside-down, exactly right way up.

The chapters in Part Two, "One Teaching Upside-Down," consider some of the up-ending and mixing-up of a formerly Asian Zen as it takes root and grows more native to the West: environmental awareness and the path of "minding the universe"; the fertile grounds for reconciliation and reciprocity between Zen and the forty-thousand-year-old traditions of Aboriginal earth-based spirituality indigenous to Australia where I make my home; the marvelous that is revealed with steady attention inside the ordinary urban world; the lively presence of the feminine in Western Zen and the challenges of maintaining a lay practice that can include relationships and the parenting of children; and how the tradition opens toward dream and the creative imagination.

From the peak of the mountain, the view opens onto range upon range of jumbled peaks and valleys. Ordinary life is the great challenge posed to any spiritual practice, which can truly open only in our actions in the blaze of things just as they are — in all the troubles and heat of life.

The final chapters in Part Three, "Lotus in the Fire," explore how we season in the Way by entering the intense fires of life; how character and karma form each other in the task of not turning away from difficulty; the intimate relationship of "mistake" and grace; and the spirit of "accepting all offers," tested and enlarged in pain, sickness, and death. The great life is not a mysterious state of mind or an ecstasy belonging to saints, but just the simple, skillful act of returning to what you really are and agreeing with that, of taking your heart's bearings from the very middle of the middle of each moment, open to all the offers of your lucky, lucky life. And when the straw sandals wear out, you just walk on.

I am grateful to my teachers, John Tarrant and Ross Bolleter, for showing how to walk the Way with rigor and generous heart and laughter and all of life included. In John Tarrant's company I fell in love with that great-hearted, inclusive Way and was initiated into the mysteries of the long koan path. I walked on through the brilliant dark of that country in Ross Bolleter's company, passing under the scrutiny of his fierce eye and loving attention to detail. With nothing left over, or as little as possible, I walk on as a teacher.

None of the play and learning that happens in teaching would be possible without good students. Many chapters had a first incarnation in talks I gave in retreats between 1997 and 2003. I am grateful to my spirited students in Sydney, Melbourne, and the United States for how much their own fierce curiosity, tenacity and love of the Way enriches me continuously. Ross Bolleter closely read an early draft of this book, which greatly benefitted the book. I am, of course, responsible for its remaining shortcomings.

A tradition is a history that makes demands on the living. My old teacher, Robert Aitken, pioneered the Zen path in the West for much of his long life, and worked with his teacher, Koun Yamada, to bring the authority of a mighty koan tradition through into the English language and ordinary Western life. For his life work, and for his many efforts to bring me into line, I offer my respect and gratitude.

With its many forks and confluences it is only one source, one long, braided river that flows from my teachers and theirs through me to my students and to teachers still to come. No one knows the outcome of this. The ocean has nothing at all to say about it.

Finally, I thank my family and friends for all that comes through mortal connectedness—love, challenge, enjoyment, and a great deal of laughter. Above all, for that great benefaction for which no explanation is possible, I thank my two children, Jack and Maeve—just for being exactly who they are. Just for being.

PART ONE

The Path
of Zen

CHAPTER 1

Breath, like mind, like water

WE LIVE BY THE SHEER GENEROSITY of a moment-by-moment miracle, and it is called the breath. Actually, we could say we live and die by this miracle. Every breath out is a practice of yielding the self to the universe; every breath in is a reincarnation event, the self reborn, fresh. Zen is the practice of agreeing to live with a mind and self as alive and fluid as breathing itself: accepting the offer of each moment, yielding to the passing of each moment.

A time comes when it is just no longer convincing to continue to live as if we had an eternity of time ahead of us. Sometimes the shift comes in the form of the right kind of trouble, which churns a restless wake of searching behind it. Sometimes it is a medical diagnosis or a relationship catastrophe that seems to present the turning moment we can't ignore, to save our life. Other times it is a more subtle and gradual but unmistakable realization that we are moving into a phase of life that recognizes and even welcomes (oh so cautiously!) our own mortality. It may be retirement, or turning forty, or beginning to hear the bones creak on the stairs. And sometimes it just ripples through us as early as our teens and early twenties, a strong call from somewhere unknown, saying, come home.

The universe breathing

And then we look for a path into the place where the water is clear and inexhaustible—yes, there are still untouched and wild places in this world, as close as your own breathing. Focus for a moment on your breath and see what I mean.

First, sitting upright but relaxed in the neck and shoulders, turn your attention to the in-breath. When you breathe in, be aware of breathing in. This is already a step outside the human habit of distractability, eating breakfast while scanning the cereal box, and mentally noting to pick up the dry-cleaning on the way home. Instead of breathing on automatic pilot, notice the quality, sensation, and sheer pleasure of air streaming in. Feel the entire pathway of breath energy into the depths of your body, like sparks in darkness. Enjoy the fullness of being that builds with the creative action of the in-breath. Receive the aware breathing-in of the universe. Consider the first breath you ever drew; with that first breath, you came forth from nowhere into this, the first spark of you. As you do with every in-breath.

Now focus on the out-breath. When you are breathing out, be aware of breathing out. Feel the yielding of your muscles and body tension as you allow the out-breath to empty out, to give, give way, release. Be aware of yielding yourself back into the vast pool of all beings, all breaths. Consider that one day, the final breath of your life will expire and take you with it back into pure unknowing, relinquishing the self forever. As you do, in a way, with every out-breath.

And now, draw your attention to the place between the in-breath and the out-breath. Extend that threshold place as long as it is comfortable, then slightly beyond that point. What does it feel like, holding the lungs and diaphragm at maximum distension and in a kind of forced but interesting stasis? What is the state of your mind and the condition of your body as the pressure builds to let go? How does it feel at that very moment when you cease to struggle and resist and just begin to let the held breath go?

And finally, focus on the place between the out-breath and the in-breath, and once more extend that to the limit of what is comfortable, and just beyond. What is the energy, tone, life of your body when you let the breath go and stay with that going, that emptying out and dwindling of the self toward nothing? And when you yield and let the tide turn once more toward drawing breath again, toward life, what is that like?

Between life and death

There are telling sensations and intuitions lying in these pauses between life and death, death and life, when we extend and inhabit them more fully. The body is usually far wiser and further along in its knowing than our conscious mind is prepared to admit and include. Meditation, an utterly embodied practice, is often an education in finally catching up and becoming consonant with your wise, wild, animal body, with its sharp keenness for life rooted in an old knowing that it dies.

Death is moment by moment. The moment before is actually dark behind us—the very dark we came from. No breath-moment can be recovered or entered ever again. Life, too, blooms moment by moment from that. To live more closely attentive to the keenness of the one moment is to find it has no limits.

Becoming the breath

In meditation we become the breath, not simply to regain the fragrance of really being alive, but to let the boundaries between "me" and "my breath" break down and fall away. When we become the breath we are not entering a trance, but the quality of our awareness shifts. It gradually includes, with the pure awareness of breath, the beating of the heart, the air on our face, the distant barking of a dog or passing of a car, the breeze stirring the leaves, and the coming and going of feelings and thoughts, but with a slow, wide sense of space around each thought. Thoughts come and go but the mind does not fasten on to them. With the subtle skill of staying afloat in water, we make the infinite tiny adjustments that are just before thought, that will allow us to rest in the condition of being, the condition of true, without forming or reaching after thoughts about it. Body and mind begin to loosen and fall away, and we grow wider and more free, wanting less, wanting nothing. The most ordinary and subtle happiness arises in this wanting nothing. We dwell for a time open to all of the offers of life, without moving toward or moving away from a single thing.

And so we begin to be more deeply at home in the universe. We fit here, exactly. To become breathing is to become more boundless, seamless, and indivisible; for breathing belongs fully to the universe and has no mind of separation at all.

A fasting of the mind

Curiously, the world leaps back alive when the mind fasts, just as the taste of water is beyond compare when we are truly thirsty. A fasting of the mind is not a matter of "not thinking." There is no such thing! Try it and you will discover it is impossible. To try to use the mind to cut off the activity of the mind is like trying to wash water away with water. What mind-fasting opens up is the possibility of knowing the mind at rest, and simplifying to meet it more fully.

Fasting the mind in meditation is not denying the mind but growing more subtle and sensitive within the natural activity of the mind, and approaching the point of choosing complete, intentional rest. The natural activity of the mind is to surge toward thought and bring things to the peculiar light of human consciousness. The mind that fasts in meditation is the mind of "me" and "mine," the mind of endless self-concern and self-defense, of have and have not, right and wrong, included and excluded. When self-concern is quiet, heaven and earth lie open in complete generosity. That is the mind of abundance, the mind of flowing. When self-concern is noisy, the world is narrow and risky, and resources for the anxious self appear perennially scarce. The Indian poet Rabindranath Tagore spoke of this when he said, "The one whom I enclose with my name is weeping in that dungeon."

Who is the one you enclose with your name? To find out, stay with your breath in seated and walking meditation. (Please see Appendix One for detailed instructions on hot to begin seated Zen meditation. When your attending to the breath of this moment grows more practiced, with the simple dedicated repetition of practice, you will find yourself beginning to grow naturally more attentive and present to the matter of this moment in everyday circumstances: driving in thick traffic, waiting in a line, picking up your child from school, bandaging a wound, noticing the pain on someone's face, hearing the quality of a pause on the telephone. Just to sit like a buddha is already to reopen the Way directly to the deep original contentment of your true nature, sometimes called buddha nature. It has never gone away. But it can be shut away from awareness for a lifetime.

An accomplice to all your wishes

Following your breath is not effortful. When you find yourself making an effort, you are adding to something that is already complete. Try giving your focused, alert awareness 50 percent less effort. The effort is brought simply to the intention and action of becoming still, so that the silt may begin naturally to settle in the stillness of the mind, like water becoming clear. Coming home is letting go, allowing resistance to drop away as it softens in the mind of breathing. Is it effortful to let go? Letting go is already dropping effort.

Jacques Lusseyrans, who became blind at the age of seven but found all of his senses, even vision, opening in an extraordinary way instead of closing down, said, "Being blind I thought I should have to go out to meet things, but I found that they came to meet me instead. I have never had to go more than halfway, and the universe became accomplice of all my wishes." He spoke of how the blind receive the exquisite return gesture of the universe in its many forms.

Whenever his fingers explored the roundness and weight of an apple, for instance, he found that soon he couldn't tell whether it was the apple or his fingers that were heavy. He didn't even know whether he was touching it or it was touching him. He adds, "As a child I spent hours leaning against objects and letting them lean against me. Any blind person can tell you that this gesture, this exchange, gives a satisfaction too deep for words."

In meditation we half-veil the eyes and let a kind of blindness open all our senses in a less knowing way. Even if you have never practiced meditation you can freely enter the experience Lusseyrans points to. Just lean over and gently press your hand to the floor. Close your eyes, if necessary, and just explore what happens. Feel the exact and absolutely reliable return of pressure from the floor to your hand. Do you feel your hand become floor and floor become your hand, in a most exquisite meeting and exchange of confidences?

Just sitting is already an experience of this kind of subtle beauty at every point where you meet the universe: the air on your face; the moisture of your eyes; the taste of your own mouth; the pressure of your buttocks and knees being returned by the floor, as you go never more than halfway, never more than 50 percent, but just allow the universe to become your most intimate accomplice.

Bathe in silence

All meditation is a bathing in silence, which was said by the fourteenth-century Christian mystic Meister Eckhart to be as much like God as anything in this world. That silence of course is full of the cries of the world—a distant plane, hammer, mutter of speech, chainsaw, or siren; the crickets in the grass; an echoing bark of a dog; a sharp exclamation, sneeze, or nose-blow; the grace of birdsong; the infinitely subtle and musical speech of the wind and the leaves—and all of them call you back to the source, long for you to hear the unpronounceable name that they sing.

To really bathe in silence, the body is still (or, in walking meditation, attuned to stillness); speech is silent and the mind is at rest or approaching rest. As the chatter of self-regard and fear dies away, the natural ground of the mind emerges as you. And so you just bathe in the presence of what is, letting yourself grow completely "wet through" with it, with no thoughts, conditions, clingings, or preferences being held onto or affirmed or pushed away. Even if you are working with pain in sitting, every breath is the possibility of entering the deep ease of offering no resistance, alight with a vivid energy of enquiry that is a willingness to accept all offers, and the subtle joy of feeling yourself becoming accomplice to the universe.

Letting be

The term *human being* suggests our true calling in this life. But it seems we have to practice with challenging and subtle adjustments of our habits of mind to become a human being instead of one addicted to human doing. Just being is *letting be*, allowing what is our condition and our circumstance to be without bothering it. A wise old Zen teacher was once asked by her student why on earth she had set up a space of meditation for people so close to a busy road. All day and night, cars and trucks whizzed by, creating a racket that never permitted quietness to settle in the room.

The student was frustrated and angry with what is, just as it was presenting itself so freely. "Oh," said the teacher. "Why don't you try not bothering the traffic so much?"

When we find out who we wall in and drown out with the drama of the self, we also find out about the nature of that endless, querulous drama that blocks so much of the light of life. Sometimes it is good to make a simple reality check about the latest edition of "The Drama" (playing on an inner screen near you). Ask yourself, "What is this, in the light of my own death? What will it be a hundred years from now?" It is extraordinary how little will truly pass through that filter, and how freeing it is to see that it is so. Let it go, let it go. You will never die of letting it go. You well may die of holding on to it like grim death.

Becoming willingness

Although sudden contact skin to skin with the boundlessness can break through from nowhere, as an act of grace, I do not pretend that it is an easy matter making ourselves more available for that lucky accident. The practice of meditation is called "practice" because you have to give yourself to it almost blindly, and put up with its difficulty, in order to grow truly accident-prone, truly skillful in the art of holding yourself open. It's called practice because you are training and habituating the mind to a radically different set of responses than it has been settled in from childhood. But it is a practice of bringing your entire intentional and focused will to bear on the infinitely delicate task of opening, becoming willing.

Childbirth is the nearest thing to this in my own experience (and not coincidentally—for what are you doing but giving birth to your true self?). To give birth, you must endure the painful softening up process, attending to it, agreeing to it, giving yourself to it almost blindly. And all kinds of new depths of will are called upon to do this, though you can't know and need not know where they come from (you reach and they are there; your sheer need provides). Once childbirth is really underway, you don't have too much energy to spare for concepts about it. Bothering traffic is dangerous enough—try bothering the process of labor!

And then, when all things have grown soft enough at last to open and let the universe come through the universe, you must get out of the way completely and become sheer willingness. The bearing down stage of labor has almost no conscious thought in it at all. Neither does the miracle of staying open and not bothering what is—in the deep forms of meditative awareness, seated or walking or lying down.

Not knowing

The miracle is not to walk on water but to walk on the *earth*—actually present to this moment that will not return.

To walk on the earth and to know it, to breathe in and breathe out and to know it, intimately, and from there to open and flow like water, without resistance—that is the real miracle of mindfulness. So meditation on the breath is offering oneself to the silence, the mind of unknowing that the breath bears us into. Unknowing is not the blankness of not having a clue, nor is it the delusion of cradling a concept as if it were direct experience. Unknowing is another word for profound willingness; it has infinite depths to show you, and there is always more to un-know.

Zen teachers are famous for saying, "If it's not tied down, I'll take it away from you!" That is a kind of odd promise they make to their students. You can struggle to keep hold of your delusions and attachments and favorite stories, but the moment your grip loosens the teacher will snatch you free of it, with a comment or a move or a laugh, or by no movement whatsoever.

Alive with death

The more you can yield toward unknowing, which is actually a state of alert openness, the more you enter what is happening at this very moment, where your life is being lived as intensely as a house on fire. When you practice this way, even your involuntary thoughts are no different from the sound of rain, or sudden birdsong cutting through. You don't try to stop them, and they can no longer stop you.

Why a house on fire? Because the present moment is the only time there is, and to be one with that is to live fiercely, accepting all offers, and leaving no trace. It's like watching a diver descend through air: the time before the diver hits the water is too short for thought. That water is rushing to meet us too.

The present moment is utterly alive to the passing away of things; you could say it is utterly alive with death, with the fact that we are here only for this moment. It is life that at last includes and can stretch to embrace even the fact of death as the most startling and mysterious fact of life. Shunryu Suzuki compared meditation to the state of nearing death—a mental state of intense yet relaxed enquiry and attention. And when are we not nearing death? This most intense enquiry opens as this mind of unknowing, that is consonant with and near to the unknown place from which we appeared and to which we return, leaving no gap at all in the universe.

The bare fact

So breath awareness is living close to the bare fact of our lives, including our limitedness. Limitedness is the gate to the most boundless and free condition; but you must go through it, you cannot go around it. To walk on the green earth in the present moment is to practice living as close to the bone of now as you dare, and now is the bone of life in accord with death, of death in accord with life, an immense and general amnesty which can only be experienced by you in your present set of bones, and nowhere else. For when we are here just as we are, making no bones about it, then there is no time at all. A brief wildflower opens eternity; a grain of sand holds the infinity of the universe.

Life and death are not two. Not one, and not two. Can you begin to see where the ground of seeing lies? The real terror is not in death, which is utterly ordinary, but in the dualism of life lived opposed to death. Life opposed to death is the grim exercise that encloses the true self, weeping, in a dungeon named after yourself. It is a life full of strain to keep the self separate from everything else that would overwhelm it—the infinite variety of the other that we effortlessly create with our thoughts and fears. In its most intimate guise, the other sometimes seems to be death, because to admit the other fully is to lose the self. And what deprives us of that more profoundly than death?

The camellia—
it dropped into the dark
of the old well.

Camellias are so heavy with their own brilliance and perfection that the stem cannot hold them long. They seem designed to fall too soon. But although all life, even the lives of the ones we love most passionately in the world, even our own life, falls in time, almost always too soon, like a perfect camellia, yet the old well is not something other than us. All life comes out of that well, and all life returns to it, just like the great well from which we draw each breath, and give it back again.

A mind like fire, a mind like water

So meditation is yielding the self until you become no different from the old well itself, and it is resting in knowing that you have never been other than this, and it is perfectly all right. All things are well and all manner of things shall be well. Only a mind like fire can catch the fire that runs through all things. Only a mind like water can rest completely in the source itself.

When you regain the marrow-bone awareness that you are that, how can you possibly be afraid of it? A very wise and unpredictable teacher, old Master Wumen, said:

> *Better than knowing the body*
> *is knowing the mind in peace;*
>
> *when the mind is realized,*
> *the body is no longer anxious.*
>
> *When body and mind are fully realized,*
> *the saintly hermit declines to become a noble.*

Better than knowing the body is becoming it so thoroughly that there is no knowing left, and this condition of deep meditative awareness is indeed "knowing the mind in peace." When the mind is realized, there is no knowing at all, just the vast waters of unknowing that moisten all of life whether we realize it or not. (Realization is just that: coming into fully aware accord with what is always present, always manifesting every thing and each action and beat of consciousness.) The body is indeed no longer anxious: it sings the song of the universe.

So why does the person of fully realized body and mind "decline to become a noble"? Well, Zen speaks with the deepest admiration of "the true person of no rank." The one we finally come to meet as us has no name, no rank, no identifying marks at all. It is not elevated or holy, but deeply at home in the nobility that is naturally ours from the beginning. Our name then is wet grass! cloud breath! dead chestnut tree! red dog running! Dandelion—that's my name!

Even in rain
the dandelions turn midday
to gold.

CHAPTER 2

One world
at a time

THIS WORD "PRACTICE" IS A STRANGE one. What does it make you think of? Music practice, perhaps? There is no other way to get to play Bach! Making perfect? Fortunately, that's impossible in this world. In fact, practice may be simply something that takes us up, something that gets our strong attention, something to test ourselves against and know ourselves by. A practice is a persistent interest in doing something difficult and strange that brings life back alive; it tends to take us up when we sense something that seems missing, mysterious, not yet in our reach. Sometimes it is brought to us by a glimpse around the corner into death. So it comes with the first sign, maybe as the first sign, of a dawning maturity.

Flowers must have bees, the ocean must have rafts of seaweed, deep space must have constellations, old trees must have mossy knotholes, and humans must have obsessions. An obsession to practice is really a form of pitting the self against its finest opponent, the self; it is a way to take a sounding and know the measure of the self. Practice is an honorable obsession, the natural outcome of the kind of consciousness that has us. Its abiding question is, Who am I *really?*

An honorable obsession

While we don't inflict our obsession on others if we can avoid it, it is perfectly fine for others to catch a glimpse of it. Even if they are too young or distracted to see very far into what we are doing (or even more interestingly, what it is that we are not doing), still they may sense a kind of fire in it, and feel themselves somehow invited further into life.

A practice is an undertaking with the self: I vow to sit once a day and do nothing, just sit and let things be completely. When we have a practice, we show up faithfully and do sincerely whatever we can to get ourselves out of the way. Hard as it often is at first, we just keep giving way to simply seeing and being what we are.

The routine of a practice is a habit with the power to break all habit. Just the act of doing something no matter what enlarges the soul. Sometimes you will long to sit; other times you won't feel in the mood. Because it is a practice, you undertake to push through mood or resistance of any other kind and just do it anyway. What happens just past the strongest point of resistance is always the interesting thing, but you cannot find this out without seriously wrestling with your resistance. And even if you have a meditation that resistance quickly dubs "bad," you just stay unmoved and grow that into humor, tolerance, curiosity—muscle for the Way. Samuel Beckett's potent advice to someone who asked how to become a more accomplished writer was stark: "Try again. Fail better." We grow by being defeated decisively by ever-greater opponents. Resistance announces, "Here I am, your greatest opponent, always on duty: yourself!"

Behind a practice consistently met grows a widening wake of satisfaction—and most satisfying of all, it gradually has less and less trace in it of you. The emphasis is on attending to your life, not on attaining

something. You have already succeeded marvelously once you have settled at the appointed time in your dedicated place and begun to simply
sit and breathe and completely be without a purpose, supposing nothing
at all. When there is no agenda of accomplishment in your way, you are
free to give yourself away with each breath, free to meet whatever appears
in that open state.

Alone and deeply comfortable

Meditation is lonely as any practice is lonely—no one can make it easier for you, no one can do it for you, and you alone can find the enduring quality within it. But that loneliness gradually reveals a subtle and
lovely flavor found nowhere else, and is oddly familiar and comfortable;
it turns out to be an enthralling solitude that teems with life, a nothing-
in-particular from which everything emerges fresh. And in solitude you
come to know more closely your own strength of unbending intent,
which also serves you well in this life. To endure without fuss is an act
of mindfulness, which is also a silent gift to others. You can give it away
with impunity and never run out.

What we repeatedly do becomes what we are. The practice of sitting
and breathing to still the mind is the practice of being just what you
are—it is enlightened being. Yet it can be hard at times to bend the will
to keep the appointment with practice. We humans seem to fear what
seems hard and we long for comfort, even though we keep discovering
that the greatest treasure is what we find in ourselves at the far end of any
really challenging process. But the difficult path is always the path of
genuine life: difficulty makes the Way genuine. Meeting with fear of difficulty is an act that sparks with creative energy. Avoiding it is finally the
more demanding and costly battle. Practice is a commitment to cease
choosing avoidance, to refuse to walk through your life as a ghost.

Until we take up a practice we are in some measure agreeing to live
in fear of the full capacity of our own heart, shrinking from the reach of

this unrepeatable life. When you find it has taken you up, a practice becomes as natural as breathing: you find yourself more inclined toward facing your fear and intercepting the reflex of avoidance, seating yourself at the middle of the middle, and letting yourself burn up more and more completely in the act.

The tiger of mindfulness

The forms of practice are not the means of obtaining the right state of mind. Just to take the posture of zazen, or seated meditation, is already to have the right state of mind. Besides, as the Heart Sutra so clearly tells us, there is nothing to attain. The forms of practice are the practice of enlightenment, are the gradual taking of the form of enlightenment. As I've said: we are, indeed, what we repeatedly do.

And we are *how* we do it—this is the practice of mindfulness. A most simple definition of mindful behavior is paying attention. This gives beauty to all things; they feel attended to. Mindfulness practice is that one-pointed attention, the mind of being right here now, that is learned and refined on the meditation cushions and gradually extended into all of the activity of your life—sleeping, waking, working, playing, eating, drinking, cleaning, tending children, making love, giving birth, enduring illness, even dying. It is not endlessly effortful. Mindfulness actually has a contained energy that is like a lazy tiger lolling on a branch, missing nothing and deeply relaxed at once.

How do you become a tiger of mindfulness? By giving all of your attention to the thing that is before you, to whatever you are doing at the time. After an old Hasidic master died, his followers sat around, talking about his life. One person wondered aloud, "What was the most important thing in the world for the master?" They all thought about it. Another responded, after a time, "Whatever he happened to be doing at the time."

With mindfulness, we see nothing can happen twice. How would that be possible, when each moment is unrepeatable? This is the secret of doing something as if your hair were on fire, of burning yourself up so completely in a task or action that you leave no trace behind. All of your being comes to meet every part of the task. If you do not reach this state of such keen aliveness, a trace of yourself is left in what you do.

A strange happiness

Is this is a stressful proposition, to burn yourself completely? No. Stress comes with resistance, with the "no" lurking in whatever we do. The effort to let go, to loosen the grip of thought and habit upon our just being, is the work of softening boundaries and keeping nothing about our life at a distance. The "no" of resistance acts like a barrier, keeping part of ourselves at bay. There is a much more taxing effort (more costly to well-being than any effort to be here more fully) hidden inside the secret contract we have with ourselves to stay aloof from our lives.

The effort of mindfulness is to become whole-hearted. When you are whole-hearted, any action is absorbing and essentially effortless, because no one is in the way, "knowing" something about what they are doing. How strange that mindfulness is a practice of knowing less and absorbing more, of always approaching that energizing and vastly interesting place of not knowing.

Not knowing is the way of mindfulness. It is very respectful. Not knowing assumes that the object of your curiosity is always new and worthy of your entire attention. The most important thing in the world is whatever you happen to be doing at the time. In this way, mindfulness constantly teaches mindfulness, just as zazen teaches zazen. Any true path is made by walking, and your path has never been seen quite like this on the earth before. Our best moments occur when we are completely extended in a voluntary effort to accomplish something difficult and worthwhile. Satisfaction, therefore, is very close and simple: the strange happiness of completely joining with whatever we are doing in this moment.

This challenging simplicity requires limiting your activity to exactly what you can do just now. Then you have no choice but to fully express your true nature. It lights up every corner of your being and your doing, even in your final illness, even in your dying. When the writer Thoreau was on his deathbed, a visitor asked him—from where you lie, so close to the brink of the dark river, can you say how the opposite shore looks to you? It is said that he replied, gently, "One world at a time."

What a vivid expression of the koan of mindfulness: *One world at a time*. The sharpest pitch of awareness is reached when you are subtly aware of the passing away of things at all times. Why would that make you happy, to remember death at all times? Because both body and mind are stretched by such awareness to the limits of their understanding. And that brings your whole life to the creative edge, the fire, the brilliance, of Zen.

The simplicity of the Way

Mindfulness is practical, as well as magically awake and alive. If we are learning to listen and to abide by our own hearts, then we are setting out on the great path of the Middle Way. The Buddha followed a path of extreme self-abnegation before he took sustenance from a woman offering alms and sat beneath the Bodhi tree to realize his self-nature. After nearly dying of spiritual extremes, he taught the Middle Way, of awareness: not wallowing in self-indulgence or self-hatred, but looking into the self, steadily, compassionately, ruthlessly; paying attention, staying at the edge of the unknown where each thing is fresh and new. This is consciousness of the self, but a probing consciousness that appraises each construction of the self with a cool eye. It is not self-consciousness, which is a foregrounding of self that blocks out all else.

Every moment is new when you are seated at the middle of it. Strangely, the Middle Way is a path of abundance, and another word for that is *flow*; in Chinese, they share the same ideogram. It is strange that wanting nothing is a door that opens to fullness. When we want nothing, we begin to notice and truly appreciate each thing that the universe offers us. Wanting nothing is not a state of surfeit, of having had enough, thank you. It is a state of awake openness to the very moment of being, a natural awareness that nothing is lacking. It is an objectless, nameless gratitude for sheer being, a most simple happiness. Whenever we approach such a state, it is hard work to be greedy, because there is no fear of any lack in the world.

The koan of orange

We are surrounded by thousands upon thousands of unsurpassed teachers of this simple state of being. Where are they? You can begin by looking in your fruit bowl. Pick up an orange, say, and ask it to teach you the mystery of being. Brian Keenan, the Irishman held hostage for many months in Lebanon during the 1980s, tells in his book *An Evil Cradling* of how an orange that found its way onto his meal tray one day, in the dark and privation of his solitary confinement, brought him to his knees in tears and wonder. He couldn't bear to eat it for a long time; for days he simply regarded it with gratitude. The whole shining world of sun, vivid color, amazing taste and fragrance that is an orange overwhelmed him in his sense-deprived state, and he truly realized orange for the first time in his life.

The Chinese phrase for "all that is" is "the ten thousand things." All sentient beings are there — in Zen we have not yet come to an end of the order of sentient beings. Trees and rocks and clouds are all vivid and alive revelations of the meaning of existence, expressing it freely as trees and rocks and clouds. It is not so strange to ask an orange for the Dharma, for the teaching of what is, and how to meet it fully.

So hold an orange in the palm of your hand and look at it, forgetting whatever you think you know about oranges. All of the story of the universe up to now, every single event, is a kind of compost dedicated to the emergence of this unrepeatable bright particular. Just like your own lucky, lucky life—every mollusk, frog, dinosaur, bird, crocodile, ante-lope, and human life up to now is laid down as a royal road of chance leading all the way to you, to this royal moment, this magisterial grace of being here.

Held within the orange is the great universe story of everything given, in birth and living, and everything asked, in seasoning and dying. Noth-ing is wasted—it is as tight as a drum, all beautifully packaged in a waxy, sharp-scented, zesty round orange, as vivid and simple as its name. Look at it carefully: although it can undergo change, it cannot be taken out of the universe. And so with just one orange, the whole universe arrives!

But look more closely at this great universe story of endless generous cause and effect: a human life, let alone the life of the universe, is not so simply reducible to a story in which this leads to that and birth leads to death. As the orange freely implies, along with the great Earth itself, maybe there's a certain roundness, too, to all things. I remember learn-ing as a child how the Mercator projection of the map of the world attempted to reduce the usual distortion, because a square map on flat paper cannot convey the whole earth with much success. A teacher told us it was like peeling the skin of an orange and pressing the peel flat to the paper. Of course there are many bulges and regrettable tears, and I remember thinking a map of the world is not a very satisfactory represen-tation of an orange!

Our understanding of causality rests on our understanding that time unfolds moment by moment. But mindfuless is the practice of entering the roundness of things through the wide open doorway of this singular moment. And then we see that it is equally round, a great round, that is not quite in reach of the mind of causality.

So—the koan of orange. Regard it well. What is it? Unblinking, like every koan, it lets you find yourself as your answer. Does an orange have buddha nature? Zen master Zhaozhou was once asked that very ques-tion about a dog. A dog would probably wag its tail, suggesting that a walk would be a good idea, or, if not, a bone, thereby settling the matter completely. No, a dog does not "have" buddha nature. An orange, too, is not subject to "have" and "have not." In fact, you could call it a potato and it would be unflinchingly happy with that! Another Zen master, Tongan Guanzhi, was asked by his student, "I wonder, what does Your Reverence love?" and he replied, "I already have become like this." A strange reply, which comes around the corner from the dark, bringing the dark with it. Like what? Like this! Have a look at the orange in your hand—like this, this!

An orange does not even have to become like this. It is already indistinguishable from it. It seems it's just we humans who undergo the amazing process of consciousness-shift—we call it suffering—in order to enter into reality, in order to suffer at last into this. We blaze with it, just as an orange does, but to know that we blaze with it we have to practice a fundamental rearrangement of awareness. An orange does not appear to share our human-shaped story, of being born in a palace, but wandering in the woods so far from home that we can only dimly recall that splendour and have to search life-long to re-establish our original birthright as our own.

No hindrance in the mind

It is as if consciousness itself, human self-consciousness, were a major interference in the direct transmission of reality. We manage to lock ourselves out of direct connection to reality. Western empiricist thought since the seventeenth century seems to have instituted this lock-out more firmly, removing us further from the fully participatory consciousness and its ceremonies that form the mind (a mind that literally "minds" the universe) enjoyed by most indigenous, traditional cultures. An Aboriginal Elder once said it very simply: "Connectedness is reality. If you're not connected, you're not in reality." And so much of the time we're not.

It is fear that keeps us outside our own minds, outside reality, held apart from what is. The Heart Sutra says, "With no hindrance in the mind, no hindrance and therefore no fear. . . ." The torsion of consciousness that creates and defends a self—that free-floating, generalized anxiety—is both ferocious and fragile. It is oddly like a two-year-old human being, curiously positioned between a dream of omnipotence and a terrifying intimation that it may be impotent, helpless.

But you may also say it is an extraordinary journey, the human journey, to become like this. Possibly worth the equally extraordinary price of admission!

An orange shows how to do it. Have a look. First of all, it just sits. Zazen is wholly natural to it, as it is to stones and trees and mountains. It just maintains the condition of true—which you actually know all about, though it looks far too simple to be ever less than deeply mysterious. Between, before and beyond self-conscious thoughts, when you are doing nothing at all, you're there. As orange as orange can be.

So, just sitting, just breathing, just coming back into that sweet, discoverable fit with your own arising and falling away beyond names, dates, conditions, addresses, stories, hurries, and worries; truly just sitting transmutes hurry and worry into true being, complete well-being.

Oranges don't form concepts that define or protect the self and then react accordingly, expending energy and even killing for concepts. They just use it wonderfully well, bringing forth roots, flowers, sky, universe, perfume, nourishment, color, and zest. Can you experience such orange-like freedom from self? Yes, in deep sleep you release yourself from your self as thoroughly as an orange. In helping another, with no thought of helping; in laughter, that sudden glory of going momentarily beyond the self; in lovemaking; in meditation; in fact in any action or moment of being not smothered or pre-lived by thought; at any such moment, wanting nothing, how wonderfully well you are using it!

What is the Mysterious?

The response of Dalong, an eighth-century Zen master, to the question "What is the Mysterious?" is a beautiful embodiment of such simplicity, revealing someone who has been deeply rearranged by the great simplicity of the mind of practice:

> *The breeze brings the water's voice*
> *close to my pillow;*
>
> *The moon carries the shadow of the mountain*
> *near to my couch.*

Dalong's simplicity of being is as unimpeded as the rain falling, and the earth getting wet. The breeze blows and the creek music comes near. The moon sinks lower and the shadow of the mountain crosses the floor to the couch where he sleeps. Clear seeing is intimate also with death and the unravelling of sickness and old age. Dalong is at ease enjoying all offers of the universe; the shadow lengthens to meet him as the moon sinks.

So this is the mystery of our journey here, the mystery of the practice of mindfulness, of learning to accept all offers with the complete grace of an orange. Things do unravel. The steadiness of real practice knows this as another face of abundance. Though orange peel is sometimes excluded from compost, we all go back to the ground of being.

Everything is divided by our human keenness of mind, but in the beginning and in the end, and in the middle of the middle, everything is not divided. If you do not believe me, one radiant orange clears up this matter completely.

CHAPTER 3

Intimacy
with the Other

YOU BEGIN TO SUSTAIN A REGULAR practice of meditation, of meeting who you are in relative stillness. You discover, in some rare moments of breathing that seem free of the intrusion of thought, "Ah! I fit here, exactly!" Every mindful breath subtly lifts you past resistance until you can sometimes enter a sea of pure breath awareness and being, where you find yourself to be more seamless and indivisible than you ever could have known. Home!

A faithful practice will begin to open this way not just in lucky moments but for whole stretches of time in which there is little or no thought of time at all.

But what do you do when you find unpleasant guests are knocking at the door of home? Some thinly disguised versions of greed, hatred, or ignorance. Of course, the guests are usually better presented than this scruffy bunch sounds, because the self does a fair bit of work to make them more presentable to itself.

Practice says a strange thing: So that you can let them go, make mindful room for them. Welcome them in as the brief guests passing through that they really are, not the long-stay tyrants we can easily turn them into. Find out who they are really, so you can know more skillfully how to let them go. The Zen Way is not about drowning in bliss but establishing freedom in every mood, condition, emotion, and belief. And so it has to be about knowing, moment by moment, our actual condition upside-down and inside-out, with an alert, curious, willing attentiveness. Sitting patiently and ungrudgingly with the way things actually are.

Compassion and insight

Zen knows *prajna*, insight, to be inseparable from *karuna*, compassion. The bodhisattva—the one who dares to seek enlightenment—doesn't seek to transcend humanity by waking up all alone, but to fulfill humanity by awakening to the exquisitely sharp sense of mutual correspondence with all beings. Human being is not cast off by such a practice but acknowledged and appreciated and lived in its real depth. We sit together with all beings and we wake together with all beings. Zen works hard to transform the habits of mind radically, right at the root; but rather than trying to cut off impurities, it takes the challenging and confronting practice of including—radical acceptance—as the way of deepest letting go. When you truly include everything, there is no trace of self to be found. Compassion flowers freely at every point where the self falls away. And so compassion, *karuna*, has its natural source in zazen, which is the practice of *prajna*, the realization of no-mind, no-self.

Although a Zen *sesshin*, or seven-day retreat, affords a powerful week-long immersion in the spare simplicity and completeness of monastic form, Western Zen is largely a lay practice. The Buddha's example of a monastic life of radical renunciation remains a potent image of the magnitude of the task of turning around our ancient habits of mind, and the ferocity needed to do so. But lay Zen practice lived in the world doesn't follow a monastic schedule behind walls; the path of including is lived right here in the monastery without walls. Ordinary life itself is the sharp needle of our practice—and don't worry, there's no shortage of acute points: our hermitage is established right here exactly where we are, in the midst of car alarms, crying babies, deadlines, domestic squabbles, traffic jams, computer crashes, news bulletins, and crowded supermarket aisles.

So realization is by its very nature a gift from all beings that is returned and placed in the service of all beings, with complete respect and gratitude. "Emptiness" has no hands or feet; that return gesture of realization, of offering "emptiness" our human feet and hands, has nothing grudging about it but simply confirms the unstinting nature of realization itself, which is interested and generous toward the all-too-human business of ordinary life. How we live our own lives in the company of others is the true gold standard of the practice. The bodhisattva path declares that we can never reach the end of the Dharma, never come to an end of unfolding ourselves to meet it. To wake up is to grow interested in turning toward freedom time and again, in every condition and encounter.

The four noble truths

The first noble truth uncovered by the Buddha holds the simple recognition that all sentient life entails suffering; and more particularly, that human consciousness entails a particular suffering. Awareness, not avoidance, of suffering is the door that swings open to waking up, to a path with integrity, a path with heart.

The second noble truth holds that the perpetual toil of contriving and shoring up the edifice of self—and every round of meditation bears witness to just how much of this there is!—is driven by a fanatical energy of clinging, of holding on for grim death. To catch sight of this labor is to see with some compassion how desperately we continually invest in the illusion of permanence. When this is discovered comprehensively as your own experience, says the second noble truth, you have already begun to soften the most obdurate and painful suffering of consciousness, and to soften that sense of separateness, which is the source of clinging, the cause of suffering, the chief impediment to freedom.

Great realization is waking up to your original state where there is nothing to cling to and no one who can cling. To wake up is to actualize the third noble truth: that there is an end to suffering. When you see clearly, there is nothing at all; every single thing, just as it is, is vivid expression of original, overflowing "emptiness."

In response, as a kind of natural praise and provision for that immensity, the fourth noble truth offers a path of practice in the world that can begin to embody no-clinging in ordinary life: the path of "right" views, resolve, speech, action, livelihood, effort, mindfulness, and concentration. Here, "right" is not opposed to "wrong," but has the sense of being aligned with the deep grain of things, true to an awakened state.

The four bodhisattva vows

Zen does not turn away from the many beings and "becomings" of the world but brings them to clarity. The first and foremost of the bodhisattva vows, the four great vows of waking up that underpin Zen practice and embody the four noble truths, is "The many beings are numberless. I vow to save them." Saving the many beings points clearly to the suffering that marks all sentient life according to the first noble truth. The Chinese character meaning "save" also carries the sense of "wake." The cause of suffering begins to show itself already. We could equally say, "I vow to wake the many beings."

There is nothing simple about maintaining genuine practice, and it is easy to backslide or drift without the guidance of a teacher and trustworthy companions of the Way. The second vow checks that subtle slippage with a deep bow to the second noble truth concerning the causes of suffering: "Greed, hatred, and ignorance rise endlessly; I vow to abandon them." The third vow, "Dharma gates are countless; I vow to enter them," is an intentional act of dedication to the third noble truth—of ending suffering by opening a more true awareness. Dharma gates are indeed countless: each thing, every gesture of the universe, invites your entry into full realization of what is. How can you count that? And finally, the fourth bodhisattva vow, "The Buddha's way is unsurpassed; I vow to embody it fully," is an undertaking to embody the fourth noble truth as your very life. No small undertaking!

Each of these great vows, in fact, is a wonderfully large and impossible proposition when set against our limited human means. Each feels like peering into a vast crater while still trembling behind the safety wire of the reasoning self, who cries, "But, but!" Saving all beings from the heavy sleep of our mind—is that even faintly possible? Finding the creative relationship with our negative states of mind; entering every opportunity to see clearly that opens in front of us; being completely who we are in this life! The safety fence of "reasonable" is necessarily missing at every point in these great vows. Each one is a kind of field of energy, and the crater in reason opened up by each vow is exactly what calls up that energy—it transmutes "unreasonable" into a passionate urge to realize the heart-mind, to encompass all that is. Each vow, like the universe itself, is inexhaustible. Don't worry—you'll never come to the end of any vow or ever run short of fuel for the fire. Just to contemplate each one is to begin to appreciate at the same moment both the puniness of ordinary human means and that transcendence is a matter that somehow requires this fragile set of bones. How we are is exactly what it takes.

To sense this is to feel an enlivening mixture of fear and courage, humility and praise, not unlike the rich moment in Herman Melville's *Moby Dick*, when Captain Ahab looks at last upon his nemesis, the great white whale, and we find he can respond with something bigger, more sober and more unexpected than fear:

We asked the captain what course of action he proposed to take toward a beast so large, terrifying, and unpredictable. He hesitated to answer, and then said judiciously, "I think that I shall praise it."

The offer of praise — of radical and daring acceptance — in the face of the overwhelming opens the magnanimity of heart that marks the great life.

Zen is not a quest for perfection, nor does it renounce any part of what is. It refuses no part of the world as unholy. Buddha nature pervades the whole universe, indiscriminately. Zen doesn't hold the world at bay but says come home right where you are, just as you are. There is no end to this adventure of arriving. Indeed, we sometimes say with a smile that the Buddha is still working hard to confirm and polish a great realization that has shone for two-and-a-half thousand years all the way to here and yet is never, by its nature, "complete"; we never give up on the adventure of becoming who we really are. This reverent piece of irreverence, just like the "impossible" bodhisattva vows, can inspire practice with a more genuine and enabling force of truly alive bodhisattva awareness than the more traditional one of the stainless and perfected Buddha.

So how do we go about "including," which means recognizing fully as no other than ourselves, such destructive forces as greed, hatred, and ignorance? The second bodhisattva vow challenges us to become mindful of the relentlessness of negative energy, to learn how not to take it up before it can take us away; instead, how to let it drop away by giving it the respect of a still, calm, unmoved kind of attention. The breath shows how it is done.

Greed

Greed seems to be the enthroned delusion recommended every day in every way in Western culture. Greed is an aggrandizing and expanding of the self at the expense of everyone and everything else. We are actively encouraged to overspill our actual needs and pursue endlessly and aggressively created wants that are designed always to outstrip satisfaction. Hungry ghosts, in traditional Chinese and Japanese lore, have a ravenous appetite coupled with a severely constricted throat. Unsurprisingly, they live in a state of extreme irritability and acute anxiety. As hungry ghosts we can never know the calm and confidence of "enough." The economy calls for the anguish of unstinting greed, calling it "consumer confidence." As hungry ghosts, we are eating up our world.

We can experience greed equally in the ceaseless movement of the mind—and find it in that longing to be diverted, looking endlessly for more, doubting what is provided, returning again and again to worry the bone of old grievances, fixed ideas. That restlessness is craving, a sense of needing something "outside" the self for completion; it can even be a needy search for momentary relief from restlessness itself. Sifting through likes and dislikes is an act of propping up the self, searching down new blind alleys for a possible way to make the self immune to change, dissolution, death. Greed is a kind of mesmerism. How can meeting the breath with all of our attention be a response powerful enough to begin to loosen and undo all the continuously arising vested interests of the self?

Every moment of appreciating the coming and going nature of the breath distils the antidote of original well-being. Consider how the breath teaches about greed: our body is filled with each freely given in-breath yet it leaves no trace as we exhale, erasing our footprints from the sand. Nothing remains again and again, yet we are filled and sustained. You can't get greedy with the breath. Try to hoard it—what happens? You have to loosen and let go in order to live. Actually, you have never stopped practicing this fact. Meditation is just agreeing to catch up with what the body has always known.

So meditation offers a safe place to meet greed in all of its arising forms with an open awareness and to grow more skilled at recognizing it, moderating it, distinguishing between the affirming forms of desire that reconcile us deeply to each other and to our great life, and the undermining forms of desire that diminish life and maroon us short of freedom.

Hatred and anger

Hatred is a more declared form of the urge to discount or override the *other* that greed accedes to more secretly. And like greed, hatred springs from ignorance, which is the primary delusion that we are limited, bounded by ourselves, separated from the *other*, from "the rest" of all that is. Hatred is an active and pronounced form of that separation: a self-imposed isolation in the self, a choosing of the condition of alienation, a degree of yielding to the urge to strike out and hurt. The self, possessed by a mood, proceeds to trample everything in its path.

Moods are actually passing shades of inwardness, as fluid as cloud reflections in a still lake, passing freely across without troubling its surface. But once we decide that we are "in a mood," we have turned that melting of the air into something solid, chosen to become its turbulence; we are content for others to weather our harsh effects. Sometimes a whole lifetime subscription to a mood appears to be on offer, and before we know it we've signed up. Later, we may call it a "family pattern," or say, as if it's nothing much to do with us, "That's just me."

Hatred and anger can be strong, energetic states and may have the appearance of warmth; but this is a fire that sheds little light and supports no life. It is in the end a cold fire, usually with a fuel of fear. It arises from some dim unease of feeling that we're missing out on something we're entitled to, something we believe is being given out to others but not to us. Often that something is love, acceptance or affirmation. Anger is horribly like a two-year-old's tantrum, an expression of fundamentally impotent omnipotence that is often very shameful to look back on later, so nakedly does it actually betray our "secret" powerlessness and sense of inadequacy.

The unwanted unease quickly finds "reasons" for itself—reasons preferably external to the self—and these stick even when the unease itself has fallen away; they become our official story. We don't like feeling discontented so someone has to be at fault—and they have to pay! As with greed, the isolated self firmly believes its own tireless propaganda and is open to very little in the way of fresh intelligence. All things constantly point to the rightness of the self, its sense of injury and its proper dues.

But when the self is "right," it's already wrong. Mild irritation, lack of affinity, subtle aversion—all can build in the echo chamber of the isolated, alienated self to become a surge of hatred actually directed at someone. Why are we so almost willingly powerless before feelings of hatred? Even when the destructiveness and pointlessness of rage and aggression is plain to us, and even when we stop short of literal violence, still we can proceed to annihilate the other savagely in our heart, creating heavy weather for ourselves and all lives touching ours.

If growing up is becoming more able to tolerate, acknowledge, and make room for the other, and grow at least as interested in a relationship with the other as in the needs of the self, then growing up is learning to experience and recognize anger, greed, hatred, and envy in a less helpless fashion. Negative emotion tends to swamp the airwaves, and leave you powerless to send or receive anything but more of the same. So maturing is growing more capacity to include such states without submitting to them and losing the natural grace and ease of your own original mind.

The offer of negative emotion

Even hatred, the emotion that is already dangerously close to being a kind of action, can be taken up as an offer to come back to the breath. Steadied by the breath, don't deny or push hatred off but dare to admit it consciously into the coming and going of breath, the welling into and out of being. Mindfully allow the moment that is presenting itself as hatred, and attend to it without feeding it or being swept away by it. Often, just to release ourselves from denial is to begin to relax the drama caught up in the strong feeling. The very act of calm attention, grounded in the fluid mystery of the life of the breath, can allow hatred to become a subtle, more intelligent and informing energy, which carries an insight into who we really are in the best sense, an insight that could never touch us as long as hatred was disowned.

Under the scrutiny of such calm, searching attentiveness, hatred often reveals a deeper underlay of fear, a self under threat from uncontrollable forces. And then compassion can come in; it is already an act of compassion to the self to bring such attention to bear. With the discovery and acknowledgment of fear, compassion for the self can grow and can form a viable bridge to the other who seems to be the threat. If you can own your fear, you have by that very act created an opening that can readmit the other to your heart. Real reconciliation can never proceed from aversion toward hatred, from blocking it or hacking it off in compounded self-hatred. It begins in acknowledgement of the actual existence of both your own feelings and the other—in vulnerability becoming a strong condition of openness.

And who is that other? Anger declares it is your enemy. Accord confirms that it is no other than your self. Hatred, whether turned outward or inward, is always an attack upon the true self.

The deeper chill that the heat of anger and hatred often masks is usually some incarnation of the fear of extinction, the primary anguish of the isolated self. The idea that anger needs to be expressed is given considerable positive press in our culture, while it is a rare idea in the cultural context from which Buddhism has emerged. A persistent question asked of Buddhism in the West is, "Well what's so wrong with anger? Isn't it healthier to express anger than to repress it?" Certainly, anger turned inward upon the self can manifest as depression and illness. But anger turned outward can manifest as violence, psychological scarring, broken relationships, even war; at the very least, it leaves a trail of shameful behavior. So how do you work with a koan like "Don't get angry"?

Not getting angry

Anger can come up again and again even when you thought you had investigated it thoroughly, and each fresh wave brings with it a lot of flotsam and jetsam. You can be left like a beach strewn with storm wrack in the wake of anger that boils and foams and finally recedes. Meditation is the decidedly more spacious opportunity to look dispassionately at all that anger has dragged up.

Some of what you find will seem frankly absurd the moment you look. Some of it may be hard to see as absurd except to others, at least at first. And among the junk, with very careful scrutiny, just one or two pearls beyond price may be found. It may be a sense of boundary violation, of someone having leant too far in, betrayed trust, denied your right to your own feelings—a breach of integrity of some kind. Equally, it may be catching sight of a pre-emptive strike of rage or sullenness that you made to cover your own shame in having breached the integrity of the other in some way.

But the valuable thing is always some kind of fresh intelligence about the real nature of the ground that lies between you and the other. Anger is a potent energy that can be appreciated for how dramatically it can raise such matters to awareness. But to act upon the fire of anger is to feed it with combustible fuel while being blinded and stupefied by its clouds of smoke. To bring the awareness raised by anger to real clarity is extremely difficult in close proximity to its hot state.

"Getting angry," then, is the mistake of acting in anger, which is falling out of connectedness. "Getting angry" is becoming anger, danced by anger, begetting anger, harboring and nurturing a self willfully condemned to its dream of separateness. Who has ever felt good or enlarged by indulging in an angry outburst? We seem to swell with so much self-importance in our anger and then feel pitiably punctured and diminished the moment we catch sight of our absurd imposture, which can then produce a whole new wave of anger generated in self-defense.

Not getting angry is more like delaying response while the tide is in flood and waiting for the chance to go beachcombing when it recedes. Not getting angry is taking the leisurely, bemused, reflective stroll through the storm wrack, curious to turn over and examine the debris deposited by anger, delighting in some things, humbled and wondering at others, marvelling at the sea change that things undergo in the depths, and taking perhaps just one or two nuggets of invaluable self-knowledge home with you. When anger cools, what you have learned from it can be more safely shared with the one who "caused" it, if that really seems necessary. (It probably will pass, anyway, simply by being in your clear and calm possession.)

So accepting the offer of strong negative emotion is never the same as venting or indulging it. Accepting the offer is the far more subtle and demanding business of not retreating and not advancing but inviting strong, negative feelings onto the ground of no separation, and interpreting it there where nothing is missing.

The original delusion

Ignorance is the fundamental delusion of separation, of thinking, "I'm in here and you're out there." Meditation constantly and creatively enquires into this sense that the self is isolated and limited—the source of fear, greed, and hatred, which are in turn the energies that proceed to feed and flesh out the original delusion. Being ignorant means not knowing the true nature of the self, obscuring our natural and innate correspondence with everything that is, and drawing a sharp line between self and other. That painful and wholly imaginary line is the fake assurance that we can do what we like: we're entitled, and there'll be no repercussions, apart from a possible smatter of applause from the imagined admirers of the self.

And with it comes the joyless hope that joy can be hoarded and does not wither and die in a strictly personal savings account; or the odd fantasy that the existence of others and the reality of their suffering may legitimately be held in doubt. The actual cost of such escape attempts is great indeed. While this way of surviving may ease you past the brutal truths and grueling needs of others that would seize your whole attention if you let them grow more real, it cuts you off from the profound joy that's available only if everyone, everything, shares in it.

True mindfulness of breath again and again repairs this endless breach of reality with consummate ease. Breath and its attendant awareness is not "out there," and even more subtly it's not even "in here." When you really attend closely, it's not "me," and it's not even "my breath." Awareness just rises like a hum of insects in the grass with the warmth of the sun. Including the breath widens out who we are; it gradually opens us to include the tires on the road outside, the ache in the shoulder blades, the nameless grief, the nameless joy—everything that is, just as it is. We truly breathe. Reunion begins. This is the moment of ignorance easing up and giving way to a more fruitful un-knowing, and with it, the beginning of the easing up of greed and hatred too.

The other, the ten-thousand things, just as they are, can be no other than myself. So what can there be to fear? It is an urgent matter to know this for yourself. As the fourteenth-century Sufi poet, Rumi, said:

> *Don't let your throat tighten*
> *with fear. Take sips of breath*
> *all day and night, before death*
> *closes your mouth.*

And yet, and yet . . .

Zen dares us never to push any part of life away. John Tarrant once suggested that you may find the great gate of the Mahayana, the compassionate Middle Way, opening in just two tiny words of a haiku that the Zen poet Issa wrote upon the death of his beloved two-year-old daughter:

> *The world of dew*
> *is the world of dew—*
> *and yet*

The first two lines of the poem bow deeply to the orthodox Buddhist teaching of impermanence and non-attachment: we must accept our place in "the world of dew," for all evanescent life is born in the morning and gone even before the afternoon—a fact strong enough to break human hearts. But in departure from orthodox Buddhism, the final line of the poem—the immensely tiny and powerful "and yet"—bows humbly and unreservedly to that ordinary breaking human heart. Issa doesn't force a choice upon us. He does not ask that we detach from our agony, grief, and longing but leaves us considering something far more challenging, something that transforms the notion of "clinging" from the inside out.

"And yet," he says, we have no choice if we are truly alive but to hold both love and grief together with the profound emptiness of all form in our own heart and bones. If we can do that—with all the rigor and courage it undoubtedly requires—then we may deeply realize as the great fact of our own sacred, mortal bodies that this limited human life and this boundless eternity are not two. Are even less than one. "This very place is the Lotus Land, this very body, the Buddha," a famous Zen poem declares. For the Zen path of practice runs right through the fertile ground of the great middle and nothing falls outside of that.

So when you are grieving, grieve just as if your life depended on it. It does. When you are grieving, lose your self in grief and let it open you beyond yourself into the immensity that is beyond self and no-self.

Just sobbing. Just laughing. Not an inch off from your unrepeatable life. And that is how to praise it.

CHAPTER 4

The great Way
of play

IT MAY SEEM STRANGE THAT RIGOR and play should be in
such close negotiation with each other, but indeed they are. The Way
of Zen is always making clear how this is so. When you look in on a still
dojo, full of adults sitting in exquisite, fluid stillness, after a time it grows
on you that this may be a place of pure play. There is a moment each
evening during Zen retreats when someone calls into the dojo, with a
voice from beyond the grave, "Life and death is a grave matter. All things
pass quickly away." What could be more a moment of pure play than
that? And we accept it with a kind of nameless gratitude. That very taking on of the grave matter that we do in a meditation practice is what
allows us to enter or to join the great Way of play—"to join the sweet
party of the most simple things," in the words of a beautiful line from a
milonga I heard recently.

We may well be the only animals that play all of our lives—or perhaps
we only think we are—and we may play all the way up to our death. We
may, in this spirit, play even with our own death, meet even that with

rigor and playfulness. It is the rigor of what we do, in practice, that raises everything to the state of play. Any seriously undertaken work is play in the deepest sense.

Zen practice is dedicated to waking us up, enlivening us, quickening us. It might seem paradoxical that the very thing that quickens us is the absolute gravity of the matter at hand. So we begin to play even with our death when we truly take on board the grave matter of what is this life.

The serious matter of play

Children know that play is a very serious matter. I remember a short story by the Australian writer Helen Garner, called "Little Helen's Sunday Afternoon." Little Helen Garner, quite possibly. I think she must have been about nine when the story takes place. It's that kind of age when you're not quite a little kid any more, and when people see you again they say things like, "Oh dear, your feet have become so big! Look at those shoes!" So she's at the ungainly stage, caught on the cusp of things, when a child begins to suspect that one day childhood may end, and adults start to hustle her towards that point. The whole long Sunday afternoon visit with some relatives is also ungainly, and on the cusp of things. There's something odd going on down in the back shed with the older cousins. In the house it's rather boring because her mother is trying on clothes in the bedroom with her aunt, and at one point her mother pops her head out and says to Little Helen, "Oh do you want to play? We're playing dress ups!" She has on nothing but her underwear and a pillbox hat with a little veil. But, the story says, Little Helen didn't really want to play with them. The problem was that when they played dress up, they tended to talk about how much the clothes cost and where they bought them, and they didn't want to talk about the serious things, like what the clothes meant in the game. Children know better than we do that the rules of a game are a very serious matter, and when someone doesn't play properly, the life goes out of the game. Practice is a path that rediscovers the seriousness of play.

How is this practice, this immensely sobering Way of meditation, also a matter of pure play? Let's look at some of the ways. First of all, it costs nothing to sit in zazen. It uses up no nonrenewable resources. It contributes absolutely nothing to the gross domestic product, unless you consider that it multiplies the figure by zero. And it has a very strict and serious sense of form, as all great games do. There are no games without rules; the rules are a kind of desirable restriction. We touch this restrictiveness in retreats. We come partly in order to accept a quite profound restrictiveness. Why do we do that? Why do we want to consign ourselves to a somewhat tight and demanding form? Sometimes I think of Zen-retreat form as trying out the coffin. You know that game? You jump in the coffin, you say, "I'll just see what it's like in here. Oooh! That's what it's like in here!"

It was the first day of the first Zen sesshin, or seven-day retreat, that I ever did, and I remember watching the minute gradations of the light from total dark through to almost dark again of one entire day and thinking at the end of that day that it had been at least as long as all of my life up to that point. It was vast. I was at a country retreat center near Sydney in a remote valley beneath sandstone cliffs, where the buildings are honest and simple. There are cracks in the timber that house frail little spider bodies. The spiders have long since passed on, but their bodies are left in the cracks of the timber and the wind reanimates them. I remember watching the minute threads of spider form just beginning to fade back into the dark, reanimated by the evening breeze, and thinking, "This is the longest day of my life, but what a feast of time." What an extraordinary abundance of time had been made available by the strictness of that form. How much had come back to life.

We truly enter into time through this restriction, and we enter into time that cannot be measured. And so we come to the point where there is a question we can ask about time that probably all great games open up for us: a sense that time is elastic, that it can't really be measured. What is the duration of a dream, or a wave falling and breaking? Or of the heat turning into the cool of evening? It can't be named, that duration. What is the time of one breath moment in which we're truly present?

The dragon of creativity

The koan path within the Zen Way is yet another whole dimension of play. It's full of that kind of creative, dragonish energy described in the first hexagram of the *I Ching*, "The Creative"—the electrically charged, dynamic, arousing force of a spring thunderstorm. And yet it is a modest, homely, simple business. Koan work is a fierce, playful form of dressing up in order to stay profoundly at home.

A koan can be a tiny story or a fragment of the record of discourse or encounter between a teacher and a student, or it may be a line from a sutra or a poem, or most simply of all, a vast and simple question. "What is it?" "Who are you really?" "Who is hearing that sound?" "What is the sound of a single hand?" "What is your original face, before even your parents were born?" In every case, it defeats the efforts of ordinary consciousness to resolve the questions it raises and we must learn to respond with wide (and wide-awake) awareness, from the depths of our heart-mind.

These fragmentary stories and images can be as secret and resistant to ordinary understanding as dreams. They present at once a barrier and a wide-open gate; they preserve a direct and actual path into the heart of reality. To resolve them they must be returned to an unknowing that lies before and beyond words; they must become part of your own flesh and bone, kidneys and gall bladder.

Intimate plainness

The word *koan* is the Japanese equivalent of the Chinese *kung an*, meaning public case, or public record. Why *public?* The word offers a kind of warning that we are not involved here in the formulation of private opinion but the apprehension of essential reality—the deepest principle, common everywhere, innate to all things, and therefore utterly "public," intimately apparent in every direction. The koan puts a merciful stop to private understanding, to conceptual thinking. You must see with the same eyes and hear with the same ears as the old teachers; and also see with the same ears and hear with the same eyes. Each point must flow out from your own breast to cover heaven and earth, in the words of Yantou.

Working on a koan closely with a teacher may require you to call up the whole great world in all its minute particularities, right there in the interview room with an abundant economy of means. The whole world is there at your disposal, so you just use it. Here it is! A tree, a buffalo, a stone from the bottom of the sea. It's also like play in that it has absolutely no purpose and makes no utilitarian sense. This is the great guarantee of a koan: it will not make sense; it will not be amenable to our usual paths of making sense. It is a little like a ball game, demanding direct throwing and catching. A koan is not a thing that you can mull over and maul and masticate. There's nothing worse than an over-masticated koan. If you cannot respond freely from your own being, it is better to remain silent and sit some more with the koan.

A koan has that directness because it is coming from stillness; it is nothing other than that vast alive stillness. If you think about an accomplished athlete or actor, there's a great quality in them of the stillness that is learned from play. It's play that teaches us so well about profound stillness. Practice, or koan work, is a game that does not involve so much moves of the mind as radical removes of the mind. It involves taking away elements that we've grown to rely on. Again, this is like play, like games, like play-acting of a certain kind. Just getting down to a bare stage and very little to rely on; in fact, nothing at all.

It's like a game, too, in the way that it is dangerous. To play a game you must put something at stake, even if it's something as slight as your dignity, your self-importance — in fact yourself. You put yourself at stake. In *Brush Mind*, Kaz Tanahashi says in relation to a calligraphic brush stroke that if it pleases the eye, it is not yet dangerous enough. The work of the Way is not about pleasing — it must be more dangerous than pleasing. The energy of this dangerous play is what undresses us and bares us to the light, and brings us home. It makes us profoundly vulnerable.

In fact, this is the gift of all of our most unstinting and rigorous play — that it bares us to the light. It's a kind of holy joy that is rarely mentioned, and so it is free to be present everywhere and to do as it pleases, just as the wind blows where it likes to blow. If such things are named too much, they start to get a bit dubious.

The green branch

Play belongs to the realm of eros, of connection, of connectedness, the green shoots of life. An old Chinese saying promises that "if you keep a green branch in your heart, the singing bird will come." The koan path offers us that. It greens the practice with its energy of connection, its creative energy. Play is like the way a wave falls: it can't be predetermined; it provides the structure for chaos, so it is as inexhaustible as clouds, flowing water, moving waves. Pablo Neruda writes in a poem, "I have never seen a wave I did not admire."

You can get some sense of this deep fund of play in the practice when you hear the kind of laughter that comes from the Zen interview room — great gusts of laughter that are somehow deeply reassuring. Like "sudden glory," which is how Thomas Hobbes described laughter. Laughter is our sudden glory. It breaks out, shines, rolls away the boulder and then it dies without trace — and that, too, is precious.

Cracking a great smile

The founding story of our Zen tradition is Buddha's realization of his own self-nature, when he looked up and saw and was seen by the morning star, low in the east. Another kind of founding story enters the tradition, some thousand years later. It is the story of Buddha twirling the flower. Even this is a form of play: a great founding story is created further down the track and our Zen tradition branches from there.

> Once in ancient times when the World-Honored One was at Mount Grdhrakata, he twirled a flower before his assembled disciples. All were silent. Only Kasyapa broke into a smile. The World-Honored One said, "I have the eye treasury of right dharma, the subtle mind of nirvana, the true form of no form, and the flawless gate of the teaching. It is not established upon words and phrases. It is a special transmission outside tradition. I now entrust this to Mahakasyapa."

This story shows how deeply we are founded in play. The Buddha twirled a flower and the whole problem started with that. One person twirls a flower; another person smiles. Actually, a truer translation of "smile," as Robert Aitken records it in his *teisho* (a kind of formal Zen talk) on this koan in *The Gateless Barrier*, would be "cracked his face." His smile cracked his face. I like the fact that there's a great crack in our face at this point; it cracks the very riddle of face itself. We spend so much of our lives and energy building up a sober, serious sense of adulthood, a most detailed play of sanity. At this moment, that vast contrivance is cracked apart by the twirling of a flower. And the twirling of a flower stops the world in this moment. Everything has stopped. The most radical play stops the world.

And when we truly stop, nothing is there.

So what is it?

Keith Johnstone's book *Impro*, a handbook for actors, is also a wonderful Dharma book, and in the next few sections I will draw several examples from his book.

Johnstone talks about our careful adult sanity, with all its suppressed misgivings about the nature of the reality to which we all agree to subscribe as a kind of sad pretence. He has a lovely story about the way people present themselves as safe, or in this case, how someone failed to present himself as safe, and so had to learn to do so.

He says that once he read in *New Society* about a man who believed he had a fish in his jaw. The fish moved about a lot and drove him crazy. Of course, the people he mentioned it to thought he was crazy, and there were violent arguments about the matter. He was hospitalized a few times but it had no effect on the fish at all, until finally someone suggested that perhaps the best thing was just not to mention the fish to anyone anymore. It was the arguments, after all, not the fish, that were getting him into so much trouble. So he kept his problem secret and led what we like to call a normal life. Johnstone points out, "His sanity is like our sanity. We may not have a fish in our jaw, but we all have its equivalent."

I presume the fish got freed when Mahakasyapa cracked a smile.

No names

Impro also talks about the way the world goes dull at a certain point in life—probably soon after the time we begin to experience Little Helen's long Sunday afternoon, in fact. Johnstone mentions that there are ways of coping with this, ways to make the world blaze up again. We have our own way in Zen practice, but his is not too dissimilar. He gets his students in an improvisation class to pace around the room and to begin to just name objects by any other name except their actual name. So any-thing your eyes light on you shout out the wrong name for it. There's probably time to shout out about ten wrong names before he says, "Stop. Stop. Now everybody. Pay attention. How do you feel now? What's going on?" And people will begin to say, "My god, everything looks sharper. Colors are brighter. People look a bit smaller, the room has changed! It's a whole different shape." They're amazed that there can be such a strong transformation brought about by such a simple, radical remove of the customary security of names and things. The effects last quite a long time. Hours afterward the world is still brighter, fresher, stranger. It has lost its habit.

Accept all offers

Johnstone tells us improvisation depends upon accepting all offers. He gives an example. Say you have two actors playing in an improvisation, with absolutely no starting point except that one decides to be a doctor, and so the other is obviously a patient. In such a situation, to say "yes" is to keep the game alive, to keep the play alive, to keep it moving. To say "no" is to begin to kill the improvisation. The trick here is to accept all offers.

So, in one of his examples, the first actor might say, "Ohh!," and clutch their leg; the second actor might say, "Oh my god, there's something wrong with your leg!" The first actor says, "Yes, I've got a pain in my leg." The second one says, "I'm afraid I'll have to remove it." The first actor then says, "Oh, don't take my leg. I'm rather attached to it." Now at that point, it's starting to go dead. "No" has been said; the offer has not been caught. But how about the second time? It goes through the same moves. "Ow, my leg!" "Oh no, not your leg! I'll have to remove it." And the second actor says, "But that's the leg you took last time!" So the first actor says, "Oh, this is serious!" The second actor says, "Not…woodworm?" And so it rolls. The play is alive because all offers are being accepted.

And it's possible even to accept an offer that hasn't been made. Johnstone gives a great example from a Groucho Marx film, a scene with a quiz show going on. Up on the stage one of the contestants freezes and can't move or say a word, which sounds like a familiar condition sometimes in the dangerous work of waking up. Groucho takes his pulse, looks at his watch anxiously and says, "Either this man is dead, or my watch has stopped!" This is accepting an offer that wasn't even being made.

Accepting all offers is a profound move to make. In a sense it is accepting suffering, too—accepting the offering of suffering, old age, death. Taking that on not as neurotic suffering but as real suffering is a kind of lightening of the burden of the entire world. Something mysteriously is lifted by that; some karmic weight is agreed to and carried by that act.

Accepting all offers, then, is what we do when we grow up, if we grow up—we become more agreeable toward discomfort, more able to accept a greater measure of discomfort. Again, this is part of the serious play of practice—learning to be at home with a measure of discomfort so that you can take that across into your life and make room in the world for the other, or for something new that needs to come into being. The ability and wish to do this is called maturity. When people say the word *tolerance*, they often think of it as, "I'm comfortable with that; I can tolerate that." But in fact tolerance asks that we accept a significant degree of discomfort. True toleration involves living with a measure of discomfort, agreeing and adjusting to make room in your mind for the other. And making room for the other is, of course, a form of intimacy with the other, whether that other be another human being or an unpleasant and unwelcome state of mind or feeling or ache of the heart.

So accepting all offers is a form of wanting nothing—it's like the other side of the one hand. On one side, it is accepting all offers; on the other side, wanting nothing. When you want nothing, when you can truly want nothing, then everything can be there at last. Just like when Mahakasyapa cracks his face.

What is there that cannot come through that great crack in the world? The great Way of play is the Way of true sorrow and true joy. Rabbi Levi Yitzhak of Berditchev was a Hasidic master, and when his only son died, the funeral bier was taken through the village and the congregation followed behind in deep silence. Of course, the Rabbi himself was walking behind his son's bier. And then to the great astonishment of his people, he began to dance. He began a slow, grave dance with his coattails flying out like great black wings. The people began to look at each other and they at last had to say something, and they said, "What are you doing? What are you doing!"

And he said to them, "A pure soul was rendered to me, and a pure soul I render back." And he rendered it back in pure play. He played, and he danced, even with heartbreak and death.

CHAPTER 5

The whole world
is medicine

A T A RALLY IN HYDE PARK, Sydney, during the terrifying blood-letting that followed the vote for independence in East Timor, I heard the words of an East Timorese poet who was listed at that time among the missing or the dead. In the crackle of loudspeakers I could not catch his name. But the koan in his tiny poem is unmistakable. Very simply:

Be here.
Be immortal.

His words speak to us not just about laying our life on the line for what we hold most dear; they are certainly a kind of koan about that. But they are equally a koan about life and spiritual practice, about living with an awareness that can be as wide and deep as the universe, in a mortal body that is wiser than we are, and knows that it will fade and die. This is the awareness that koan practice awakens and refines in us: "Be here. Be immortal."

When we are fully present, truly here, we have some taste of how eternity opens in a fragile wildflower, an ordinary grain of sand. We touch our entirely human immortality right in the midst of a mortal life, when eternity touches us. This poet offers it as an urgent invitation, an injunction. Be here! Don't miss it. The kingdom of God is always right here. And sometimes, you will find, you can enter.

But the strange fact is that it is difficult to turn that way. There is a human resistance to being here, being immortal. "Be here" is, after all, a koan, a barrier, a matter to be resolved. To be present just as you are in this very moment is a challenge, a risk to be taken with your whole life in your hands, not a simple article of faith. The sharp poignancy of the barrier presented by "Be immortal" is offered to us again and again. And not only when we turn on to hear the latest news about how things are in East Timor or the Middle East. It is offered, moment by moment, in every piece of gross or subtle evidence of our own failing, our falling short, our fading, our falling.

Bring forth that mind

Why is it so difficult to be here? Why is it seemingly easier to evade eternity, during our days here, than to offer ourselves to it? Even when we know for ourselves the sweetness and homecoming of daily practice, still we so lightly take a little holiday from it. Just today I won't get up early enough to sit and make being here the foundation of the whole day, when in fact the holiday is to sit! Every koan awakens the most fundamental awareness, and turn us back to being here.

Koans began to be collected, published, and used in a systematic way in tenth-century China. Before that, teachers created koans by their immediate exchanges in words and actions, and student faced these in their immediacy, when the teacher would demand, Speak! Speak! Or even less than that. Dwelling nowhere, bring that forth! As the records of these great teachers began to be consolidated by their students, and great collections of the most noteworthy exchanges were assembled by later important teachers, the compilers attached commentaries and verses, which in turn also became koans and were handed down that way. In all, around seventeen hundred koans form the basis of the formal koan path in Zen. Every one of them demands our wholeness; there is no other way to approach them.

We have bodies that inhabit time, and rise and fall in that. And in the very condition of mortality itself, we have the possibility of an awareness that can reveal the universe itself! This is our human condition, and this strange and unlikely combination is all that we need, all the basic equipment, for realization. This is a kind of exulting realization just in itself. And it is mysterious. Somehow, profound limitation is a doorway to boundless freedom. The limitation is, by some secret agreement of human nature, commensurate with the freedom itself. The path to "Be immortal," touch eternity, lies right through the very middle of "Be here," and there's no way to do that except in a mortal body. Every koan realizes this fact, makes it vivid and real.

If you argue "right" and "wrong"

The whole world is profoundly endangered right now — not just from the ravages of exploitation of its "resources," but from the contending ideologies of politicized religion, armed with weapons of devastation that threaten the entire natural world. Buddhism offers some antidote to the ravages of ideology. And the Zen koan takes that challenge to ideological thinking—indeed, to all the commonplace habits of thought—to a radical and luminously clear place.

Human life is filled with contradiction, which is so much its natural condition that even to speak of contradiction begins to be conceptual, to shift from the direct experience of the whole. Life is neither good nor bad, right nor wrong; it just is as it is. Buddhism is cosmological in its reach, asking us to stand and be exactly where we truly are, to embody the whole that we perceive with the entire reach of body, mind, imagination, heart, heart-mind. A cosmological impulse embraces all that is, the whole, whereas any ideology picks and chooses, selects and discards. Ideologies seek to "perfect" the world through the elimination of whatever they judge to be bad or wrong. Ideological reformers see themselves as right, and opposed to those who are wrong.

Yet when you look deeply into yourself you will find that life and death, good and evil, all transect your human heart. In a life that is fully realized, wisdom and insight and apprehension of the whole are round and also crooked, and not able to lie down straight and narrow and logical. From the point of view of physics, says Neils Bohm, the opposite of a true statement is a false one, but the opposite of one great truth may well turn out to be another equally great truth. "If you argue right and wrong, you are a person of right and wrong," says Master Wumen. That is a bitter discovery to make of yourself, from a Zen point of view. Condemned!

A mere ideology feels too dangerously marooned from the life of the whole body of mind to be of use to a world in peril. It is too locked into an adversarial politics to be able to risk seeing any kind of whole, or even to admit that the whole is vitally missing from the picture; too remote from embodied mind and being to grasp and be accountable to experience. An embodied mind has no choice but to perceive cosmologically — it is, by virtue of its original and unshakable nature, mind in the image of cosmos, the entire universe itself. How could it be anything else?

Minding the universe

How do you arouse and refine an awareness and mind that directly corresponds to the universe in its unfolding, and discover how to bring this directly into your thinking and acting in the world? How do you intentionally join the cosmos in its revelation of itself? The koan path is a path into that. And it is an urgent matter.

In the three centuries since the eighteenth-century shift in Western thought toward rationalism (referred to, without irony, as the Enlightenment), many have pointed out that the older, indigenous, cosmological casts of mind of the European West and elsewhere have been demoted, paralyzed, and "progressively" abandoned, and we have paid for this dearly. We have paid in alienation, estrangement, unease, homelessness; we have become marooned in ideology, imprisoned in language, impaired at the level of the imagination.

Flowing from this is the state of the planet: the exploitation and extinction of species and forests, the despoiling of oceans and rivers and lakes, the paving over of the green Earth, the loss of the genuinely local. This is a miserable fate. How can you know who and where you are if there is no way to be comprehensively here? We need a framework for truly being here, in all our particularity and profound relatedness, and an ideology is a sorry and impoverishing substitute. Ideologies offer only the hope of being "right," and "winning," which is anywhere but right here.

Just to move toward a mind grounded in the whole — in a world that has so painstakingly decommissioned most of its ancient images and imaginings of the whole — is a radical, enlarging, and dissonant move. It runs against the grain of our time. Such a move asks us to bring much more of ourselves than just intellect to bear on the human task of minding the universe.

We speak of the eye growing adapted to light or dark, as the iris opens or contracts to the intensity of light. The "eye" of the understanding mind is trained by human language, experience, and almost every step of education to distinguish this from that, to analyze this part as opposed to that part, and to theorize how the parts work together as a whole. But the koan "eye" can see and express the whole, perceived beyond all categories of mind, apprehended at once.

The eye of insight is a whole-adapted eye, and radically relativizes the seeing of the conditioned, part-adapted mind. The most radical, imaginative, and creative insights spring from the sense of the whole. Such insights open upstream from understanding, in the fertile darkness of unknowing, intimate with the source—the nothing from which we endlessly come. Wholeness can hold loss within its imaginative grasp, without being diminished. It embraces the co-arising and disappearing of life within the field of death, of life not opposed to death. And this is the very business of koans—opening doors that cannot be entered except from such radical wholeness. Koans invite us into minding the universe, into mind as direct experience of the universe, unmediated and unrestricted by language and concept.

Medicine and sickness mutually correspond

The great tenth-century Zen master Yunmen posed the koan "What is it?" this way: "Medicine and sickness mutually correspond. The whole world is medicine. What is the self?" Medicine and sickness, he suggests, are so intimate with each other they are not two; in fact, they are not even one. It flows from this, in some way that you must see into with your own life, that the whole world is medicine. And this, in turn, in some way that you must discover for yourself, both provokes and responds completely to the question, and this, in turn, in some way that you must discover for yourself, both provokes the question "What is the self?" and responds to it completely.

Each of these statements of Yunmen's together form a mysterious field in which all your notions of your self and the world are utterly revised, as an electromagnetic current passing through a dish of iron filings rearranges them completely.

This koan, like all koans, reflects every other koan in its depths, just as the jewel tied into every knot in the mythic Net of Indra is utterly individual, yet picks up and reflects in every one of its facets every other jewel in the net. Every koan asks us, at the deepest level it can find in us, What is it? What is the true nature of this? What is the true nature of the self?

You can "think" about the implicit question lying in the statement that "The whole world is medicine" and the explicit question "What is the self?" that arises from a realization of how the whole world is medicine. But thinking will not get you very far. The gate of a koan opens when you can let go of what you know with your mind, and open a kind of passionate unknowing that lies beyond the grip of mind. You don't understand a great koan so much as allow it to understand you; you allow it to resolve the koan of yourself. So in some way, not to be sought from "outside," but allowed to arise from the depths of your still mind, "The whole world is medicine" can put to rest the uneasiness in the self that holds us at bay from our own lives.

Unknowing

Wumen, who compiled the magisterial koan treasury called *The Gateless Barrier*, said, "Knowing is delusion; not knowing is blankness." His words open up a space between the conceptual mind of knowing that, from a koan point of view, is badly in the way, and the mental impotence of a mind that is simply blank and mute. Lying in the space between is quite another thing altogether, a potent unknowing that the fourteenth-century anonymous Christian author of *The Cloud of Unknowing* says is the mind that knows God. Unknowing is a state of making yourself available without the self in the way. Artists intuitively find some way to this mind; every authentic and original creative impulse of mind springs from it.

To think you know something is already to have missed the fundamental point; to think you know nothing is just blankness. Unknowing is like brooding over an egg of indefinable possibility—you must agree to sit patiently and passionately with the egg until something starts to stir. The hatching of the chicken is unmistakable; it is unstoppable when it happens. This condition of brooding is a kind of darkening of the mind, allowing it to become fertile. What you think you know is already of limited value in the realm of the koan. It might get you to the point where you dare at last to walk into the dark, that's about all.

The koan path travels right through the human heart. And so to enter into a koan is to fully admit to the fact of connectedness; to put aside all of the ordinary moods and instincts or habits of mind, and to completely admit the fundamental connectedness that was there all along. It gave birth to you, it will give death to you, and it gives you your life, moment by moment.

The koan path must travel right through the human heart, or it will be something else. You bring your life just as it is through the eye of the needle. If not, koan training risks becoming a mere gymnastic of consciousness. Zen is a whole-body, whole-hearted, whole-life practice. The koan path undertaken without placing your life at stake is not the koan path. Later on, you will not thank the teacher who lets you get away with less.

The koan *Mu*

The first koan or "gate" in Wumen's collection, *The Gateless Gate*, is the koan *Mu*. You cannot walk through it without an intense practice of passionate doubt that undoes your knowing completely.

When the old teacher Zhaozhou was asked by his student, "Does a dog have buddha nature?" he responded with the utterly simple "Mu," which has the sense of "no," "un-," "does not," or "has not." A strange response, since even the smallest child in Buddhist culture will understand that all sentient beings are nothing but buddha nature. To walk through the barrier of Mu that Zhaozhou presents, to meet Zhaozhou eye to eye, you must find the vast shout of "Yes!" inside yourself that dissolves the apparent barrier of "No."

You can't get there by talking or thinking it through. Mu seals your lips, it blinds you, gives you nowhere to turn. Anything you can come up with, short of an unmistakable opening of your being way beyond all boundaries of self, will be taken by the teacher and put aside. "Not that way." "Not yet intimate." You must realize Mu for yourself, realize it as yourself and the great Earth. Then Zhaozhou's refusal of all "meaning" is vividly clear to you as a wide-open invitation. An old song like, "Yes! we have no bananas!" suddenly makes new, joyous sense.

Working with Mu involves rigorously accepting every offer of the universe as not this, not yet *this*, until *this* is at last suddenly so tremendously apparent that your heart overflows with vast gratitude, wanting nothing.

Realization experience—extraordinary "peak experience" though it may be—is just putting your head through the gate. From this point, the crooked koan path of wisdom opens before you in the moonlight of that experience, a kind of royal road of beautiful difficulty, and with every step, every koan, we make it more our own, allow what we have glimpsed to become more lucidly ourselves. It never stops opening.

And after that? There is a long seasoning in the Way, of truly learning to allow self and other to be exactly what they really are—of living life with a clear mind, and a free and magnanimous heart.

True Zen practice leaves no trace of special "enlightened" behavior in its wake. The wake of enlightenment seals over as naturally as that of a boat in water.

You may well sense something unusual in the presence of someone who has taken that long, arduous, and passionate journey, but if they are indeed walking the Way, you will detect no "stink" of holiness or piety. The long maturation in the Way is exactly the work of always realizing and living this "no trace," with less and less strain and stain of self in all the gestures of your life.

The silence of koans

"It speaks in silence. In speech, you hear its silence," says a line in the old eighth-century Zen poem by Yongjia Xuanjue, known in Japanese as *shodoka*. It speaks, it roars, it effortlessly expresses itself even in the speech of human beings caught up in concepts, delusions, and attachments. How could it not? Can you take anything out of the universe? But to realize this for yourself, first you must see through words and phrases, hear all the way through to that which is unimpeded even by the buzz of human thought. Koans free things from their names, freeing us back into original ancient stillness and timelessness. And then each thing is standing up alive, right now, brand new. The whole world is medicine.

Les Murray's poem, "The Meaning of the Universe," begins:

Everything except language
knows the meaning of existence.
Trees, planets, rivers, time
know nothing else. They express it
moment by moment as the universe.

The path of seeing into koans is a path that leads into the core of reality. It gradually imparts as your own native tongue the language that speaks into being whales and stars and liver flukes and volcanoes. To respond to a koan you must let the koan align you with the nature of things, the deepest fact of reality. It is traditional to say that someone "has the eye," meaning a Dharma eye of insight. This "eye" is opened by a direct experience of your original nature, which is no different from the self-nature or buddha nature of all things, of all "Dharmas"—including whales and stars and liver flukes and volcanoes.

To understand and begin to use language that directly knows and expresses the universe, you must shake the mud of words and concepts off your feet and walk freely right through the very center of words, not eschewing language, not dependent upon it. Actually, language expresses the meaning of existence as the universe just as wonderfully well as birdsong does, or the movement of the branches shaken by a spring wind, or the chewed bone left under the bushes by the dog. But to hear its real expression you cannot be caught by words and phrases! How is this possible? To find out, you must truly taste some koans for yourself, and let them show you how you already know it. I can draw you to the gate of a koan; it is up to you what happens after that.

A wise fool

A koan is a barrier to every part-adapted way of seeing, and brings us up against the limits of that habitual cast of mind, which has no purchase on a koan. The only way through the barrier is to fully become what has always been true, but obscured by what we add, almost imperceptibly, to the bare fact, and almost immediately mistake for the real nature of things. That adding is a kind of theft. Meditation is slowing down awareness enough to catch sight of that tiny, fleeting pickpocket move of mind that steals us endlessly from reality.

When it does break open, there is no barrier at all—that is why Mu is called the gateless gate. When you see clearly there is nothing at all. And everything is realized in its original freedom to be exactly what it is. Murray's poem goes on to say:

Even this fool of a body
lives it in part, and would
have full dignity within it
but for the ignorant freedom
of my talking mind.

Of course the wise fool of the body does not live "in part," except as it falls under the sway of the brilliantly part-adapted mind. Indeed, it knows better than we do that all things pass quickly away, but that each moment of life is edgeless and wide as awareness can be in a mortal body—as wide and unlimited as the universe. For the body belongs without apology to the universe. Only the mind resists admitting that it is equally guilty as charged!

When people "break open" in this way, it is sometimes called an opening experience, or an enlightenment experience. Joy and sorrow are indistinguishable; laughter and tears are interchangeable. These can be the hallmarks of an opening experience as it rolls through a person, shaking us free for a time from all the categories of knowing that seemed to exist before.

To understand this better, consider how great paintings rearrange us. You don't so much look at a great painting and figure it out as stand before it and, with a sense of the self dropping away, let it reorganize you from the center of your being. In the same way, great koans are not understood, but rearrange us into buddha mind.

Shikantaza: the koan of just being

Shikantaza means "nothing but sitting." Just sitting is a matter of sinking into one's bones and sinews and facing the bare ground of mind. Each thing that arises is allowed to come and go, within the one who sits. What comes and goes there—that too is gradually more empty and clear, like the one who sits. Who is it? Nothing sticks to that one. And nothing is clung to. Is it you? It seems to have no name, and to be far wider than the one called by your name. Attending to the breath is the way in, then that too falls away from prominence in the state of brightly alert attention that opens, directed to no object, attached to no content.

To practice just sitting and just breathing is already to be brushed by a powerful koan, a matter to be resolved. When you look, you see at every point the question, What is this? What is this breath? And that is a koan. Each breath is in a sense a koan, a matter to be resolved as who you really are. In this light, it has an energy that is alive with the curiosity that is so particular to the Zen Way. How do you do nothing but sitting? How do you do nothing but walking? Already, the attention you pay in zazen and shikantaza is the same keen attention that the koan path will sharpen in you. It is the mind of facing life, the mind of facing death, adding nothing at all to what is.

And whatever your path at this moment, every single step is equal in substance. Every step actualizes the true self. Every moment of practice is always the koan of having to agree to your condition, to bring unlimited friendliness to what you are, just as you are, right now. Even your obnoxiousness, your failures, your rank inadequacy is it. Your best revenge is to include it as you.

When we dare to accept and really meet our own narrowness of being, just as it is, without moving toward or away and without adding a single defense, then the very constriction in our lives subtly opens as its own way through. Suffering, which has the sense of "allowing" in its older usage (as in Christ's "suffer the little children to come unto me"), reveals itself as the secret architecture of our liberation, when it is accepted. There is no other way to be free than to be free within suffering. We don't know why this is so, but no life lived on this planet has ever contradicted it. Oddly enough, only by accepting your condition can you stop clinging to it. Then in some strange way the question of who you are and how to be is no longer a barrier. The world is at peace. To resolve the koan is to dissolve yourself, and always brings the taste of freedom, subtly different in every great koan, although every koan opens from and to the same great matter.

A direct path into reality

Practice is a continual journey into reality, into becoming a true human being. Without saying good, without saying bad, we agree again to remember and allow our experience. That passionate and compassionate curiosity of practice and alive acceptance toward our own hardship is already a change. It is already our changing. It does what it came for and we become more whole for having lived deep into that reality.

And so a sense of hardship is a question not yet lived into, a koan not yet resolved as the ground of being. To resolve the koan of a particular hardship is not to arrive at an "answer" that cures the "problem," but to fully align with what really is, what you really are. To agree to suffer or allow the hardship until the truth of your hardship may emerge. And it doesn't emerge even then as, "That's what I should do!"; it emerges as, "That's what I am!" It emerges as us.

When we don't refuse reality we are subtly released. Most spiritual disciplines say that the Way is very difficult until we accept that we will keep walking it even if it is very difficult. That very acceptance — lying somewhere between rigor, daring, and love — is a kind of opening. It changes immediately and by infinite degree who we are and how we stand in this world.

Trusted by the unknown

Holding a koan and working to resolve it with all your being builds your capacity to meet and bear with doubt. It grows tenacity, tolerance of your own inability to see, trust in sitting with the unknown. This capacity for tolerance of difficulty kindles Great Doubt — not the small, day-lit kind of doubt but something more strange that grows in you as you walk further into the dark of no longer fully "knowing." Gradually, it is more like great ripeness, great willingness, great yielding, great precariousness — indeed, great unknowing. Great Doubt is the state of letting go what it was you thought you knew, and passionately inquiring into the condition and the nature of your being with no expectations, just as the hen can hatch her egg because her heart is always listening. And so we brood upon the koan, waiting and listening it into its own precise season of breaking open; knowing nothing about the egg except roundness and a kind of attentive, objectless patience.

Becoming what it wants

To meet your true self-nature you must yield yourself and align with what is, unflinchingly. It is a matter that is, at once, as public as the stars at night, and intensely personal in its realization and in how it discloses your original being. The koan is the gateway that swings open in the dark to that experience. So it is very simple, really. It is just a matter of becoming able to do and be what it wants.

A friend of mine was walking on a beach when she came upon an Australian Aboriginal man gathering pipis from the sand. Pipis are lovely hinged shellfish that open to the shape of a butterfly—purple, blue, and pink; they are found in the littoral zone of the beach where the tide crosses the sand each day. Pipis are used by fishermen as bait, but have been an indigenous food source for thousands of generations. While fishermen may gather only twenty, this man was entitled to fill his bucket—which he did, with ease. Pipis were abundant in the stretch of sand he had carefully chosen from his reading of the current, time of day, tide, and season. They seemed to want to be available to him.

They fell to talking about fish and the drought, and how in times of drought and such low river levels, saltwater fish travel far up into the rivers and stay there. My friend was intrigued and dug for the facts, in the way that we have all learned to do. "Why don't the fish come back down the river?" she asked, perhaps waiting for a scientific explanation. He simply looked at her, almost sorry for her, as though she were missing the obvious. "Because they don't *want* to," he replied.

Because they don't want to. How simple. How hard to see, when you are trained toward the analytical cast of mind. Looking for the pieces of a puzzle, we miss the whole, the grain of things, the Tao, the innate sense, apparent everywhere in the universe, of what it wants.

So working with koans, letting them have their way with you completely, you become what it wants. Simple as that. The mind trained to see parts seeks for medicine that would defeat the "diseased part" of the universe; the mind revised to its original wholeness sees very differently: the whole world is medicine. The self and all its secret misery of separateness and fear of extinction is resolved completely into that endless, indivisible whole.

Every "why" on earth melts into that great fact of wholeness. Every koan demands our own dissolving of the self into that great fact. It wants to. There is no other way to be here, be immortal, than to join with what is, which is entirely what it wants.

CHAPTER 6

"He is me"

THE HEART OF THE ZEN PATH is the relationship between teacher and student, a relationship not quite like any other, although master and apprentice comes close. It is not a guru relationship, of self-surrender through surrender to the teacher, and not a psychotherapy relationship. It is an intimate guiding and testing process that very closely observes, encourages, and challenges the student's attempts to experience who they really are. Teacher and student completely meet and recognize each other in the student's experience of buddha nature, self-nature.

Every stage of this process—subtle and low-lit, or dramatic and radiant—can be said to be the transmission of buddha-mind, or mirror-mind, which receives each thing just as it is. Accord deepens throughout the years of training, until student and teacher can truly say they are of one mind. At such a point, transmission can be said to have become a clear and public matter.

Receiving transmission is not the same as saying that the student takes on the mind of the teacher. We meet in one mind that is not you and not me. Self-nature has been yours from the beginning, just as the Buddha said in his moment of enlightenment, "All beings are already Buddha, already awake." But that does not mean you can recognize it, just as the Buddha added, "but only their delusions and attachments prevent them from knowing it."

An initiatory path

Coleman Barks is a fine translator of Rumi's poetry. I once heard that Barks was once asked by an interviewer, "Do you love Rumi?" Everything in his work displays passionate recognition of Rumi; and yet, or and so, he replied, after a pause, "I love what Rumi loved." This is a fine way to understand the true nature of the bond between Zen student and teacher. It is the shared love of something gradually held more and more clearly in common—at the beginning, incipient in the student and unimpeded in the teacher, and aroused to full awareness by the teacher in the student by every means available. When at last they see completely with the same eyes, there is the profound congruence of "I love what Rumi loves." They share one eye, one understanding. (Barks has since told me he is not responsible for this gem, but he's nonetheless pleased to be wrongly attributed with it.)

The journey of teacher and student together on the path, like any true initiatory adventure or process of apprenticeship and mastery, usually extends over many years, or sometimes decades, of life. It has phases of forming, maturing, weathering, seasoning, and subtly completing, and there are important obligations of tending and bringing things to consciousness on the side of the student as well as the teacher. One of the marks of maturity in a Zen student is the awareness that, just as it is only your own self-nature that can blossom into full awareness and life, your practice is your own responsibility to maintain, your bodhicitta fire is finally yours to tend. If you forget this and seek to be carried, a teacher will bring you back to awareness at a moment he or she judges to be ripe, refusing your projection, turning your assumptions back to you, raising a shout that echoes back into the dark of you and chases your life and spirit and daring out from hiding.

Transmission mind to mind

Transmission means literally "passing across." Zen speaks of a direct transmission of the actual nature of reality that can be received by the mind laid open and bare in stillness. The Buddha twirls a flower, and his student Mahakasyapa smiles. This transmission lies beyond all scriptures, beyond all explanation, beyond all teaching: it is directly experienced, or passed by until your brooding ripens you further. Another name for it is "realization." The teacher is a vital partner in the process of helping you open yourself to this gift from the universe, in whatever form it triggers your recognition of what you are, what you have been from the very beginning.

Then the teacher's long and patient work is to walk with you into a deeper, more sustained and lucid appreciation of what you have seen in that moment of great concordance, guiding, testing, and opening your eye—the singular eye of realization that sees into the Dharma and each moment with unswerving confidence. The koan path seems to be the best means of refining and polishing your understanding in this subtle and mysterious matter of opening your eye. That long journey is taken together through your own life and the riches of the tradition—the two are finally inseparable.

This initiatory journey is also your gradual initiation by the teacher into the treasury of experience and practice of the past, which is a history that makes demands on the living. In the ceremony of transmission that marks the formal beginning of teaching, the old teacher presents to the new teacher a document that says this person is deemed fit to be a holder and transmitter of an incomparable tradition, a tradition for which great teachers of the past have given their lives. It will be passed on through this person. Its continuing strength and integrity is in the hands of the new teacher.

So you reach a point where you can feel and know beyond doubt that there is one mind, one realization, although in an important sense this congruence is happening all the way through this intense relationship. But full unanimity may be reached. Then, in one sense, an ardent and arduous phase of training is complete; in another sense, practice has just begun at last. The long maturation in the Way opens from here.

Transmission in the wider sense is openness itself, and in that state transmission never stops happening; the gift is always in motion. It is intimacy itself, a state of such complete accord with all things that there is no fixed and separate self to be found. So that moment when the habits of the world are suddenly broken is the moment where the nature of transmission is laid bare, as Dongshan's enlightenment story clearly shows.

The master's likeness

Together with Caoshan, Dongshan is the great ancestor of the Caodong (in Chinese) or Soto (in Japan) line of Zen. The telling I'm offering here is based on William Powell's translation of *The Record of Dongshan*.

Dongshan had worked with the great Guishan for some time, but Guishan felt that his heart was not yet at rest, and Dongshan agreed with him. Guishan sent him to seek out his own former student, Yunyan—a crusty and difficult old hermit living in a series of linked caves—saying, "Living in those caves is a man of the Way. If you are able to push aside the grasses and gaze into the wind, then you will find him worthy of your respect." Dongshan stayed with Yunyan for some time, and the record includes some memorable encounters with Yunyan, encounters full of the roaring wind that has always been blowing. Dongshan's great doubt deepened through this time. And then Dongshan prepared to move on in his search.

But just before leaving he asked Yunyan a question. "If, after many years, someone should ask if I am able to portray the master's likeness, how should I respond?"

After remaining quiet for a while, Yunyan said, "Just this person."

Dongshan was lost in thought. Yunyan said, "Chieh Acarya, having assumed the burden of this Great Matter, you must be very cautious."

Dongshan remained dubious about what Yunyan had said. But later, while crossing a river, he caught sight of his reflected image and experienced a great awakening to the meaning of the previous exchange. He composed the following poem in gratitude:

> *Earnestly avoid seeking without,*
> *Lest it recede far from you.*
> *Today I am walking alone,*
> *Yet everywhere I meet him.*
> *He is now no other than myself,*
> *But I am not now him.*
> *It must be understood in this way,*
> *In order to become intimate.*

Saying that you have your teacher's portrait is a way of saying that you have their likeness, that you have seen with the same eye. When you have truly caught a powerful glimpse of your own original face, you will have your teacher's likeness. There's no choice in that matter.

So whose face is that? And in any case, what is a face? And why does it call so clearly to us from our first days of life? How is it that we can read such an incredible array of subtlety, meaning, and recognition from such a tiny vocabulary of possibilities as are there in the elements of face? What is it about a face that leaves so deep an impression upon the heart?

Just this person

This moment of parting was in fact the last face-to-face encounter between Dongshan and Yunyan, because Powell notes that the opening words, "Just before leaving Yunyan," can equally be translated as "Just before the master's death," "just before Yunyan's death." So this is not a casual goodbye but a parting at the core, with Yunyan very sick and close to death.

Yunyan remained quiet for a while, and then he said, "Just this person." What is this "remaining quiet"? Thinking it over? Surely not. Dongshan has asked a Dharma question. Everything is alive in the field of that question, pierced as it is by Yunyan's fast-approaching death. It cannot be thought over. But it is vividly presented, moment by moment, and here it is, in bare, plain form. He remained quiet. And then he said, "Just this person."

Zen, like poetry, is hard on words, insisting that the core of reality lies beyond words and phrases, yet resorting to words and phrases, as human beings do—and not as makeshift gesture or explanation or apology, but as an immediate disclosure of that reality. Yunyan offers Dongshan, and us, subtle and rigorous words of silence. He dwells nowhere and brings forth that mind—he remains quiet for a while, and then says, "Just this person." Here is my likeness that I would have you convey, says Yunyan.

Now there's another interesting translator's note at this point. "Just this person" is a variant on the common phrase, in ninth-century China, "Just this man of Han." And "Just this man of Han," in medieval Chinese legal custom, is the phrase in which a criminal formally confessed his guilt in court. Guilty as charged, says Yunyan. I take full responsibility; no teacher can take less. Stripped back to the true person of no rank whatsoever.

Yunyan's reply left Dongshan lost in thought. I do not think he was thinking deeply so much as losing his way from thought. Another kind of profound quiet has descended, as Dongshan unfolds more of himself to try to meet the simplicity of self that Yunyan has offered him, so barely, so plainly. Another koan tells us, "Not knowing is most intimate." When you have almost slipped beyond the mooring of thought and can only point at the slowly rising sun or a little flower in the grass, you are very near, the ground is fertile.

The work of compassion

Yunyan watches Dongshan very closely through this. I imagine him lying down on his sickbed, watching. He sees this fertile doubt, sees something moving, and he says, "You must be very careful." Having "assumed the burden of this Great Matter," you must be very careful, very cautious. Dongshan is great with it at this moment. But "assuming the burden" also has a double meaning here; when a criminal acknowledged his crime in old China and personally assumed responsibility for it, he was said to "have assumed the burden." Guilty!

This double play of meanings is very beautiful, and wise. His humor has serious depth. The old Chan masters like Yunyan had a very Australian sense of humor: dry, dark, a little bit wicked. So there's an aspect of "Now you begin to share my guilt, so take care. . . ." But you know there really is a karmic weight to seeing into the Great Matter: from now on you must continually work to align with that in all the parts of your being or be dragged by a feeling of failure, a sense of being out of the Tao, of cheapening the Way. Wumen called it "climbing a mountain of swords with bare feet." Painful, the travail of compassion. So your share of the weight of the world must be carried, and carried consciously. To see this way is dangerous work. Great work, if you can get it.

"You must be very cautious," Yunyan warns Dongshan. Why cautious? Dongshan is not quite through the gate; not quite pecked free of the shell. A most delicate moment: if you cling to what you think you have found, then you have lost it; if you try for it, it has eluded you immediately. Remaining willing, open, curious, alive, without a thought of attaining or losing anything at all—this is feeling your way along a wall in the dark. Cautious. Very cautious.

The dark waters

So Dongshan went away, full of alive brooding, live doubt. Feeling his way in the dark of it. And then, as he was crossing a stream, he caught sight of something: his own face in the water. Just that fleeting glimpse broke him open to the presentation of his teacher. Indeed, he awoke, when he saw his own face, to the very portrait of his own teacher. Now he understood Yunyan remaining quiet for awhile and then saying, "Just this person."

To see the flash of himself in the water at this moment was to see, and to love, what his teacher loved. He saw it—whatever you may wish to call it. It may have many names, and it has no name at all. But how beautiful it is.

And to catch sight of it while crossing the stream, the source, as it is called in French: this is not unlike looking upstream into the dark from which we come and to which we will return, the source of each breath; each speck of dust; each mountain, ocean, and single blade of grass; each dream, artwork, gesture, toenail; and every unrepeatable human face.

In this moment, transmission between teacher and student is complete. Yunyan may well have been dead by this moment, but Dongshan looked down and saw his face, and his teacher was vividly alive right there, in that dark, rippling water of the source. He was utterly in possession of his teacher's likeness.

So he saw his face, he saw no face at all, and he wrote a gatha of thanks. It begins: "*Earnestly avoid seeking without.*" This is the fundamental and enduring undertaking of Zen meditation. Don't move an inch away from it. Don't look outside. Don't have inside or outside; let that go free, lest it recede far from you. "*Today I am walking alone, but everywhere I meet him.*" This is a beautiful phrase. It has more than the sense of walking alone—it *means* walking alone, completely accompanied, the small self gone. The universe roars, the small self falls away, we are joined at last by all beings, "*yet everywhere I meet him.*" I'll leave you to ponder who "he" is at this point, when you meet him. There are a thousand ways to be met, at last. Then Dongshan takes a beautiful turn. "*He is now no other than myself, but I am not now him. It must be understood in this way in order to become intimate.*"

You could say that some distinctions save your life: "*He is now no other than myself, but I am not now him.*" Dongshan's poem lets you feel the force of this complete intimacy that is your birthright from the very beginning. His word for it here is *me*, or *myself.* Do you know that one? Just watching the cedar wattle fronds move in silvery light and shadow, with no thought of anything at all; just smelling the sharp scent of rain on warm pavements; just stroking the cat's fur, watching the flames. Truly, nothing is missing. Every day is full of such moments, before and beyond thought. These are tiny intimations of the overwhelming wave that breaks as realization and shows you your true face.

And then he delicately teases that complete intimacy ("he," "myself") out, from "I," that very self-important, singularly capitalized letter in the English language. I can clearly recall the moment sitting on the back steps of my childhood house in Queensland when I discovered the word "I," at the age of three. I was reading a story and I kept seeing this strange, slightly alarming stick-insect of a word, "I." I went and asked my father about it. "Oh," he said, "That's *you.*" *Oh!*

It was an amazing moment, because it carved me out of the universe, and for that reason it was also a terrible one, and it is a long, hard road back from there. Yet Dongshan recalled himself completely at last with one accidental glance to his reflection in the river. "*He is no other than myself, but I am not now him.*" The most intimate and private thing of all turns out to be held in common, in profound agreement, with all beings everywhere: it is the same in everyone. We all receive evanescent, momentary intimations of the true "I" whether we can yet bring that to vivid realization or not.

St. Francis of Assisi said, "What you are looking for is what is looking." Christ, in the Gospel of Thomas says, "You can never take hold of it but you can never lose it." It looks through you as through a window. And sometimes by sheer act of grace, sometimes by dint of exquisite and prolonged concentration, you catch its face in the dark waters and can never be the same again.

He is me . . . and yet . . .

Dongshan's delicate teasing out of "he" from "I" also points back into his heartfelt question to Yunyan: "Do I have your likeness?" Am I your true descendant? Have I yet seen deeply enough? Another koan says this of the teacher-student relationship: "We are born on the same stem, but we do not die on it." What is this about?

There is a place in the stem where the leaf fits exactly — a perfect meeting. As you begin to see into the Dharma, you see at last what your teacher sees; your insight opens to one Dharma, that which your teacher also sees. No realization experience is the same as any other and yet there is just one realization, a perfect coinciding. But at the same time that place in the stem where the leaf fits exactly is shaped, as all life is shaped, by death, by the great succession of time in which each thing becomes completely itself. We unfurl and live and finally fall. That place in the stem that meets the leaf exactly is where all things interchange and nothing bumps into anything else. The meeting place of leaf and stem is also perfectly formed for the departure of the leaf. There is just one Dharma, one realization; but your expression of the Dharma is as distinct and individual as the lines on your own face. So it is that we are born on the same stem, but we do not die on it. Every death, utterly distict.

Is death a barrier to that free interchange? In an earlier exchange, when Dongshan said that he was planning to leave, Yunyan asked him when he would return. "I'll wait until you have a fixed address," said Dongshan to his beloved hermit teacher, who was obviously close to death in his cave in the wilderness. What fixed address is to be found in a universe where all things pass quickly away? Where is the fixed address in vast emptiness? Yunyan said, and we can hear a lot of feeling in his words, "After your departure, it will be hard to meet again." Whose departure is that? And where can you go? Dongshan said, "It will be hard *not* to meet."

There at that place where the breath out becomes complete and takes its mysterious turn toward the breath in, when we are one with that, there is no base to rely on, nothing is fixed, and there are no barriers at all. Everything meets at the source of all peace. Indeed it is hard not to meet, when you have realized one mind. Every point in the universe is it.

A teacher has nothing to offer

If you ask for a teacher's teaching, he or she can offer you nothing but what is yours already—your own essential nature. It has never been anything but your own. Teacher and student are the same: the true you, exactly like the true me, is alone in the universe and there is no one to transmit to you and nothing to transmit. We all share the one word, "I." What you are looking for is realized as the one who looks. You can never take hold of it and equally, for that very reason, you can never lose it.

But teacher and student are at first very different in their relationship to this abiding fact. The long and subtly changing relationship with a teacher is dedicated to waking you to your birthright by every skillful means available. When you know it for yourself with complete equality, when the teacher's Dharma is no other than your own unrepeatable realization, then you have the likeness of your teacher, the likeness of the whole universe. You come at last into full possession of your inheritance.

PART TWO

One teaching
upside-down

CHAPTER 7

The tiger's kindness

To PRACTICE ZEN MEDITATION IS to settle and touch and convey the heart-mind—that dark eye of seeing into your true self-nature. And to continue more deeply on the path is to agree to grow more and more accountable to what we glimpse when we shatter the habitual glaze that protects us from the real condition of our being. Until we know this for ourselves, we are bumblebees bumping the glass of a windowpane, longing for the field and flower beyond, but firmly investing in the enduring resistance of the glass.

When we practice becoming more porous and boundless, the full intensity of the natural world can both gradually and suddenly break through—and then there is no glass! That amazing discovery can feel like being in love with all beings and the whole world, just as it is. This is a very expansive state of interchange, where terror or loneliness have no purchase.

Such an expansive state brings to light and rests upon a kind of confidence in our place at the heart of things—the confidence of seeing who you really are, what this really is. At the same moment it rests on the absolute clarity that there is no base to rely on, nothing at all to cling to. From this no-base grows a fearlessness that does not depend on personal reassurance; a fearlessness like tiger.

How can this fearlessness grow so that we join more fully in the human task of minding the universe? Of sharing, with all that is, a mind shaped as universe is shaped?

The fearlessness of the tiger

Let's walk into this matter through an old Korean Zen koan in honor of the fearlessness of "Tiger," who burns bright in the forest of every human being on the path of liberation and, mercifully, stalks every one of us. I first encountered this marvelous koan in the presence of an Australian Korean-Zen nun, Chi Kwung:

> *The tiger fears the human heart.*
> *The human fears the tiger's kindness.*

I notice in myself a tiny contraction of fear just hearing that the human heart is fearful to the tiger. I've always loved knowing there are tigers; I've been made curiously hopeful by their strolling presence in the world. So what is there about the human heart that could be fearful to the tiger?

We may be living at a time when the last natural-born wild tigers still prowl the earth. That this could be allowed to happen or considered acceptable is one of the things I fear about the human heart. Tiger is important. Animals have made us human; they are perhaps the germ of the earliest ideas we ever had as a species. We have observed them, learned to understand their superb specializations, and built on that inner human knowing through metaphor, dance, and art. Tiger ways are a deep part of becoming human. No doubt there are still some saber-teeth marks sunk deep in the memory of my neck and yours—you can feel them when you watch a tiger moving, intent and relaxed, rippling with such conserved energy and unerring musculature. Even my own small house cat carries the noble swagger of tiger and conveys it to my grateful eye. If we don't know tiger any more, we lose our "tigerishness."

Fear of tiger is perhaps not so far from what some call the fear of God: that healthy, vivid fear—if I don't wake up, I am losing my life!—that can wake us with a roar. This is fear to the brink of gladness. Practice for me has always had that edge of almost lovely fear and powerful intent, both of which I associate with the tiger.

But the koan tells us that the tiger fears the human heart. It fears the contracted, scared human heart, which cannot yield completely and be consumed, be the feast, "the sweet party of the most simple things." It seems to me the one thing to be truly feared in this world is that contraction of the scared human heart, that shrinkage into careful separateness—the ground of all violence and destructiveness. If anything is going to obstruct or ruin the unfolding of this earth it is probably something to be found in that fearful human heart, its ungenerosity and lack of imagination.

The carefully repressed and contracted heart polices its objects of love, subscribes to a "reality" of scarcity (which may also be called greed and hatred), and may well be the greatest threat to our planet. Once we had "citizens"; now we have "consumers." There is such fear driving "the consumer": not "eat or be eaten" but "devour incessantly or you may not exist at all." This is a costly business. Recently I learned that the ecological footprint of how we live here in Australia is such that for every person on Earth to live as we do, seven more Earths are needed. Nobody yet has indicated where these are to be found. It is of little consolation to learn that the way of life in the United States requires eleven more Earths.

There seems good reason for the tiger to fear the human heart.

The strange offer of fear

Fear. That is our most retarded place. The secret of creativity is inti-mately tied to it. Look into your deepest fear. Is it loss? old age? sickness? death, of the one dearest to you, or of yourself? Is it being unloved? being all alone? Whatever it is, there you will find your storehouse of locked-up energy. And the key to the storehouse: turn toward your sharpest fear. Accept its strange, surprisingly empowering offer. Can you include your source of dread as if it might be your most valuable treasure, your secret joy? Fear makes us clench our life into the contorted shape that appears to avoid contact with all our sources of fear, but the anguished shape we form in doing so is the negative impress of that fear, stamped upon every-thing we do. It is such a great strain to maintain the posture of fear. And fear keeps us living so close to transformation and yet doggedly turned away from it. ("Doggedly"—that seems unfair to dogs, who show much bravery toward reality. *Humanly* turned away!)

The Sufi poet Rumi tells of the farmer who goes out to check his ox in the dark barn without a light. A lion has lain down in the place of the ox. The farmer unwittingly feels the shoulder of the lion in the utter darkness. His heart strangely stirred to beat faster, he reassuringly pats the shoulder of God. If he could see what he was doing, he would die. The unknown is the roaring in us all and in every leaf coming forth in the light; to hear it is to be devoured by it, torn free from all habitual familiarity into a familiarity far more profound and terrifying. We may even catch a glimpse of it in our own familiar faces—the mystery of not-knowing.

So this may be one clue to the tiger's kindness: that kindness is the great freedom itself, life coming awake with a roar—a wonderfully dan-gerous idea!

Once when I was around twelve years old my brother and sister and I sat up around the kitchen table nearly an entire night speculating about the fate of the planet. We pulled on that thread until it gradually unravelled the entire potential catastrophe: overpopulation, destruction of habitat, loss of species, nuclear waste, and "Mutually Assured Destruction." It was frightening and yet it was spellbinding, a kind of initiation toward adulthood, to take on the weight of such things, to begin to take on the weight of the world. I went to bed close to daybreak, devastated, exhilarated, flattened.

The next day, deeply tired, I walked into the kitchen, pulled out the same chair as the night before, and sat down at the table. It is impossible to say what happened in that most simple of ordinary miracles—pulling out a chair, sitting down, touching the table—but I do know that what sat down as me was abruptly an utter flood of assurance and gratitude for the perfection of everything that is, just as it is, beyond all doubt. I touched the chair, sat down, rested my hands on the table, and each of these miraculous actions cleared the whole matter up. It is all okay. How closely these two nestle in, limitedness and unlimitedness, one the very shape of the other.

The tiger's kindness: Dogen called it "body and mind dropped away." There is a ruthless quality to this matter. As the old Chinese poets liked to remind us, heaven and earth are ruthless.

Ruthlessness

Barry Lopez, a nature writer, once spent hundreds of days travelling in the bellies of freight 747s, with the vast array of things we believe we need—and apparently need *now!* These planes carry assorted loads, but the things the pilots remember are the very costly: an absurdly priced Bentley; 70,000 pounds of gold; animals, from Vietnamese potbelly pigs to draughthorses, bulls, goats, and ostriches. One pilot told him about going down into the hold one night to take a look at a white tiger. This animal charged as ferociously as the cage permitted, and sent the pilot reeling onto his back. The animal's roar drowned out the sound of the engines and nearly stopped his heart.

One day the tiger's kindness will stop our hearts. The roar that wakes us and saves us from all our doubts is complete intimacy with life, inseparable from intimacy with death. It might be the Buddha's glimpse of the morning star, the fleeting sight of a plum tree in blossom, or a twig breaking underfoot. The old teachers spoke of realization, of seeing into the core of our own being, which is the core of the universe, as the Great Death. It is an intimation of death, cessation, stopping, that opens up our great life. "Body and mind dropped away."

The old Hebrew prophets sang of it: "For ye shall go out with joy, and be led forth with peace, the mountains and the hills shall break forth before you into singing, and all the trees of the field shall clap their hands." The mystery at the heart of each blade of grass, pebble, cloud, dream, and human body is intimate with death, lit by death, flooded with life. Right now!

The *Tao Te Ching* tells us that the softest thing on Earth overcomes the hardest thing on Earth. So coming back again and again to mindfulness, to agreeing to be here with what really is, overcomes the stubborn human heart. The heart must break completely open so that everything may be here, fully itself, at last. It's said that until you've wept deeply, you haven't meditated. Tears can be the first sign of grace.

The tiger's kindness is not offered as a bland reassurance; it guarantees precisely nothing. The wild reality at the heart of the universe and the core of ourselves both generously ushers us into this amazing life, and is absolutely dangerous to us, promising our extinction; we are completely dependent on its terrifying whim for our existence. Mortality, mutability, and infinite variety are our terrifying condition and the place in which we make our home. The cliff-edge of birth and death, the shoulder of the lion in the apparently familiar and hospitable dark— that's where we live.

Life cycle, gift cycle

Another way of looking into the tiger's kindness is to think about the way this life is an endless cycle of giving and receiving. Human life itself is granted as an extraordinary gift—as far as we know one of the rarest gifts that anyone can have anywhere in the universe. And everything until this point, from the Big Bang through eons of pure energy, then eons of matter, then eons of life coming into being, life after life after life, has yielded to open the way to you and to this moment. Everything that has ever lived is laying down its life all the way, like a great royal road leading exactly to this life, this consciousness, and this rarest of human chances. What a gift! If you look into a newborn baby's eyes, you can see the gift there still so clearly, the planets and the stars still turning in the baby's eyes. Everything is given. Where it comes from, nobody knows.

When you open yourself to the falling away of a life, there's the other revelation of the true nature of the universe, that everything is also asked. The gift is passed on entirely; it leaves our hands and goes around the corner back into the dark. We don't know where it goes—or need to know. This too is the nature of the tiger's kindness.

This wild animal body that we walk about in is simple and ultimately fearless in how it meets suffering. It is here for all kinds of suffering and all kinds of joy. It doesn't hold back. It knows how to do it: how to be born, how to continue to be born deeper and deeper into life, more and more richly layered by experience. And then, how to let go, to give way and disappear back into that dark. But something blocks us from truly knowing what the body knows. Something balks in us and says, "No, not me! I believe I've been granted an exception." This is the comfort path of misery, which has little true curiosity, or lasting joy, or real creativity.

Why is the comfort path a secret misery? It looks so easy and beguiling, and sells so well that the great Earth and most of our fellow species have been placed under duress or outright notice. Cosmologist Brian Swimme's parable of the quality of "hawkness" is helpful here. The "hawkness of the hawk" depends upon the extraordinary speed of the mouse. If it were easy to catch mice, if mice were fatter and slower, and tended to walk past hawks, gradually hawks would become fatter and more roly-poly, their eyes would go dim and they would need spectacles after a while; then even the ability to lurch toward a passing mouse would diminish, until we would have to ask—bereft somehow of a deep part of our own strength—where is the quality of hawkness? Gone, disappeared into that secret misery of comfort.

Loss and creativity

In a strange and interesting way the tiger's kindness is deeply connected to both loss and fear. In this universe a truly radical creativity somehow seems to need the companionship of fear and loss, the inevitability of relinquishment. You see it in the universe itself. It came into being from an extraordinary sacrificial fire like none seen before; and it is destined to extinguish itself, which is the fate of all individual lives. Individuality, consciousness of self, this unrepeatable you, is born of sexuality and mortality—consciousness cannot come into its exquisitely differentiated forms without these two. Ungendered, and so bypassing sexual reproduction, an amoeba repeats the same amoeba endlessly. There are no two individuals giving rise to a third unrepeatable individual who will reproduce, and die, and make way for new individuals, never seen before or since.

So sex and death, the karmic round, is essential to our kind of consciousness itself, a consciousness that may get caught behind glass of its own making, but is also free to fly unhindered in reality. Our condition is not a regrettable, accidental interruption of holiness: it is holiness. It is it. The blade of this life is so keen and sharp. It wounds.

Sitting deeply in zazen is a way of working your way back to the roaring inside each thing. We come back to the freedom of emptiness by unpicking all the locks we put between us and it. It's also a way of coming back to real suffering: not doctored reality, but what really is. Life is constantly undoing everything we believe we truly want. Newton called it the Second Law of Thermodynamics, Shakespeare's Edgar in *King Lear* called it "Ripeness is all." Life itself is in time the undoing of everything we passionately believe we want. It continually separates us from that obscure or obvious object of desire that never truly settles. It's going to do that in any case—have you noticed?

So why not join it? Why not join its endless doing and undoing? Every time we do agree to accept difficulty, irritation, or subtle or demanding offers from the universe, even our own decline, failure, and death, we are lending ourselves to the deep current of it all; we are practicing truly being, without hedging anything. This is not the same as giving in to collapse or despair, but more like riding the swell of the moment, choosing the moment to catch the wave to shore. Like a bodysurfer, completely entering the one wave, unimpeded. The clearest actions in response to the profound threat of planetary ecological disaster, whether from indifference and slow ruin or catastrophe, must begin by entering what is, just as we truly are. We agree to the deep movement of the Tao, and from there each graceful, useful, timely, and helpful action can open, as naturally as grass bends to the wind.

No glass

Anna Kamienska, an obscure Polish poet about whom little is known, wrote "A Prayer That Will Be Answered." It begins, "Lord let me suffer much / and then die." That is possibly the one prayer that will always be answered. She continues: "Let me walk through silence / and leave nothing behind not even fear"; and she ends by asking, "And let my poem stand clear as a windowpane / bumped by a bumblebee's head."

In every condition of the world's unfolding, we have only this moment now to be who we truly are. And part of who we truly are, very recognizably, is that insistent bumblebee-bumping of the head against this strange pane of glass we call *mind*. Practice asks you, What if there were no glass? What if that were the true nature and boundless generosity of the universe?

At that place where the breath out becomes complete, and being takes its mysterious turn back toward the breath in, when we are one with that, there is no barrier, no glass at all. Everything meets exactly with everything else at this dimensionless point that is the source of all peace.

This is a meeting place way beyond all limitation. I feel confident that we know a great deal about it through our wild animal bodies that know how to live, to die, to give birth, to grow old, to make love, and to dream us endlessly into our unimaginable lives. All we have to do, in a sense, is sit still and catch up with the deep slow knowing this body already has coded within every cell: that it is all okay. Every contact we make with that forms antibodies to the comfort path and its secret misery. Not that comfortable complacency ever stops banging its tambourine on every street corner. "Join the Consolation Army now!" it urges. "Enrollments always open!"

Martin Buber quotes words of the Baal Shem Tov, the original Hasidic master, words that make it so plain it stings the heart: "Alas! the world is full of enormous lights and mysteries, and we shut them out with one small hand!" Is that small hand over our eyes, I wonder? Or is it held out before us, a gesture of "No, stop!" trying fruitlessly to hold it all at bay?

But grace can break through, and does. We find that we share one mind with the universe itself, and that we have always shared that mind since before even our parents were born. To fully achieve the grace of our own minds is to realign decisively with that, continually resisting the pull of habitual consciousness.

And yet, how strong that pull is. Raymond Carver's poem "The Window" describes how it is when a storm blows in and knocks out the electricity, setting everything back into original simplicity in the vast calm that follows: trees translucent, covered with an icy rime. The deep rearrangement of everything penetrates all the way into the poet's own heart. "I knew better," he says, "But at that moment, I felt I'd never in my life made any false promises…My thoughts were virtuous." But later on that morning, as it usually is, electricity was restored. The sun comes out and dissolves the hoarfrost, the spell of the extraordinary is dispelled, the weight of habit duly restored to all things, and the poem ends back inside the dull, unspoken ache of ordinary consciousness. "And things stood as they had before." All of it, back again.

Who doesn't recognize that disappointing moment when we find we have traded in our birthright once more for the ramified little defense case tirelessly presented by the ego?

The kindliness of all beings

The tiger's unbidden and inexhaustible kindness brushes us at every moment. We're drowning in it even while we insist on thinking we're swimming somewhere. But sometimes we accept the offer, and the name for that in some parts is "grace." Grace is the moment when we understand the kindliness of all beings, including the tiger that will snatch our life and all our certainties away, when we accept all offers for all eternity. It is like seeing with the eyes of a hawk above the river of time: all time at once, not just the tight little bend we're rounding now.

So this is the human condition—that one of us sees this, and the other one resolutely does not. The one who is not afraid of the tiger's kindness—"myself"—recognizes in it the deepest communion, central to the entire universe, all beings intersecting at once. Every point in the universe is the center, and it radiates from here, from myself. It is a kind of gratitude, but one that has no object, no name, no tongue. It is pure giving, yielding, joining. All of us freely burn up in the fire of this communion, the fire that runs through all things. "Myself" occupies no space whatsoever. The other one—"I"—walks the karmic world of "I am born; I pay taxes. One day they reckon I will die, but I refuse to believe it." That one is capable of eating at the feast while resolutely not believing in it for a moment.

And yet all of us walk out at the end; snow has stopped falling for a blessed moment, the sky is full of stars. We gather round the old well, hold hands and sing, before dispersing into the dark.

The long work of ripening in Zen is the ongoing work of bringing the demands of the ego back into proportion with this. The great life is one that takes part in minding the universe, participating in its flow, making room for the other, bending to the roundness of a life. To begin to save all beings, you must wake up to this.

The old Chan teachers lived freely in this fifty-fifty human condition, reconciling this in every gesture, every word, every rigorous act of awareness. Being blind, we think we have to go out and meet things. But being truly blind, we find that they come to meet us instead. Remember? You never have to go more than halfway, and the universe becomes the accomplice of all your wishes.

So, each one, each thing, longing to be recognized by everything else—that is the heart's longing for rest, and sometimes we call it "saving all beings." We know that the Earth yearns for the Sun, though we call it gravity. And grave it is—grave as the tiger's kindness. Dante, emerging from the underworld in the *Inferno*, called it "the love that moves the stars and the other planets," and we have our own gate to it, hidden right here in this mortal human body. The longing for recognition: mountains feel it, and clouds, stars, creaking floorboards, sudden laughter, singing crickets in the grass—all long for that utterly open recognition and boundless acceptance, as just who we truly are, just as we truly are.

Our own original face, recognizable at last. Don't resist. Insist on not resisting.

CHAPTER 8

Songlines
of the Way

L IVING AND TEACHING IN AUSTRALIA, it feels increasingly
important to me to begin to seek out and walk the songlines of the
Way, to explore the affinities and resonance between two traditions, two
spiritualities, the Australian Aboriginal and Zen, as they meet in this
country we share. To reconcile practice with the place where we are, to
fully realize reciprocity, all the way down.

That conversation seems natural over time in the reverberant field
between these two, deepening us and widening the Dharma. It can't be
hurried along.

But if the rain falls, the earth can't help but get wet. Some intimacy
with an Aboriginal sense of being here, and some tending of that awareness, can only green Zen practice here in the ancient red continent, can
only make it more truly itself. It will not be the first time that Zen has been
enlarged and refined by the more ancient earth-based spirituality that
awaits it in a particular place. The Dharma is waiting to stand up here in
olive-grey saltbush and red earth, grey kangaroos and satin bowerbirds.

Does the Dharma come from somewhere?

On a night of heavy snow in the winter of 642 C.E., an old Chan hermit called Huiman took refuge in an ancient tomb in the grounds of the Hui Shan temple of Loyang. He was a man who traveled light, keeping just two pennies as insurance in winter, and throwing them away in summer. Going into the temple early the next morning, he met the abbot, who wondered at his presence and asked—and I'm not sure that this was entirely a Dharma question—"Where did you come from?" The master answered, "Does the Dharma come from somewhere?"

The abbot was intrigued and sent a man to search for his tracks and bring him back, but he only found snow piled up five feet in every direction. He remarked, wondering deeply, "The depth of this cannot be fathomed."

Indeed it can't, and anything we might say about it is pretty limited. Huiman left no trace behind him in the deep snow. Realization does not linger and explain itself to anyone or show itself in special ways. It leaves no trace, and this no trace continues forever.

But does the Dharma come from somewhere? Do we come from somewhere, for that matter? Where is that? And where do we go?

It speaks in silence

The depth of this is truly beyond fathoming. Red earth goes on for more than a thousand kilometers in the center of Australia, sandhill after sandhill. Tiny finches dart between the tussock grasses. After rain, flowers shake in the spiky bushes, and rainbows appear even at midday. Near sunset, a human shadow can stretch for fifty meters across the finely textured ground. The depth of this is unfathomable. The little dream of who we think we are can pose the question, "Where does the Dharma come from?" but Dream answers in the eloquence of olive-grey saltbush, of old rocks in the sun. It speaks in silence. And yet in speech you hear its silence too.

The abbot registered that immense silence a little late and sent for the old hermit, but there was too little coming or going left in the old hermit to leave a trace in snow five feet deep.

Still, we can trace some of the tracks and travels of the Dharma in the historic sense that we might make of its journey here, and notice its many intimate meetings and marriages from the earliest moment with indigenous Earth-based spiritualities. In India, Buddhism was founded by a wandering, forest-dwelling yogi who sat under a tree and was enlightened by the dawn star. The very tradition of forest-dwelling monks aligns earliest Buddhism in part with a return to the old ways of the indigenous forest-dwelling tribes of the subcontinent. Buddhism journeyed on from India to China, where a profound meeting and melding with Taoism took place in the emergence of Chan; to Japan, where Chan flowered as Zen in intimate contact with older Shinto roots; to Tibet, where Buddhism and Bon spirituality entwined in the Dharma that arose there; and now to Australia, where there is the most ancient unbroken line of Earth-based spirituality, still alive in various ways and forms despite its collision two hundred years ago with post-Enlightenment Western culture, in its most aggressively colonizing mode.

The Zen we inherit here, now, brings all of this richness and proclivity with it: the affinity with the natural world in its minute and immense particularities; the sensitivity to spirits of place and the language that is spoken by mountains and rivers, rocks and clouds, Tasmanian tigers and blue wrens—it all comes in the bundle we inherit, a medicine bundle. How will we unfold it? How will it unfold us, here in this Australian corner of our magical planet?

The place that lives us

Nobody lives "somewhere in general," though much of our electronic culture might like to persuade us that we do, or can. Every breath breathed, every step taken from birth to death, is lived somewhere sharply in particular. To overlook this and to live in vagueness toward where we live, the place that lives us, is to place our living place in peril. There is a real urgency here that Dogen echoes when he says that when you know the place where you are, practice begins. Exactly then.

Here, "knowing" means knowing as lovers know each other, knowing and being known by a place as intimately as is humanly possible. When I returned recently to my childhood country of Cairns, North Queensland, I was almost shocked by the power of seeing the mountains that had ringed my childhood, front and back, even out to sea across the bay, the hills of the Yarrabah community; the power of feeling how well they know me, how their forms endure as the shape of my heart.

We have to put our ear against the body of the Earth to really know the place where we are. The Zen tradition forms us in a way that makes that listening relatively natural and instinctive, although the clamor of information, facts, opinions, and counter-opinions can cloud what speaks through our bodies and the knowing in our bones, the feel of things, our intuition.

Belonging

"Ownership" is a legal matter, and can be a powerful social fact; but "belonging" lies much deeper, and is a matter to be won, like respect. When we sit deeply in zazen, we enter ancient time; we lose our edges and realize with a joyful shock that we sit not just together with mountains, rivers, and the great Earth, but as each thing, each unrepeatable arising of being. This is to realize—literally, to "make real"—our Great Body. That faintly singing cricket by the door is this very body walking, sitting, talking; those blue-green mountains capped with low cloud, too; and that weed in the cracks of the pavement—that too is our body. After we come into the birthright of our Great Body, which has been ours from the beginning, the next step is to begin to take on our own human part in minding the universe.

If we can sense the promise of an affinity and shared ground between the Dharma apparently coming from "elsewhere," and the Dreaming or Law that is already anciently revealed here, are we entitled to act upon this recognition (in a respectful way)? Eugene Stockton, an Australian Catholic priest and prehistorian, has boldly suggested that a graft can "take" (and endlessly has done so up to now) between cultures. And so, as a branch is grafted onto mature stock, we can respectfully seek to be grafted onto the ancient heritage of this land, so that its life might flow through ours. And, I would add, so that our lives and imaginations and dreaming may form a taproot into the deep time of this place—for indeed, the deepest theme of place is time.

It feels very promising, this image of patiently and assiduously doing all we can do to assist a graft of our culture or cultures that will "take," that will join us to the tree of human knowing and being long known in this place and share its taproot deep in time. There's such longing in the word "belonging." But then an awkwardness arises: a painful pause, full of history. Even if you could put aside the apparent gulf of difference between the two worlds that collided at time of first contact, the consequences have been huge: the history of dispossession enacted by violence or indifference; and the indelible injuries of rupture, theft, removal, obliteration, ignorance, and official amnesia. It seems extraordinary to me that the injured party to this encounter, the Aboriginal people themselves, have been prepared even to speak of "reconciliation."

Reconciliation as a word has suffered becoming almost meaningless in its overuse, and the rhetorical contortions it has been forced to perform have been painful to watch in the recent past. Yet a substantial act of reconciliation must lie on the path between where we are and where we long to be able to go and freely meet. Actively reconciling your spiritual path with the most ancient Way in this land may be a good beginning.

Reconciliation with *this!*

When Aboriginal elder of the Yuin people, Dulumunmun, is asked to say a few words about reconciliation, what he says is surprising at first for some: "I don't like this word reconciliation. I don't approve this word. How can there be reconciliation between us mob and the other mob when there never was a partnership put there in the first place! You can't reconcile a broken down relationship if there never was one in the first place."

He lets the silence deepen. Then he continues. "So I don't talk to people about reconciliation. What I'm trying to do is get both mobs to reconcile back with the Mother. You know—*This!*" And he picks up a handful of earth and pours it from one hand to the other, then holds it out. "That's what reconciliation is about for me!"

This skillful teaching slips past every barrier erected by politics or views of history, straight to the essential. And by the time that both indigenous and non-indigenous Australians have truly reconciled with the earth herself, you can bet they will have found themselves encountering, acknowledging, accommodating, and learning from each other in penetrating and reciprocal ways.

Dulumunmun wisely moves the center of gravity from reconciliation to reciprocity. Real reconciliation is the sharing spirit that arises from belonging and recognizing "all my relations"—trees, birds, animals, rocks, water, sky, sun, moon, and people, too. It is unforced respect that grows from recognizing what this reality is, and that rises in us, as naturally as water in a well, when self-concern grows quiet; it rises as a sense of accord we might call love.

It's a very revealing question, to find out what it is that someone loves.

Recall the old Chan teacher who was asked by his student, "I wonder, what does Your Reverence love?" No doubt he was expecting to hear it affirmed that he had put all love of the world aside. The teacher confirmed something else entirely, coming from around the corner out of the dark to the student's implicit question. He responded entirely upon his own ground of being, confirmed in him by countless years of unstinting practice: "I have already become *like this*."

Again, we hear, see, and feel this come forth: just exactly what is. That "I" is not the I of self-concern with its fixed address in karma, though it shares an abode with it. When "I" have become "like this," the simplicity is so profound it is both hard to miss and hard to see. Love appears in a new light, when reciprocity is realized at such depth as this.

Dreaming country

To begin to reconcile the Dharma apparently coming from "elsewhere," and the Dreaming that is anciently revealed here, we must first journey some way into an indigenous sense of "country," sit down on the ground and sift the dust in our own hands. "Dreaming" has been widely accepted as a good English equivalent for words like *djukurppa*, but some prefer "Law," which is also how *Dharma* can translate. Another suggested sense is "originating from eternity," which is equally resonant with *Dharma*. The anthropologist W. E. H. Stanner suggested that the Dreaming cannot be fixed in time. It is, in a word he coined, *everywhen*, and many things in one. It points to a story of things that once happened, a kind of charter of things that still and will always happen, and a fundamental principle of order transcending all other considerations for Australian Aboriginal people. It tells how things came into being, and how that forms, in turn, an ordered system of human relationships, including physical, spiritual, moral, and social matters.

A later anthropologist, Deborah Bird Rose, offers a brilliant metaphor for the kinds of time subtended by Dreaming:

If we were to locate ourselves, hypothetically, in Dreaming, we would see a great sea of endurance, on the edges of which are the sands of ordinary time. If, by contrast, we locate ourselves in ordinary time and look toward the past, we see a period of about 100 years—a present ordinary time marked by changes which do not endure…Dreaming can be conceptualized as a great wave that follows along behind us obliterating the debris of our existence and illuminating, as a synchronous set of images, those things that endure.

These words get as close to the heart of the matter as words can go: the immensity of Dreaming, like buddha nature, is fully present in each moment and detail of ordinary time and circumstance, closer than breathing. However, some particularities of country are more strongly marked by Dreaming traces than others. The Dreaming of a country is sung—which means tended in ceremony, minded—to maintain the whole order of relationships that keeps things whole, and healed. No amount of obliteration and forgetting can take the song out of the land.

Singing the land

Song sung to country, for country, is deeply at home, deep in Dreaming. An example is a Groote Eylandt clan song for the West Wind, sung in accord with the flat, treeless Ekilyangba country. The West Wind is visiting, rising, testing its strength as the song is tossed, wind and song tossed together, a gift to the bare, flat, treeless land, from the sandy flats all the way down to the tiny pebbles and tiny heaps of gravel of the ant's path and the wind's path. All the ants—red ants, meat ants, tiny ants—are greeted by name. So are the parrots that screech low over the heads of their ant friends. And so is the wind, the same wind that the singer's grandfather— all his ancestors from the beginning—sang, which is also tiny ants' wind and thin ants' wind, rustling, striking, parting the grass until it veers away. The singer is the song and the song is the country. No difference.

Such intensely localized knowledge is already, vividly, the Law made clear. A very Buddhist sense of interdependency or co-arising leaps straight from the song, and so does complete confidence in the natural order of being. The wind, spirit wind, ancestor's wind, has direct confidence in the singer. When we see deeply, the universe confides in us directly. When we trust so completely, we are entrusted.

Quiet country

"Country" in Australian Aboriginal terms is surrounded by other unique and inviolable countries, which are not politically formed or separated but richly related in clusters of alliance networks, Dreaming tracks and ceremonies, trade networks, tracks of winds, and movements of animals. No one can know the whole of this network because knowing of country is of necessity intensely local. The whole is rested in the lap of connectedness, entrusted to the intricate tracks of interdependence, not sought to be grasped. As anthropologist Deborah Bird Rose says, nothing in this system invites people to assume that they can or should know everything, or commends itself to people who believe that they can (or already do) know everything.

One time she was travelling in the 1980s with a senior man, Daly Pulkarra, when she was working in Yarralin country with people in the Victoria River district of the Northern Territory. They stopped so that she could film some of the most spectacular erosion she had seen in the district. She asked Daly what he called this country. He looked at it long and heavily. Then he said, "It's the wild. Just the wild." He went on to speak of quiet country—the country in which all the care of generations of people is evident to those who know how to see it. It stands in stark contrast to "the wild." They were gazing at an eroded wild resulting from a "land-use" of tree clearing and cattle grazing, in which the life of the country was visibly "falling down into the gullies and washing away with the rains."

I notice how all my old notions about wilderness and the relationship between humans and nature are utterly revised by this. Something drops away and a new understanding—a much older one—is recovered. Quiet country is like awareness tended by mindfulness: it is country entered into and cared for by a modest and profound sense of connectedness and reciprocity.

"Country" entails direct kinship of people with country: people are born for country and their bones are powerful food for country later on, fertilizing it with power to draw life into being and meaning for those who follow. "Wildness," then, is the folly of standing outside your life and failing to grasp the mutual custodianship of where you are, which is what you are. All around you are all your relations—tree, mountain, wind, river, fish, ant, dingo, emu, possum, wombat, furry caterpillar. Failing to know it is actually failing to be in reality.

Quiet country—it's the country that begins to open to us when we truly stop, where we truly stop. Stanner says:

> When we took what we called "land" we took what to them meant hearth, home, the source and locus of life, and everlastingness of spirit. At the same time it left each local group bereft of an essential constant that made their plan and code of living intelligible…What I describe as "homelessness," then, means that the Aborigines faced a kind of vertigo in living. They had no stable base of life; every personal affiliation was lamed; every group structure was put out of kilter; no social network had a point of fixture left.

The epidemic of alcoholism, petrol-sniffing, community breakdown, violence, and despair that some Aboriginal people are now suffering so keenly, the tearing that's happening more keenly than ever, right now, is shameful in equal measure for both *mobs*, as the Australian usage would have it, of indigenous and non-indigenous Australians. It is easier to understand the grief and shame that is acted out or covered up in a wide variety of reactions, as well as being silently borne, when you understand what has been torn. For what was here on this continent, as profound spiritual reality lived in every action of people congruent with a Law that made people so congruent with country, was shockingly invisible to European eyes at first contact. That inability to see ruptured a world and began to tear the intricate web of country.

The late Kimberley law-man David Mowaljarlai puts flesh and blood onto this loss, this "vertigo in living":

> Disturbing sacred sites and land is agony for our people. Land and mountains and spring water—the heart of sacred sites—is really our body. Graders, bulldozers are pressing down on our body, liver, kidney, bleeding. The spirit of the landowners is sickened. Graders are scraping the skin off our flesh—a sore that will not heal up: in my language, *wilu*, killing us.

But when you are alive to country, completely awake in alive, quiet country, you are realizing *yorro yorro*, which Mowaljarlai translates as "everything standing up, alive, brand new!"

> Morning gives you the flow of a new day—aah!...You go out now, see animals moving, see trees, a river...Your vision has opened and you start learning now...Your presence and their presence meet together and you recognize each other. These things recognize you. They give their wisdom and their understanding to you when you come close to them...You got country as far as the eye can see, and it's yours. But because of this consciousness, you are going through it reverently, quietly....

Realization is a vast moment of infinite wideness that lets everything stand up again alive, brand new, in its eternal now. Indeed, you recognize things, animals, trees, a river; your presence and their presence meet so exactly there is no difference at all. Dogen's way of expressing yorro yorro was to say that when the ten thousand things advance and confirm the self, that is enlightenment. And it is a matter of humble reverence.

Yorro yorro is fullness, ripeness. When you become like this, Mowal-jarlai says, then every day one more day is added to your life; you will be one day richer.

Resonance

All the best teachers give the gift away so openly and freely, like this, like original abundance. Dulumunmun says, "The only way to keep a gift is to give it away. Just keep on giving it away." Our Zen tradition calls this generosity "Dana," the giving away that restores life right at the source. Aboriginal tradition and life expresses belonging as a network of giving and indebtedness.

A willingness to accept all the amazing offers of life, even hard times, insult, difficulty, sickness, old age, and death, without self-pity, is also very strong in Aboriginal culture, not unlike the Zen spirit of accepting all offers and being completely alive in every condition of living and dying. This refined and enduring equanimity can improvise well with a lot of humor and limited means. Sometimes the black humor of the old Chan masters seems extraordinarily close to the testing, playful Australian sense of humor, which I think may be one of the great gifts of black Australia to have entered the culture at large — a humor indigenous to the very rocks.

Shikantaza ("just sitting," just meeting what is, breath by breath) has close kinship with *dadirri*, Miriam-Rose Ungunmerr's traditional word for the practice of quiet, still awareness, listening, waiting. In time, foods will ripen, children will grow stage by stage, grief will mature and heal, death will come. Inside this time of connectedness, you don't mind waiting because you want things to be done with care. Mindfulness grows out of this quiet still awareness, just as seasons turn, becoming like this, needing no forcing. The ritual of mindfulness maintains us as quiet country.

Ancestors are an important element of spiritual transmission in both traditions. The Zen ancestors, like the Aboriginal ancestors of the Dreaming and the recent past, are right here now—not so much behind us in a linear kind of time, but walking ahead, drawing us deeper in through the gate of unknowing. When we deeply recognize and become intimate with the teaching of an "ancestor" in the Dharma in koan practice, we walk and talk with them and see eye to eye, with the same eye. This changes the very nature of time, as does all intense and sustained spiritual practice; when we see it this way, the extraordinary temporal fluidity of the Dreaming opens to us as simple and evident: everywhen.

The deepest expression of reconciliation is the open sharing of difficulties and riches—the action of relatedness. The impulse or energy of conciliation is recognition and affinity: general amnesty. This whole business of a dialogue between our "two" traditions is basic reconciliation business: coming home in this very place. Zen places at its threshold a ceremony of atonement, of bringing us to the condition of being at one again. We say, together, at the beginning of any ceremony: "All the harm and suffering ever created by me since of old, on account of my beginningless greed, hatred, and ignorance, born of my actions, speech, and thought, I now acknowledge openly and fully."

This is a conscious move to release the estranged self and take fresh personal responsibility for our own impact on the world. If we say these words mindful of the history of European impact on Aboriginal people, they offer a gesture toward acknowledging the deep hurts running through the soul of this country, running through us wherever we are alienated from our own true nature. An act of atonement is also a prayer for release. When we hold this self in a state of "at-one-ment," we can learn to feel with greater sensitivity into the heart-mind of this country, all of these countries, this very place beneath our feet, where practice begins.

Affinity

Just sitting, and being, and listening, and holding the self open is an element of practice and living intrinsic to both traditions. In Zen we sit on the ground and a different kind of time and relatedness opens here: it is a place where children roll and tumble, a place where there is no rank. When he was most sorely tested and tempted to abandon his great effort to wake up, the Buddha drew on the strength of his connectedness with the earth; he touched the earth to call upon it as witness and sanction, and so could remain in a state of profound affinity, unmoved by the blandishments of self-deception and self-contrivance. The entire Earth Sangha sat in solidarity with him in that moment.

Respect for place, the specific place where you engage with the mysteries of what is, is important to Zen: just look at its tradition of poetry, culminating perhaps in haiku, able to glimpse the face of eternity in the most inconsequential and fleeting thing. The spirit of place, indeed, the spirits of place, are alive in sometimes convergent ways in both traditions. Sensing them more keenly, treating them with respect, seems to arise naturally with awakening, just as awareness of the sentience of rocks and clouds and bushes and mountains, as well as all living beings, grows with that natural respect. Meditation itself is a ritual action of respect, recollecting the true self, looking again and again, without moving toward and without moving away. Respect structures the spiritual authority through which teaching is offered and transmitted; and respect—a kind of nameless gratitude—marks every mindful gesture and breath, gradually maturing into minding the universe, distinct in each human being.

Sacred sites are especially powerful "doorways" into deeper seeing and participation in the Dreaming. The full force of the creative urge of the universe is still lodged in these places, and can be felt by the person prepared to open themselves with sensitivity or ritual care to that place. Such places become important ritual and teaching places. The Zen *bodhi-mandala*, the place of dedicated meditation practice, is usually a dojo or temple, but it can be a rock, a cave, a mountain, or the shelter of a tree. It can never be other than the place beneath your own two feet. From a Zen perspective, any place where you sit or stand completely open and aware becomes alive to its own sacredness through your own willingness to open and include. Even ordinary, nondescript city places are completely awake and responsive to this kind of attention.

In both traditions, story is a vital instrument of transmission of the teaching, and of testing how deeply you see. Dreaming stories are song-lines of story that "make" the world, containing multiple levels of entry depending on initiation. The koan path also offers a Way of stories, which make little literal sense but open in a vastly different light when entered upon the ground of "emptiness." Koans, like songlines, are the footprints of the ancestors. They do not create the physical world as the Dreaming does; but like the dreaming, they bring us to a state where we can see its true face, at last.

Reciprocity

If we are born in Australia or drawn here to live, reciprocity starts with finding ways to learn respectfully in the tradition of our Aboriginal ances-tors. This depends on the generosity of Aboriginal teachers, and on our courage and desire to seek out opportunities for learning. Always ask. Even tongue-tied by shyness or ignorance, always ask. Even the silent spirits of place will respond to a cry from the heart.

When Odysseus was cast out in the final, hideous shipwreck that drowned all his men, he found himself unable to get ashore in the pul-verizing surf breaking on jagged rocks, caught up in powerful currents that refused to release their grip on him. Homer's *Odyssey* was composed at a time when old ways were breaking down and the spirits of place were losing familiarity, no longer regularly propitiated. "Quiet country" returning to the wild. So Odysseus found himself tongue-tied, unable to call out and appeal to the gods of that unknown island to help him get around the headland to the sanctuary of the river mouth beyond. At last his need grew so great that he cried out loud to the unknown river god of that place, begging for help with his last breath. And then the current ran differently, he was swept at last past the rocks that would dash out his brains and into the calm of the river, and a beach where he could be washed ashore, almost lifeless, still breathing.

So another gesture is finding the forms to offer respect to land and country and its caretakers, animals and spirits—all its sentient beings in deep time right now—especially when you practice. Knowing where you practice, in every possible modality of knowing that you can open to, is part of this respect. Learning the local birdsong and flower language, being in on the intimate gossip at that level, knowing the flow of rivers and waterways, even if they are now buried underground, and feeling the bioregional shift, the change of country, when you cross borders. This is a journey toward becoming in some measure custodial. So too with the place where we abide, take refuge, and practice. What can we learn about being here from the people who have been here for thousands of generations? What a gift, to be able to tap in just a little to the conversation happening in the secret forms of mountains, rivers, rocks, and trees!

Zen ceremonies and forms grow richer when they are open and sensitive toward the original tradition, people, and spirits of the place where we are, beginning with formal acknowledgment of traditional country and its landowners. This impulse to let ceremony become shaped by *here* is a kind of dance that follows place—letting it lead; responding to its lightest touch; yielding moment by moment from a deep confidence founded in the millennia of Zen tradition and, even more fundamentally, in our original nature touched in stillness.

Custodial mind, the mind that longs to sing alive the land and law that sing us alive, can deepen our sense of the reciprocity in all the forms that shape the passion of our practice. For example, the precepts of right action in Buddhism are not just a lot of rules to prevent harmful action, but can be seen as a whole country of aliveness and interconnection, of veneration of all my relations. We speak of taking refuge in Buddha, Dharma, and Sangha. A refuge is also a home place, a place we tend as well as retreat to, a place that nourishes life and must also be nourished with custodial mind. The gift cycle, always in motion.

Each of these propensities, and all of them together, is a willingness to let the tradition be sung by this continent as country is "sung" when it's maintained by attention, ceremony, and affinity. Waking up itself is not unlike singing ourselves awake, creating ourselves again and again all the way through, just as "sung" country—quiet country—is properly awake and tended all the way through by the cycle of ceremony. Then the ancestors are satisfied, and we and the ancestors meet exactly "like this." And so reconciliation, edged with so much shame for us, might shift over in the end into reciprocity, an open-ended exchange of gifts that includes a readiness to share hardship and difficulty. Mistakes will be made on the way, but these will be the instructive moments, the growing edges themselves, invaluable.

Singing ourselves awake

It takes time to absorb tradition—time for intuition to register its light touch and suggest the way, time to learn the songs of a place, and time to enter the singing and being sung. Martin Buber tells a koan-like Hasidic tale that knows something of this matter. After the Great Maggid's death, his disciples came together to mourn, and talk about the things he had done. When it was Rabbi Schneur Zalman's turn to speak, he asked them: "Do you know why the master went to the pond every day at dawn and stayed there for a little while before coming home again?" No one knew why. Rabbi Zalman explained that he was learning the song with which the frogs praise God. "It takes a very long time to learn that song," he said.

You can't rush the song of the frogs, and you can't absorb it in just a few visits to the pond. Patience is the willingness to come back and listen again and again. It is mindfulness, *dadirri*. What is that song with which the frogs praise God, with which buddha nature sings the frogs and us and the dawn star?

Here's one small stone, red with dust, that points the Way—a Zen koan native to this continent. In Arnhem Land a man named Maralung was sleeping. In a dream, a master song man came to him and said, "Wake up, I have a song to teach you." At first there was a *min-min* light approaching through the trees. But when the light approached it was a human being. The dreamer woke up within the dream and the master taught him the song. But then the dreamer went back to sleep and forgot the song. Next day, a musicologist asked him for the song. So the next night, Maralung dreamed again and it happened the same way. Again the master came into his dream and woke him and taught him the song, and again he fell asleep afterwards. But in the morning he remembered the song.

So, what is the song? Why do we go back to sleep and forget it again and again? And when you wake, knowing it at last, who wakes?

CHAPTER 9

The hermitage
in the street

HAVE YOU EVER GONE WANDERING slowly, with all the time
in the world, through the nooks and crannies of a large city, attending to its unlikely beauties and aspects of the marvelous hidden right
there in the ordinary, right under your nose? It is possible to celebrate the
ordinary, under-loved city streets and lanes with the eye and mind of Zen,
curious and alive to the presence and the sentience of even the most
humble things of the human world. Each act of complete attention offers
a custodial gesture of responsiveness and responsibility toward a small
fragment of the human "Dreaming," which is a true antidote to terrorism.

The poet Gary Snyder has suggested that those who look with a natu-
ralist's kind of loving eye at the things of towns and cities are able to
see many marvelous things in the ordinary: cities are old fallen tree trunks
and their hosts of opportunistic life forms springing up in the
remains; they are paper wasp nests and beehives, the debris and wash-
aways left behind after floods (of traffic, demolition, people, road-making);
they are also guano heaps, courting and strutting bowerbirds, look-out

rocks, solitary caves, sacred groves, and coral colonies. "And for a few people, they are also palaces," he says, echoing Dogen in the Mountain and Waters Sutra, who contends that dragons can see water as a palace or a pavilion, though hungry ghosts may see it as raging fire or pus and blood.

Most of us live in towns and cities. What would it be like to see our familiar places like this? How can we perceive these riches we're swimming in, and reinhabit the palace that was always here?

Feel free to look around

In old-fashioned stores (sometimes still found in country towns), you used to see a sign in the window that reassured you: "Feel free to look around. No obligation to buy." This was in an era that still respected dreaming forms of awareness, and still respected people; in fact, an era that had not yet invented "consumers." Let us pay homage to that old vanishing courtesy by taking its invitation much further, out of the shop and into the street.

Zen literature is replete with exquisite imagery extending deep recognition to the natural world—both because of the kind of barely urban world in which Taoism, Chan, and Zen arose, and because of the kinds of places in which monasteries, temples, and hermitages tend to be built. Mountains, rivers, rocks, trees, grasses, clouds, blossoms, and moon richly elaborate and differentiate our own most intimate self—more readily, maybe, than the world of streets, fire hydrants, and electricity substations.

The flower in the grass may point the way with humble ease, but what about wall rubble and discarded plastic toys and a broken tile in the weeds? That too is where we live; it is a fragment of our regular world of human trouble and riches, and it waits to meet with us. I suggest we can well afford to love it, tend it with our open attention, redeem it with our full imagination. To fail to truly attend to it is to lay waste the place right where we are, where we live our lives. It is to agree to live with indifference.

Is indifference so bad? Well, strange as it may first sound, it is a kind of terrorism, which from one angle of view may be thought of as the extreme expression of contemptuous indifference for the human world. A friend who is an eco-philosopher has suggested that the only truly dangerous places in our human world are the only truly unloved ones. The concrete canyon of a freeway, the dark, fluoro-lit intestines of a grease-stained parking lot, the urine-desecrated stairwell—is it possible to feel the propensity of things, to lean into contentment, even here?

Counter-terrorism

When we recognize a place, or an aspect of a place; when we bless it with our inner recognition; then we know it to be part of us, and something can begin to live there. A home is made, a haven, in the most unlikely place. Until then, we dump there everything we don't like about ourselves, and it will seep back into our dreams like toxic waste.

Counter-terrorism, in this sense, is to actively take up the practice of loving the order of matter generally. This is not the act of shopping—of turning compulsively toward material goods as though suffering and loss may be magically eased by that hankering. It is more subtly the act of not turning away, of not breaking faith with the things of this world. It is feeling for the mysteries beneath appearances, without picking and choosing—in other words, the far side of shopping.

The grain of the world

You can wander across an abandoned lot and begin to discover the suggestive fragments and relics of human life preserved in it, partly breaking the surface, moulded into ephemeral sculpture; or an improbable cluster of objects strange to one another but embedded together in an

odd kinship and richly art-directed by time. You can become an afi-
cionado of outback goldfield rubbish tips, where gadgets grown extraordinary and unintelligible by time have become welded and melded by
rust into things both beautiful and so gone they can never be explained.
When you feel free to look around, many of the beauties arise through
a secret love of ruins, and fascination with the sea change of time; and
others come with the sheen of nostalgia, but in its perverse mode,
unsentimental.

A flattened tin can, as blood-red in its rust as the red dust that the
heart so loves out there among the olive-grey saltbushes, can be a treasure to take home with you—on its upturned base, an imprint of the
map of Australia. When you handle it, the dust as fine as incense ash, a
silt-layered memory of an ancient sea, lightly coats your fingers. The
word *nostalgia* has, in its older, Latin roots, the sense of "our old
(sweet) shared pain": the ability to hold the bitter until it joins up with
all sweetness.

Each treasure starts with a sense of the world as distinct and penetrating, a little piece of the world's grit trapped in the soft, wet open eye.
It is something like a pearl. The grit or grain of the world washes in to
the tender open oyster of the embodied self and leaves its residue—a
kind of suffering accepted. Then it can suffer a slow sea change, in the
depths of psyche, memory, and imagination, and the abrasions of the
world become gradually pearlescent, many layered, spun around the
embedded injury to make it no longer alien but tolerable, included,
and strangely beautiful over time. This receptiveness to the world is a
powerful practice—accepting the pain of openness in a human body,
and turning that way.

A storehouse of treasures is opening of its own accord inside your self.
Just letting it in is part of that opening; the rest is the willingness to play.
That is the fantastic, uncalled-for, inspired movement back toward the
suffering, the forgotten or unloved or overlooked thing; that's the real
meeting.

Such a sense of play is a true antidote to terrorism and its mortal fear of life, its aloofness from the complexity and duration of suffering, and its deadly disrespect for the comical and lovely human effort of making a world. I want to call our common comical, lovely, ugly human world "the street," the shared social space we build and desecrate together. And I want to ask, What happens if we agree to fully live in the glorious mixed feast of the street? What secret dimension of play, what unexpected homecoming, might that open up in us?

The secret life of the street

There is a kind of attentiveness that can be cultivated and deeply relished, and a whole secret life of the street that it brings to light. It gives to the human-made world almost the same kind of delight that the lover of the natural world (and I am also one of those) might take in lizard eggs, bird colonies, feathers, droppings, rocks, and lichens. It does not oppose the wild and the made worlds but conjoins them, finds their overlap and resonance, sees the wild in the made, pays to the rust stains on an old corrugated iron wall the same receptivity it gives to dewdrops delicately strung in a spider's web. It includes but goes beyond spotting and classifying.

Just as you might dream your way into the inner life of a honeysucker hatchling by entering the downy inside of a tiny abandoned nest with your finger, you might dream and play your way into the imaginative resonance of the street. To take up the street with your imagination and follow its back ways into time is to allow the overlooked, overgrown, and half-ruined faces of the street to become the topography of your most intimate being.

In my own looking around I have met people who walked the stormwater tunnels; people who walked the underground train system in the quiet between midnight and 3 A.M. on Sunday mornings, searching for the "false starts," the abandoned tracks, the odd buildings said to remain in obscure places; people who visited disused gasworks, brick-pits, the underneath of old wharves; people who boat up old industrial canals, who comb landfill sites and take tours through sewage treatment plants; people in Sydney who know about the underground passageways linking old mental asylums with landing-stages on the harbor. There's a lovely freedom in momentarily stepping back into the privilege freely taken by children, finding the gap in the cyclone wire fence and sauntering along in that heightened state of casual alertness, just having a good look around.

Knipls

There are other denizens of this layer of the street world. In Ben Katchor's cartoon strips, Julius Knipl, a hatted Jewish New York real-estate photographer, walks the streets, his camera on his back. Knipl has a sixth sense for obscure bus routes facing extinction; notices how the telephone books in public places begin to yellow and roll their leaves as their replacement date approaches with its inexorable season; finds comfort in the sight of a remnant smokestack standing useless and abandoned in a corner of the city because no one can afford to demolish it; notices how the scar of a sidewalk excavation takes years to completely heal.

Knipl is a Yiddish word meaning a little treasure to put away for a rainy day, a nest egg that can be held in the palm of your mind. Anything can hatch from it. Julius Knipl has an eye that can see New York all the way down to the turn-of-century strata of the street. His creator, Ben Katchor, says that the best knipls are the suddenly apparent things that he "never saw the interest in before." Just walking down the street, for example, he may see a faded, tattered, only semi-legible old sign from maybe fifty years ago, warning about rat poison. *Think about it,* he invites us. The rats are long gone, the people who posted the notice are gone, and the people they are warning are gone. But the sign's still there—just. Once you've noticed it, it's taken an interest in you. It's a knipl!

Knipls are always touched by time; they carry evidence of its secret tidal shifts. And each one offers a tiny private joy. When you recognize a knipl, you'll notice that the very act opens a private lair for dreaming right there inside the moment, on even the most bleak or shelterless street.

The midden of the human world

Architects and planners are only the inaugural dreamers of the built environment; what they make are merely the props for all the other dreamers.

All of us have a right of way on the street; all of us have a share in it. There is a deep well-being in this. The streets, even the most unlovely ones, are brilliantly art-designed stages for our dreaming minds. And streets have a life of their own that we share in but do not own. It is a special joy, on the street, to be only one of the many dreamers. In it, you blend your dreams with those of strangers. Some kinds of street are less alive to you than others, but a street has life the moment it grows interested in you. Then it will talk to you, waft smells at you, set off trains of inner connection and dreaming.

The street is a midden of the human world, and every thing in the midden has its proper place in our attention as it descends through the layers of time, acquiring "pearlescence." Each thing in the human midden belongs to a natural poetry that the great Yunmen spoke word for word when he challenged his monks with "Everyone has his own light. If you want to see it, you can't," and then responded to his own implicit question with "The store-room. The gate." The kerosene lamp on the kitchen bench. The box of cabbages. The veranda. The front step. No one can go past poetry of this force (and every day we do, we pass over it as if it were not the breath of God on our faces!).

Administered reality

A shopping mall is not quite a free place for feeling free to look around, for dreaming. On that air-conditioned privatized "street," your rights are restricted. The fluorescent bath of denatured light (in which we're all suspects) is a part of the trauma; the trapped effluvium of electronic sound is another. You can't sit down on a bench there. You can't escape the forced muzak and announcements. In fact it is often frustratingly difficult to escape at all—the rare exits are marked in such very small print. Real choice, real surprise, real discovery is very limited—is this why sleepiness falls like a pall? Something has been fatally pre-digested, like the "imagination" called for by a video game. You are welcomed by the Cheshire Cat of commerce just as long as you consume, and present a willingness to be consumed.

Feeling free does not take kindly to being badgered by too much administered reality, the kind you feel in a "mall." However, it can take up even the bullying of administered reality as a perverse pleasure when there really is no escape from the shopping. Even in the mall, if you look you will see that a ruin is in progress, that the maintenance deficit is growing and interesting little compromises or inventive stopgaps are creeping in. Perhaps a tile has fallen off, revealing the texture of mortar and its unintended punctuation effect; perhaps no one has bothered to replace the ceiling panel because the air conditioning breaks down every day and continually needs adjustment.

And you can always walk decisively through any nondescript door marked "Exit" to enter a vertiginous, bland maze belonging to the realm of Services, Deliveries, and Security. A rabbit-hole in Wonderland. A true exit to the street is almost impossible to find. Instead, you may stumble into a loading dock; but you may also have a door slam one-way behind you and a lot of time to explore the smells, the strange hot air, the scuffed white walls, the echoey steps and passageways, before one of the attendants of administered reality finds you and shepherds you disapprovingly back to the public side of things like a stray — indeed, a bit of a suspect.

Walking meditation on the pavement

The proper pace of feeling free to look around is lazily slow, idiosyncratically detailed, and half-entranced. It is the pace at which you might stop and stare and see the almost unseeable gap between two buildings, a gap big enough to let your eye look in and grow dark-adapted and begin to see, and your nose to register the dankness of things down near the mystery area where a building meets the earth.

In the 1930s, Walter Benjamin explored Baudelaire's Paris through the eyes of the flanêur, the idle stroller whose slow and purposeless peregrinations brought the city into being. The flanêur goes botanizing on the pavement, said Benjamin. And then he noted (astonishingly!) that around 1840 it was briefly fashionable to take turtles for a walk in the arcades, saying that the flanêurs liked to have the turtles set the pace for them.

The slow, mindful pace of walking meditation is the proper pace for feeling free to look around, for your feet to pay their loving dues, step by step, to the earth that is completely there under the brief asphalt. This is the pace when the trance of looking and noticing can overtake your errand, your small sense of self-importance; and this is the pace in which the inventory of loved things has a chance to grow.

The plainest poetry

The deepest level of play with the spirits of place, in the streets you live on, always knows each thing is sacred and speaks the strongest, plainest poetry: a fast-dripping tap heard in the too-thick grass on an abandoned lot; the old tracery of bathroom tiles on a slab lost in weeds; the shape of a smokestack in the last light; the half-inch forest growing thick in the crack that marks where the tram tracks used to be.

When you touch such an intimate inner perspective, a nest for dreaming, right there on the homeless street, even the most routine city moment becomes a journey. Once you place one foot into the unknown and the other in the most deeply recessed self, you are in liminal space, travelling, any day of the week, right in your own home town.

There's a pilgrimage aspect to this, too. The little "stations" of discovery can be revisited and celebrated—a small and secret homage to a crack in ordinary banality through which the light has shown itself. You can take other pilgrims to share your arcane joys, to strengthen the sacred as it stands up in the ordinary. Walking is a pilgrim's wisdom. The categories of the "ordinary marvelous" opened up on foot cannot be praised enough.

The hermitage of the everyday

Letting the streets flow like water, mutable and empty, and entering the flow, mutable and empty as water—this is to encounter walls, tiles, and pebbles as mind. "They passed eons living alone in the mountains and forests; only then did they unite with the Way and use mountains and rivers for words, raise the wind and rain for a tongue, and explain the great void," says Dogen of the old Zen hermits and teachers. In the hermitage of the everyday, we have to learn to talk the language and become the silence not just of mountains and rivers, but also the median strip between the sucking slipstreams of the traffic, the flare of neon in the mist, the rain staining a concrete apartment block, the broken tile in the weeds.

And then the plastic bag pirouetting beside the grinding tires of a semi-trailer is redeemed in a most profound act of counter-terrorism; indifference is dropped away; boredom is a sheer impossibility; and general amnesty is proclaimed by each thing that is cherished just as it is.

Follow the little tug of curious interest somewhere in your chest, and curl your palm inward around the knipls as they collect you into the treasury of the ten thousand things. It takes little more than missing your bus or train and walking in the rain those five blocks, finding the streets are black mirrors and the rain light deforms each thing just beyond its habitual invisibility.

Enter there.

CHAPTER 10

Can the Buddha be a mother?

ONCE A MONK WENT TO CALL on a teacher, Mi Hu. On the way, he met a woman living in a hut. The monk asked, "Do you have any followers?"

She said, "Yes."

The monk said, "Where are they?"

She said, "The mountains, rivers, and the whole Earth, the plants and trees, are all my followers."

The monk said, "Aren't you a nun?"

She said, "What do you see me as?"

The monk said, "A layperson."

She said, "You can't be a monk!"

The monk said, "You shouldn't mix up Buddhism."

She said, "I'm not mixing up Buddhism."

The monk said, "Aren't you mixing up Buddhism this way?"

She said, "You're a man, I'm a woman. Where has there ever been any mix-up?"

This little story is drawn from an informal collection of koans that circulates in enderingly pale, mimeographed form, made by women members of the Zen Diamond Sangha in Hawaii in the 1980s, which they called *The Kahawaii Koans*. *Kahawaii* means "sudden little stream that can move boulders." The women wanted to make a gesture to redress the weighting of Zen—of all Buddhism—toward the masculine: almost entirely male teachers, male lineages, and a wonderful koan tradition that makes hardly any mention of women. The few exceptions were often anonymous tea-ladies serving refreshments to unwary monks passing by, and throwing in a crooked kind of question that left the monks chewing hard. The women searched every nook and cranny of the tradition and collected every obscure koan that centered on the enlightenment or spiritual search of a woman.

Like the nameless nun in this story, many of the women they found were unnamed. Of course, our deepest affiliation is with something so vast it can have no name at all; Linji called it "the true person of no rank." And clearly the women who restored this koan to the record knew very well that the deceptively meek little creeks in the ravines of Oahu can roar with tumbling boulders any time they feel inclined.

A nameless hermit nun, defying the social order, living alone in her hut with all her followers—in accord with the mountains, rivers, and the whole Earth, the plants and trees—lets the monk hear the roar of the Dharma in this encounter. All his habits of mind are overturned, like the boulders in the path of deceptively small streams when they choose to roar with floodwater. The monk is stuck in "man" and "woman," "layperson" and "nun," "mixing up" and "not mixing up"; he is seeing only through the part-adapted eye of the conceptual mind, and missing entirely the whole that she lays out so helpfully right under his nose.

Contraband

This is very like the legendary story of the frustrated border officials who were always trying to work out what the old Sufi trickster Nasrudin was smuggling each time he crossed the border. The whole world knew Nasrudin was a smuggler, but nobody could ever find the loot, however hard they searched his donkeys and panniers and many pockets. The officials despaired in the end and gave up. They knew they could never pin down this one...And all the time, Nasrudin was smuggling donkeys.

We are so adept at interposing concepts that we miss the very point that everything in the world presents, right under our own noses. We are too busy supposing something ever to detect the contraband. And all the time, it's nothing but donkeys! cabbages! morning glories! the wind in the leaves! How beautifully each one bears the load, with grace and freedom: the light on your own hand, the silver sky, the rooftops. When you see this, you share the complete freedom of the nun in the story: "Where has there ever been any mix-up?"

The Zen tradition still has relatively few women teachers. People sometimes ask me what it is like to be a woman in such a male-dominated tradition. Well, as the unknown nun makes clear, in essential nature there is no male and female, no teacher and student. And yet, as a woman who came of age with feminism, of course I know that there are interesting questions lying here. A female Zen teacher, with children, a relationship, and a demanding lay life that can sometimes contend sharply with the work of teaching, is herself a kind of question posed to the tradition. The female body and its particular mysteries and passions, and the role of women in bringing life into the world and tending it to maturity, challenges by its very presence and powers what was for many centuries a mainly all-male preserve of monastic spiritual practice. Some traditions within Buddhism even insist that a woman cannot, by her nature, realize her own self-nature, but must wait to be reborn as a man for that to become a possibility. Meanwhile, presumably, she can make herself useful in the kitchen and labor in the field.

Yet this fearless nun, clear as a bell, asks, "Where has there ever been any mix-up?" You will not find mix-up in the affairs of mountains, rivers, and the whole Earth, the plants and trees. But you may discover it here and there in the concepts and contrivances of human beings.

All the unknown women

Some years ago, John Tarrant offered a sutra dedication to help name how powerfully the feminine, by its very absence, structures practice. The feminine is an untidy fit in this present world, which gives it a strange, ungainly, and unbounded power. The dedication made in our sutra service to acknowledge this powerful absence is, "All the unknown women, centuries of enlightened women, who hold our zazen in their arms, *dai osho.*" (*Dai osho* means "great teacher" or great priest, now dead.)

Zen is founded in the practice of seated meditation and one-pointed attention—alert, awake, wide open, attached precisely to nothing. When you look closely, the image of being held in this endeavor in the arms of the unknown women is not just maternal; we are also held in the arms of a lover. We are indeed held in zazen in the arms of all beings, those ten thousand mysterious "unknown" others who support and are supported by our life. We are "interbeings," whirling together in the dance of life and sex and death.

Words can be like hatchways: we can fall through them into depth the moment we cease to take them for granted. The words "unknown women" have the power of anomaly, the prick of a needle in them. Along with consciously celebrating something often in danger of being carefully "overlooked" by the last few thousand years of human culture, they also test our toleration, our preparedness to live with a measure of discomfort. The koan that hides in the words of the dedication opens here.

If "All the unknown women" was a koan, how would you respond?

One woman's response was "Emptiness bleeds." Indeed, it does. Embodied consciousness suffers, weeps, is born, and finally dies. If the bleeding of women may be an expression of great emptiness too, then perhaps it is in the nature of women also to wake up in this lifetime. Emptiness also flowers and makes love and gives birth to universe after universe. Every single birth is a revelation of how the universe brings forth something from nothing (among blood and loud cries); the body that bleeds knows this most intimately.

Lineage

So who are all the unknown women? "Generations" implies a lineage. There is one in the charts at the back of some Zen books: Shakyamuni Buddha, Mahakasyapa, Ananda; on to Bodhidharma; down to Dogen, Keizan, Hakuin; and right on down to the present head of this temple. All men up to now. And yet—from a deeper, wider perspective, there's a fine array of unknown women already! Where has there ever been any mix-up? "Men," "women"—where is that distinction in our heart of hearts? At the deepest level of deepest practice, with that water of unknowing on your lips, can you say if you are a man, or a woman?

Moving in a little closer to your own set of bones: Who are your generations of enlightened women? I would want to include my huge old fierce Aunt Kay, for example, who never married but who once ran down seven flights of steps and then up a very steep path to a cliff-edge to save my twelve-year-old brother Michael from being pushed off the cliff by the toughs who had invaded our little beach. (In fact, they'd already grown bored with the idea by then and were simply throwing sticks and insults at him. I forget, if I ever knew, what he had done to deserve this. Some tiny premature assertion of his fledgling masculine self, no doubt.)

A case could be made for the four pink sinuous angophora trees that hold hands together down by the creek at the back of my house. And the hands of your lover—yes! now there are infinite generations of enlightened women who hold your zazen in their hands. Rumi has a lovely expression for the ecstatic unknown somewhere in the Mathnawi, calling it up as a spring wind greening the ground, birdsong beginning in the egg. His image in turn calls up that extraordinary dream within a dream that is the human ovary. Once I learned that in the microscopic ovaries of a female fetus, some four hundred ova are already formed and assembled in patient succession within the spiral folds of the ovaries, each of them already a potential female life with its own minute spiral nebula in time, and back and back. Or is that "and forward and forward"? The birdsong beginning in the egg, indeed.

All true human beings are unknown, but some human beings' stories are more untold than others. That "unknown" is historic, karmically regrettable, and must be mourned. The Buddhist bodhisattva of compassion, Kuan Yin, listens also to all the untold stories and hears all the cries of all the silenced women, and everyone else besides. Which returns it to the deeper "unknown," that vast reverberant fertile ground that fills us all, trees and clouds and we ourselves, and can be filled by all of us. It leaves nothing out.

Spring wind

Here's another unknown woman from the Kahawaii collection of koans, sweeping through like a spring wind, known only as "The station lady."

A woman at the station in Hakuin's district called on Hakuin, who was the greatest Zen teacher of eighteenth-century Japan, and was greatly enlightened. Her name is unknown, and it is not known when she was born or died.

She once attended a lecture by Hakuin, in which he spoke of the Pure Land and asked, "Since it is the Pure Land of mind only, what kind of embellishments does it have? Since it is the Amida of your own body, what kind of distinguishing marks does Amida have?" Hearing this, the woman said to herself, "This is not such a hard thing." Returning to her home, she meditated day and night, bringing this to mind in both wakefulness and sleep. One day as she was washing a pot she suddenly broke through. Tossing the pot aside, she rushed to see Hakuin. She said, "I've run across Amida in my own body—everything on Earth is emanating a great light. How wonderful!" She danced with joy.

Hakuin said, "So you say, but what about a cess-pool—does it also emanate light?" The woman went up to him, gave him a slap, and said, "This old guy still hasn't realized!" Hakuin roared with laughter.

And he was probably still laughing when he went to meet Asan, another female lay student, in Shinano. Hakuin confronted her with the koan, "the sound of one hand." It is said that Asan immediately spoke an extemporaneous verse, saying, "Even better than hearing Hakuin's sound of one hand, clap both hands and do business!" Hakuin, who was also a master artist and calligrapher of his time, promptly drew a picture of a bamboo broom and gave it to Asan. She immediately wrote on it, "sweeping away all the bad teachers in Japan—first of all, Hakuin!" Hakuin smiled.

Can you hear the spirit of fierce practice here, of fear taken all the way to the brink of glad and beyond, turned to praise and sheer play? Deep practice can reach all the way down to the child, still there, who knew she was a girl but was more profoundly a human child—not male, not female. The woman who has lost a breast to cancer incarnates that mystery: one side seven years old and free of sexual meaning; the other unmistakably woman, weighted with that karma. That breast is itself a mystery: it is a sweat gland transformed that itself transforms blood (greed, hatred, ignorance) to milk (life, love, sustenance, compassion). Yet the chests of a seven-year-old girl or boy, with the same tender blue rivers of blood pulsing beneath the skin, cannot be told apart: another mystery!

A covenant with the unknown

All true human beings are, most intimately speaking, as unknown as all the unknown women not recorded in the lineage. The mystery of this is clearly met face to face in the firelight of *dokusan*, the practice of direct, one-to-one encounter with a Zen teacher. Transmission of the Dharma between teacher and student, teaching itself, is utterly direct, from unknown person to unknown person. All the strong relationships of our lives—with our parents, our children, our partners, our dearest friends—are formed in a covenant with the unknown. In joining ourselves to one another we join ourselves to the unknown. We can truly join one another only by joining the unknown. We do not know what this moment of opening to the other will lead to, and love is the risk of opening to the mystery, the unknownness, of the other.

The other may acquire in time a deep familiarity, but any truly alive relationship works hard not to extinguish the unknownness of the other. The pull into relationship is the unknown in the other, and relationship becomes the conscious tending of this mystery. Mysterious affinity, that powerful attractor that arranges all our karma as if in advance, may be, paradoxically, this very recognition of the unknownness of the other. We recognize it in the other because we have met in some degree our own portion of this mystery, which is Dante's "love that moves the stars and the other planets," and which circulates in our own veins.

This is not offered as bland reassurance of anything at all. It guarantees precisely nothing. At that moment of being brushed by the hands of the Beloved, who on earth are we? No one knows. No one is there to know.

Home-leaving without leaving home

Dedicated lay Buddhist practice in the West is open at all of its edges to ordinary life, to the householding life and the parenting life. And we are all pioneers here, doing the impossible—bringing a two-and-a-half thousand year monastic tradition into all the corners of our ordinary, sacred lives. In one sense every step of practice, every step on the Way, is pioneering. We make the path by walking; even those of us who are not literally parents but are including, in various ways, parenting relationships with others, are making the path of practice right through the center of ordinary life. (Though what life was ever ordinary!)

The Buddha asked his disciples to "leave home" in order to find their true repose and refuge away from the householding life. If you are mother or father to a dependent child, guardian of the household that shelters and nurtures their life, how do you contemplate this matter of "leaving home"? Does it mean you must put such deep concerns aside, until they leave home?

Home-leavers gave up the shelter and comfort of home to wander in the world, with two alms-bowls and a threadbare robe as all that was left of "home." And of course they also gave up all the discomforts of home life — the exquisitely challenging business of weighing and balancing your own needs and wishes against those you live with and care for, people you are so closely tied to by bonds of love that it is not always easy to see clearly.

The arrival of a child is an extraordinary business. It is among the greatest revolutions that can happen in a life, as powerful in its transformative force as falling deeply in love. What am I saying? It is falling deeply in love! Almost everything that applied yesterday no longer applies. All your own priorities are converted into the singular one of the baby being satisfied in enough ways to make life possible — and all of this accompanied by extraordinary intensities of feeling. What happens to practice in all of this?

Not mixing up Buddhism

Not long ago I asked a friend who has maintained a passionate Zen practice for six or seven years, and who now has a fifteen-month-old baby, what she could say about not mixing up Buddhism and mothering. She smiled. "Well, falling into quietude is no longer a worry," she replied, laughing at the idea that her practice might retreat behind the outward form of sitting, into a kind of self-deceptive quiet of nothing happening. The challenge has become a very different and demanding one in her present circumstances of mothering an infant: staying on that alive edge that practice hones in you, that receptive and creative edge of your being that can entertain true intimacy with the other while being sufficiently grounded in some spaciousness. The challenge, indeed, becomes maintaining any ground of spacious mind and being at all, and securing a now scarce opportunity for the meditative practice that sustains it.

But the opportunities for exploring that edge when you become a parent are boundless! What a pity the Buddha missed them. He called his child Rahula (the word means "obstacle"), and did his home-leaving on the very night of the child's birth. The morning star that would later free him from all his doubts was shining right there in the eyes of his own child, but he looked for realization elsewhere. Of course, generations of Buddhist monastics have followed him in this: to cut deeply, they say, you must break radically with your life of attachments, including partner and children, and dedicate yourself completely to the Dharma.

So the human being who includes parenting others at the core of their lives must "leave home," must radically and subtly loosen and break the habits and reactions of mind, in order to truly come home, right in the midst of the fortunate and ongoing disaster of ordinary householding life. How can we go about this obvious impossibility?

Dongshan points the way unwaveringly in his verse on the "Jewel Mirror Samadhi," echoing his own enlightenment experience while crossing the creek, when he said "He is me, but I am now not him":

Like gazing into the jewel mirror,
form and reflection view each other;

You are not him, but he is clearly you.

Just as in the common infant,
the five characteristics are complete;

No going, no coming, no arising, no abiding,

Ba-ba wa-wa, *speaking without speaking…*

A newborn baby can wail the Dharma in its fullness and complete-ness, with an ancient eloquence never caught in words and phrases, with no arising and no abiding, no coming and no going—and what's more, it is impossible not to attend! *Ba-ba wa-wa!*

The teacher of your life

If you are a new mother or father you are someone who has just been given the teacher of your lifetime; the teacher of your life itself. Some-one has entered an intensive teaching contract with you that will last for the next twenty years unabated, the terms only slightly renegotiated for the rest of your life after that. Someone has arrived who will grow you up, season you, teach you to let go at every stage of the most profound attach-ment. What a gift! To be in the presence of a new baby is to be vividly presented with the great matter unimpeded, unembellished, uncon-trived. In their eyes, the stars and the vastness are still slowly turning. The newborn can lie so quiet and attentive, their attention free of judgment or expectation, in a state of naked awareness. Just look into that mirror of your own original nature (you can't resist it anyway)—there it is!

The mirroring changes as the child begins to grow into its distinctive human character, its unmistakable beauties and blind spots (it seems we must have both), but still there is that constant invitation into presence, play, and unlimited friendliness. Remember how it is when you get down on the rug and enter into the child's world? There's no time at all down there, around two feet from the floor or less, and all the time in the world. You are endowed, in their presence, with a most healthy laziness:

be here, enjoy yourself. You are invited and allowed and even *required* to have no purpose. What a teaching!

In the adolescent years, the child makes one last valiant attempt to grow you up as they struggle, themselves, to be born as a rudimentary adult. Now the jewel-mirror samadhi of parenting faithfully presents the very image of your own transition or struggle to find some yielding toward the change that is called "old age and death." You can't miss it. You have the ringside seat at this wonderful drama, so relentlessly true to life, so deeply funny (though we may miss this fact at the time), and so deeply poignant. Opportunity after opportunity to let go, know less, and grow more mature in wisdom. The adolescent is a teacher who knows our every weakness and never spares an opportunity for our realization!

One insult after another

"We have children in order to torment ourselves," someone once said, "and we succeed beyond our wildest expectations." I'm reminded of Chögyam Trungpa's famous adage that meditation is just one insult after another! Oddly enough, this is not a warning but a recommendation. Parenting is the darkly funny, savage, grim, and amazing agreement we form with the universe to be present to this "just one insult after another" and not turn away or abandon the child. This will call into question virtually everything we think we know, beginning with who we think we are. (How quickly we find out who we're not, under the light of this most searching and visceral relationship.) Children have an extraordinary talent for undoing our customary roles, and forming our souls in the crucible of right now, demanding again and again that we meet them right in the moment, meet our lives, meet difficulty, moment by moment meet and resolve the extraordinary koan of "the other." To do this, we must lose our precious adult facades and regain access to the mysterious and creative core that has no name, the source that we brush again and again in meditation.

So this is the hermitage of everyday practice for the Buddhist who is a parent. People who are carrying out full-time the tasks of parenting are generally not monks and nuns. Instead, what normally comes with parenting in a Buddhist context in the West is sexual partnerships, wider family responsibilities, paid work, mortgages, all the pressures of ordinary life. How can you hold all of these together with the mind of practice? How do you hold in one mind "the baby" (especially when the baby is a teenager!) and your own intention to practice assiduously? Is it even possible?

The mind of "Is that so?"

There's an answer to be found in a folk-story attributed to Hakuin, who suffered and relished an unplanned excursion into parenting right in the midst of his devout life as a monk. It is a wonderful mixing up of Buddhism and of traditional gender roles; it is possibly also a way to understand his great openness to female students in a time when monasticism prevailed.

Hakuin was living in a small hut outside a village, dependent on village alms to sustain his fiercely intense practice. He was startled one day by a sudden loud and angry knocking at his door. He rose from meditation and opened it to a furious woman who had dragged along her reluctant daughter, and who thrust forward a newborn baby. "Here!" she said. "She's told us everything. We know it's your baby. You look after it, you imposter monk!" What should he do? Hakuin opened his arms to the baby. To take the baby was to take on a mantle of shame as a monk, and also the burden of looking after a tiny baby (while also maintaining, as best he could, his unswerving practice). He simply said, "Oh, is that so?" and took the baby.

Was this an ironic question? We hear it with ears tuned to irony, but don't miss the wonder in his voice, and also no doubt the heaviness of heart. But Hakuin received the baby with the freshness of no-mind, no-views, just wonder and wondering.

Life no doubt grew very, very complicated. Somehow he managed as one has to manage, as every new parent can attest to. The basis for this is not duty but love. Hakuin duly fell in love with this baby—the baby sees to this as a matter of its own survival. Months passed, then there was another loud knocking at the door. It was the angry woman again. This time, she held her own arms out for the baby in Hakuin's arms. "She's told us everything. We know it's not your baby. It was the boy at the fish-market. Give us back the baby!"

"Oh, is that so?" said Hakuin once more, and with his heart both relieved and breaking, he handed the baby back.

There are three important things to notice in this story from the point of view of practice and parenting. The first is the marvelous mind of "Is that so?"; it is a jewel of Buddhism. It is the mind of open inquiry, a willing-ness to receive insult after insult without "knowing" that it is insult but accepting it with non-blaming curiosity as mysterious potential, a "baby" full of unknown unfoldings. Expectation powerfully shapes our reality. But if we hold open the mind of "Oh, is that so?" we relieve the world of the weight of our own expectation and "knowing" and neurotic suffer-ing. We create room for the other, which frees us as well. Mindfulness is practical, as well as magically awake and alive.

The second is that every child is in the deepest sense also our own child, and that every child is simply passing through our lives—a being in dramatically perpetual change—and the great task of love is to learn to let go. A child presents that at every moment: love me, and love me enough to keep looking for how to finally loosen the bonds as the last and greatest act of love. Some people go into graveyards to meditate for a span of nights on non-attachment, and others work on that most exacting task across the span of all the years of parenting. We may have many more than Hakuin's several months of parenting; but still the world will come by degrees and say, "Give us back the baby" and we must find the way to hold all the opposing feelings in one mind. The mind of "Oh, is that so?" is the very space of that dynamic work.

The third thing to notice is that every child, every woman, every human being, is indeed profoundly unknown. This is the source of our deepest love and respect for the other, in the parental bond—indeed, in any bond. "Oh, is that so?" marks the depth of respect, which is to say the agreement to look again (to re-spect), to hold in the mind considerately, to forgo "knowing."

This is the letting go free of all striving to let go; a profound unknownness and unknowing is at its heart. When we recollect it completely as ourselves, we follow the mountains, rivers, and the whole Earth, the plants and trees.

Far beyond any mix-up.

CHAPTER 11

The koan
of dream

A T FIRST GLANCE IT MIGHT SEEM STRANGE even to think of putting dream together with the urgent matter of waking up in our life, but "dream," or *yume*, is a character often displayed on the walls of a Zen temple, a matter accorded deep respect and even gratitude. Why would this be so? And what is the nature of this fertile halfway zone of consciousness?

Chuang Tzu's famous story tells of a person who lay down in a field of grass under a gentle sun and fell into a dream of being a butterfly flitting from stem to stem of the warm, grassy field. Waking up, the sleeper could not say if he were a butterfly waking into the dream of being human, or a human being waking from a dream of being a butterfly.

Who doesn't recognize this half-state between dream and waking, this pregnant place between where all worlds lie open, the place of profound exchange between all things? The human mind is a kind of original egg, endlessly hatching. Extraordinary and intimate transformations are continually secreted beneath the curved white bones of the cranium. They are always rippling beneath our thoughts, gestating within the oyster folds of the brain. Metaphor surges toward thought; dream becomes perception, perception becomes dream. Endless rich becomings that dream themselves serenely as one thing becoming another; this fluid state can be glimpsed underneath and in between the agitations of all the little schemes and notions of the self, the person we call "I."

Some of the ripples and murmurings we catch in daylight are associations, wordplay, puns, jokes, daydreams, fantasies, creative mishearings, mistaken glimpses, memories, hummed phrases, and those rich reflective thoughts you catch sight of as you step from the shower and reach for your towel. Other more deliberative footprints we might call novels, plays, films, paintings, sonatas.

The fertile "place between" is always alive in us whether we are conscious of it or not, but we can't force entry to it. Dreams are largely involuntary tickets of leave to return home to it. Koans are more like voluntary tickets of leave, but they return us to a home beyond dream and waking; Dogen called it *dream*. Metaphor and the strong language of poetry leap into life here in the "place between." Language itself seems born in this medial realm.

The space between

In the place between, all things are equal and have the power of interchange; dreams blow like the weather. Under the scrutiny of dream work, virtually any dream, however slight in appearance, proves to be a complete architecture with its foundations deep in psyche, and even deeper in self-nature. Some dreams are recognizably big dreams; they have foundations in the deepest weave of our existence, and hold intimate conversation with us on our journey on the path. Such dreams can even present us with koans, and we can learn how to enter them, fully awake and lucid.

I am using "dream" here to refer to sleeping dreams. Another sense of dream is *mara*, in traditional Buddhism the delusory half-sleep that can steal our lives even while we dream we are awake and aware. We all know about that sleep that can steal whole seasons of our lives, and long to wake from it into something more alive. But this valuable cautionary and salutary sense of "dream" leaves out and attempts to leave behind much of the complexity and poetry of human experience; and it does not reach far enough into the true nature of that waking up experience. It may also encourage us to think of working hard to attain some pure condition of awakening in which such dark dreams as anger, fear, envy, grief, or regret may no longer have any relationship to us. That pure condition is itself a dream, and beneath its bright mirror, self-deception can lengthen in the shadows, undisturbed. It may seem a lovely dream, but it is a dream nonetheless. To confine yourself to dream as mara is to miss the deeper grounds for the obvious respect and gratitude in which Zen holds the matter of "dream."

For we wake from dream into another kind of Dream, into the profound dreaming of the universe, in which we have always most intimately belonged. We are that great Dream, together with the bird tracing its dream across the sky, the concrete freeway crawling with its dream of slow traffic, the dreaming grass blades nestled against the brick wall.

At that moment the conditioned dream of our lives is like a husk that falls away from the kernel of true life. And yet, even our attachments, vulnerabilities, daydreams, and desires are, from the truly radical view of Dream, blessed too. Buddha nature pervades the whole universe and is only to be found right here now. When we see clearly, all three aspects of "dream"—delusion, night dreams, the Dream of reality—present one buddha nature, one indivisible reality. As Dogen says in "Within a Dream, Expressing the Dream": "the dream is the entire great earth; the entire great earth is stable"; this matter is utterly at rest; and so just turning your head and actualizing freedom—and knowing that beyond any kind of knowing—is nothing but your own awakening of the dream within a dream. Waking up is the business of walking deeper, ever deeper, into lucid Dream, the actual brilliance of reality.

So Dream is a life koan, a matter to be resolved as complete intimacy with each thing, each moment. The journey into this dream is a journey into reality. Dream work is that journey into dreams; zazen is that journey into Dream. It is not uncommon to receive dreams that seem to inform the mysterious course of practice—"Big Dreams"—that help unfold whole stretches of your lifelong journey of waking up.

Equally great dreams

The mystery of this is sprouting and branching in every direction, rooted right here now. When we are awake, for a moment or two at least, we can see with very different eyes. We notice then that we wake from dream into Dream, the one that forms the universe and speaks in whales, liver flukes, avalanches, creek-beds, pebbles, blue wrens, and ocean currents. It also issues forth in *Hamlet,* "The Well-Tempered Clavier," unicorns, dragons, *The Blue Cliff Record,* and the songline of Green Ant Dreaming. And in the dream of walking backwards up a hill in Switzerland, from three nights ago.

Koans are windows straight into Dream, and the koan path is the path of learning to speak the language of the extraordinary condition that Wumen speaks of in his commentary on the koan "Mu," the first barrier, the root koan of Zen. "You are like a mute person who has had a dream—you know it for yourself alone," says Wumen. You could say that every other koan is a chance to grow more lucid and less mute in Mu. *Mu,* in Greek, by happy coincidence, is the root syllable of the word "mystery," and means "to seal the lips" in mute wonder, which is certainly what Mu does for us! And then Mu begins to speak, to walk about, to grow lucid within Dream.

Dogen's "Within a Dream, Expressing the Dream" speaks vividly to the strangeness—and yet wonderful familiarity—of Dream, which conjoins the interchangeable dream of enlightenment and the enlightenment of dream as one pure play in vast emptiness:

Thus, a tree with no roots, the ground where no light or shade falls, and a valley where no shouts echo are no other than the actualized expressions of the dream within a dream. As unsurpassable enlightenment is unsurpassable enlightenment, so dream calls it dream.

Dream calls it dream because what we confidently call everyday reality is a dark dream made dim in the actual blaze of reality. Until we encounter and realize our true nature, we see only "through a glass darkly," as St. Paul put it in I Corinthians 13:12. "For now we see through a glass darkly; but then, face to face; now I know in part; but then shall I know even as I am known." The Buddha in his great moment of awakening knew the morning star exactly as he was known, through and through, by it.

It is not surprising that dream calls it dream. There is no dream and no waking up, at the heart of the matter; no dreamer, no closer in or further away states of mind. There is no object of knowledge to be found here at all. "Supreme enlightenment" is nothing but the experience of seeing with the eye that sees you, just as you are. And yet it is not even a hair's breadth separate from us, just as we are, with our strange and various bodies that life dreams us into, and our even stranger and even more various dreams of consciousness.

The koan of being conscious in a human body is like this: when we see clearly, we see into the unborn, our own original nature, by the means of an ordinary, magical human body that will dream, itch, ache, fail, and fall away. It will also settle into stillness, convey deep wisdom, sip water, walk about, and perform a thousand miraculous acts each day. We are born, we grow to full size, we sit and stand and move about, and one day we will die—a very great dream. Another great dream is a tree, and the space beneath a tree, a single blade of grass in the light. And still another, from long ago and right here now, is the dream of a human being sitting under the shelter of a tree and, after deep meditation, glancing up at the morning star in the east, and being pierced by the very Dream of the universe.

Dream and Dharma

The dreams we meet in sleep occupy more than half our conscious life. They are interesting guides and potentially wonderful teachers, which move between realities with ease and can help us open to that mind. They cannot be decoded like riddles (though we may flatter ourselves with trying); yet they can help decode our own riddle, and their substance is the same no-base that utterly holds up and brings forth our life.

So the dream mediates in some way, conducts its own strange conversation between the self and God, as Carl Jung has said. Tibetan dream yoga teaches a way of practicing with dream and incubating dreams that directly convey the Dharma; Zen steps more lightly over dreams and any other visionary experiences, making little of them. Yet a monk like the great twelfth-century Shingon monk Myoe Koben honored and recorded his dreams for the forty years of his life as a monk, and that remarkable document opens up a window into the depths of a life of profound practice, with many teaching dreams appearing. Such dreams can visit us and offer great encouragement, but every dream, like every other thing in the universe, goes all the way down, pervades the whole universe.

Even a tiny fragment of a dream can reveal itself as the great architecture of the whole when you steadily look into it and learn the discipline of holding its polarities in one mind. And sometimes dream work that focuses its gaze through the lens of the sensing body can open, like meditation itself, to a state of communion with the fertile dark from which each thing comes forth.

I remember, or perhaps creatively misremember, a scene in the film *Antonia's Line*, tracing a line of mothers and daughters in rural Holland after World War II. Antonia is riding through their farm on her huge stately mare, with her ten-year-old granddaughter propped in front of her. The granddaughter, precociously intelligent, has been reading Kierkegaard under the tutelage of a gloomy, gentle misanthropic neighbor. "Isn't it terrible," the granddaughter remarks, "that everything is nothing!" The horse plods on some more. Antonia's broad face is calm. "Yes," she replies after a moment. Plod, plod, plod. "And isn't it wonderful, that everything comes of that!"

Even in a dream

Dreams open from the place where boundaries are already soft and can readily fall away. Dreams offer themselves as *upaya* (skillful means) to loosen our boundaries even when the dream is not obviously a visionary dream, a koanlike or practice-related dream. Dreams don't lie. They open the Way in an inward direction. They don't follow the logic of literal meaning. The language of psyche shares vocabulary with the waking world, but observes a different syntax. It is good practice to enter a new syntax of reality.

Dream also does not lie, draws no distinctions, and cannot be approached in any literal way, because the deep dream of reality does not conform to the habits of our ordinary conscious minds. Concepts cannot hold that great dream, can only withhold it. The deep Dream of reality also does not conform with the habits of our ordinary conscious minds. To become more versed in dream work will not in any way harm your chances of becoming accident-prone enough to fall into Dream itself.

Notice how the dream is exact in the detail it chooses: The rabbit on the roof is pink. The double-adaptors in the corner of the room sings hot gospel. Each blade of grass cuts the air precisely in its own angle and shape. The rain falls exactly where it falls. The back of your own hand would be familiar even in a dream.

Snow in a silver bowl

The Zen koan, and the way it works on us and in us, is bordered by the country of dream. The koan, like the dream, is compact, even chaste. It is enigmatic, resistant to daylit explanation, demanding the most serious thing to draw it out, pure play. Take this koan, to taste the dream in it:

> In a well that has not been dug,
> water ripples from a stream that does not flow.
> Someone with no shadow or form
> is drawing the water.

Xuefeng said, "When I pick it up, this great earth is like a grain of rice in size." This is only possible in Dream. "Each branch of the coral holds up the moon." "What is Zen? Snow in a silver bowl." "What is the sound of one hand?" "Someone comes to you in a dream and asks, 'What is Zen?' If you do not answer, you neglect your duty. How do you reply?"

Dreams, koans, and poetry have an affinity; they tap a partly shared deep well of mind, which may be why so few koans refer literally to dream. The states of deep samadhi somewhere between waking and Dream may be a zone of *makyo,* or waking vision, especially when they come to you in deep wakefulness. Zen tradition does not make too much of makyo, treating such experience as the little stream, not yet the great ocean. But even the little stream leads that way, and can help keep the practice alive and green.

The great dream body of the Buddha

The Three Bodies of the Buddha, a kind of mystery map of awareness, may help us grasp the wholeness of Dream. Keep in mind that the map and the actual territory, as with any map, have an approximate and semi-magical association: no more than that, and no less. Do not make the error of regarding these as categorical distinctions. Even to call them aspects or facets of each other is to push too hard to separate them; each one illuminates the others. There is one realization, three "bodies" manifesting that unified awareness. And yet just one ephemeral and imperfect ordinary human body realizes Buddha! This one!

And don't grow too attached to ones, twos, and threes. In Japanese, "not always so" is expressed in just two characters, in English it takes three words; Shunryu Suzuki liked to warn his students that the great secret of Zen lies in just two words, "Not always so." Truly, it cannot be counted.

The first era of Buddhist thought identified two "bodies" of the Buddha. *Dharmakaya* (body of the great order) is the realization of fundamental, all-pervading emptiness—unbounded, unspellable, pure, and clear. This is the gateless gate of realization. *Nirmanakaya* (body of transformation) is each form coming forth in its place in karma, in the realm of cause and effect, the whole marvelous "error" of each particularity of existence—moth! redwood! dust! human hand! These two "bodies" are even less than one. Everything falls away, and by that great fact everything stands up as itself, alive, brand-new.

The Mahayana identifies a third "body" of the Buddha, like the mysterious third in alchemy which is never given but endlessly actualized. A third cuts many fathoms deeper than a duality. The Indian philosophers of the early Buddhist period loved to break through dualisms by multiplying them beyond mind-blowing limit-point. But three is immediately a more alive and challenging dynamic than two. *Sambhogakaya* (body of delight or bliss body) is the middle of the middle, unhindered by opposites, a samadhi of form and emptiness in frolic and play. It is sometimes called the great dream body of the Buddha.

Dharmakaya is unbounded emptiness: the dark empty sky, the formless field of benefaction. Nirmanakaya is the unrepeatable face of each thing embodying for its own brief time its own minutely particular self: the great waking dream of each thing. Flower! Toe! Rabbit! You and me,

human beings in bodily form! Sambhogakaya is complete reconciliation: insight *(prajna)* meeting exactly at every point with compassion
(karuna), healing the split that ordinary human consciousness creates
between form and emptiness, life and death, dream and waking life.
Sambhogakaya is embodied realization.

Literature and art share some affinity with this medial consciousness.
Story, poetry, and koans are sometimes the only means of holding the
unsayable, short of silence, which holds everything. Synchronicity, the
sense of insistent and unlikely pattern in events that alert us to the deeper
grain of things, seems to arise here. In fact, all forms of field awareness—
intuition, dream, acts of creative imagination, and profound insight—
form on the natural ground of the mind that is beyond and before all
thought, that knows no-separation as itself.

It may be that language, the great human medial form, was born and
endlessly reinvents itself here. Speech itself may have begun when
human use of fire extended the day into darkness. In the dark of night,
when the world grew vague and hidden beyond the wavering line of firelight, language could reconstitute it. It's as though language were pulled
into being by the shape-shifting lines, the hypnotic moving figures and
the momentary visions created by fire. The possibility of extending the
time for human social interaction through the medium of firelight,
together with the sheer need of a growingly instrumental consciousness
to communicate that which could not be directly pointed at, demanded,
and called into being a language beyond grunts and gestures. Fire
revealed how the world could be spoken, told, visualized, recreated.
Now, what are words of fire?

Ordinary pebbles

In dreams, as in language, story, koans, and the cycle of life and human
consciousness itself, one thing is open and free to become another; each
moment is a new flicker of the original fire. Each thing is a conversation

between the self and God. And each thing that mediates this conversation—story, metaphor, dreams, and koans, things themselves—can dissolve the apparent gulf between form and emptiness; dream and waking life; life and death; day and night. There is no gulf! The Sambhogakaya, the bliss body of awake and medial awareness, is that no-gulf.

The poet Charles Simic recalled his childhood memory of lying in a ditch and looking at some pebbles while German bombers were flying over his head. He could no longer remember the face of his mother, nor the faces of the people who were there with him, but decades later he found he could still see the perfectly ordinary pebbles. And you can rely on it that perfectly ordinary pebbles will always staunchly convey a clear mind, a free and magnanimous heart to human beings, even while inhuman bombs rain down on human heads.

Dream pierces and manifests all three bodies of the Buddha, at once. Just pick up a fallen leaf, or a perfectly ordinary pebble, and you will have it.

Dream and death

Through deep and sustained practice, we come to look into the dark where we are not: dream is a bridge to that place. Realization, dream, and death share a deep and telling kinship. According to the ancient Greek philosopher Hesiod, among the nine children of the Titan goddess, Night, are the twins, Sleep and Death, and their sibling is Dream. In Zen, realization is often referred to as "the great death," although you might equally say "the great life": the momentary death of the small self opens a wide-open glimpse beyond the habitual form of this. Our practice asks us to include death, loss, and impermanence and the falling away of all things in time. Every opening toward it, degree by degree, enlivens our lives.

During a two-day workshop I was leading on the Dharma of dream,

the dream of a participant effortlessly conveyed this healing of all oppo-
sitions, and I reproduce it here with her permission:

> In the dream, my partner, his young daughter, and I are walking deep
> in the bush when a strong storm comes up. In my dream-self, the fear
> arises around finding shelter. Down the path, I see a large stone cylin-
> der, open on both ends—it looks like a stormwater pipe, but I know
> it to be a natural formation. We rush to it, enter and huddle inside,
> glad to be safe. The inside of the stone formation is covered with soft
> green moss, and though it's very cozy and womb-like in here, I'm
> aware of the storm raging outside. The light at each end of the cylin-
> der has its own unique quality—translucent at one end and opaque
> at the other.
>
> Suddenly the light within changes, and I wonder if that's caused
> by lightning outside. Then a sudden worry: How will we know which
> end to go out by when the storm subsides? I somehow know that one
> end is birth and the other death. But I have no idea which is which.
> What if we choose wrongly? Terror!
>
> At that moment an understanding—not exactly a voice, but a
> knowing—enters the stone womb with the words, "It doesn't matter.
> Birth and death are the same." I feel tremendous relief. I know it to
> be the truth. And that is when I "wake up," in the dream, and in my
> dreamer's bed.

How far beyond our waking fears and little knowings a dream like this
can reach! With such astonishing economy of means, it frees us from our
mooring in time, and for a moment reveals the whole ocean of being,
not just the narrow bend of the river we dream we're rounding now on
our way to the sea.

Psychologist James Hillman suggests that the most telling question to
ask of a mysterious or impenetrable dream element, even an apparently
trivial one, is always, What does this mean in the light of my death? The

capaciousness of dreams, of even the smallest dream fragment, opens from there. Even to ask this question is to begin to loosen the habit of life barely lived, liberating a certain energy of playfulness and courage. We can dare to begin to accept even the offer of the dark dream: the fact or fear of loss, grief, abandonment, insignificance; the final act of disappearing from the world of phenomena.

Contemplate your dream

The Dalai Lama has aligned the three bodies of the Buddha with three states of being: death (*Dharmakaya:* falling away of body and mind); the bardo or intermediate state (*Sambhogakaya:* unrestricted awareness); and rebirth (*Nirmanakaya:* each particular coming forth in the world of form, and karma). Accordingly, the Dharmakaya, as a state of pure cessation of the proliferation of all phenomena, aligns with death, when the gross levels of mind, and all the proliferations of phenomena, have dissolved into "the fundamental clear light"—which the Dalai Lama calls "the very nature of the sphere of ultimate reality."

The intermediate state of Sambhogakaya—rather like the interval between two lives—aligns with the bardo realm between death and rebirth, the "place" that mediates between ultimate reality and all the abundance of phenomenal life. It can be simply the interval between two breaths, in that slowed meditative awareness that stops the world, and catches sight of the flux in progress. In Tibetan Buddhist terms, this is the realm of the subtle body, the primordial body, arising from the experience of realizing the Dharmakaya. And "rebirth" aligns with Nirmanakaya, the multiple forms of the embodied universe, the movement from subtle body into the gross body and its energies.

Furthermore, dreamless sleep aligns with Dharmakaya and death, dream with Sambhogakaya and bardo, and waking with Nirmanakaya and rebirth. This is entirely true to the experience of anybody who has sat long and deeply, contemplating nothing but the bare ground of being that grows aware in us through meditation with the breath.

Dreams turn us inward; but koans turn us even further in, to turn us all the way inside-out and upside-down. The more we wake up, the softer all the boundaries begin to grow. Living, dying, sleeping, dreaming, waking: which is which? There is no separation, no gulf. There is nothing to mediate. They are the same.

So, contemplate your dream, and let the great Dream contemplate you.

PART THREE

Lotus in the fire

CHAPTER 12

The Way of character

THE WRITER D.H. LAWRENCE SAID somewhere that you can get to heaven in a single leap but you will leave a devil in your place. It is like that. You can experience a sudden realization and begin to open the eye of insight, but if you hoped that might keep you safe from all subsequent human messiness and frailty, you will leave a devil in the very place you vacated for heaven.

That "devil" is the energy of unacknowledged shadow. The people we love best stand to know far more about the disowned dark or difficult aspects of personality we may leave behind us in our leap to heaven than we ever will—after all, they're the ones left bearing its weight. It takes a valiant effort to catch sight of our own shadow, to look before any such leap. That effort is the character-work side of the matter of waking up. How does the lotus that blossomed in realization fare when it meets the other fire, the fire of ordinary life and all of its difficulties?

Character: a work in progress

One teacher said that the true goal of Zen practice is the perfection of character, the work of becoming who you really are. Don't be misled by the word "perfection." Like housework, perfection is never finished with us. We are all, without exception, its works in progress. This is the work of becoming genuine, a willingness to be more whole in every moment and condition that presents itself.

The quest for the "perfection" of character is not a quest for purity but for the great elegance of simplicity. It begins the moment we start to sit and notice our lives more intently, and the transforming fire is embodied awareness itself. The sudden great blaze of realization is wonderful and transforming but it does not end the quest. It just begins it in a new way. At every point, practice is the art of integrating all that you are into a calm awareness that is not preoccupied with the self, yet is alert to the nature of your actions and mistakes, and alive to how they affect others. After an experience of opening far beyond your limited self, you can glimpse the lifelong work of actualizing the compassion implicit in that experience of insight ("I am that!"), and seasoning into its wisdom. Insight and compassion cannot be separated from each other but may be sought and found only in each other's company. A truly clear mind is a magnanimous heart.

Enlightenment understood as separable from the mind of compassion is not enlightenment. Insight without compassion would be little more than an unusual and intriguing turn of mind. Compassion is not pity, which is actually a disguised form of fear. Compassion by its nature is fearless and uncondescending—it is clarified and resolved in the matter of self and other. Our true self is recognized in the other. The most natural compassion draws its reserves of no-fear from insight into what truly is, which begins with profound realization that we are not limited to our small, frightened ego selves, despite all press releases to the contrary issued by our hard-working Bureau of the Ego. Compassion and insight arise together on a path with heart.

Direct experience of your own self-nature opens you wide and is a great happiness worth all the steps of a long, hard journey; but it is not a leap to the safety of heaven, and will not relieve you of all further obligation to your life. On the contrary, it opens up to view new vistas of connectedness and consequence — it is like climbing a great mountain only to discover range upon range of jumbled peaks crowding away into the blue.

When we see truly, we see that black is also not black, and white is also not white, and that this is perfection. Likewise, ordinary life may present situations that seem black or white yet it is finally neither black nor white but the wonderfully piebald mixing up of every conceivable tonality. Its sacredness cannot be separate from its mixed and broken nature. Its sacredness can only be realized as you as you really are, in the mixed and broken condition of this life as it really is.

There's nowhere else to look for perfection.

To forget the self

There is no curriculum for work on character except life, and no graduation from it except death. How we die is just the final articulation of our character spoken in the hearts of those we leave behind. The whole matter is properly a modest business. Good character is not expounded, it is merely lived. And shame, not praise, is its compass. Perfection of character is indeed a koan, like the bodhisattva vows — we must resolve what it may be as moment by moment enquiry into who we really are, and what that wants of us.

Descartes famously said, "I think, therefore I am," seeming to express in seed form the Western Enlightenment view of the primacy of consciousness and reason in the making of the world. But meditation practice, and the exploration of the nature of awareness it opens up in us, soon discovers that while something about us may be defined by thought and reason, it is not even remotely the whole of what we seem to be. Who are we between or before or below thought, in sleep, or in deep states of meditation when the ordinary sense of the self dwindles to a small speck in vast space? Dogen said, "To enter the Way is to study the self. To study the self is to forget the self." How interesting: a meticulous study that becomes a meticulous "forgetting."

What is this forgetting of the self?

Paying attention

Ego lives a lot of the time in a state of susceptibility and abrasion toward things as they are. Yet this is not a matter to be solved by killing off the ego, which would be in any case an egotistical idea, and also an unrealistic one, for reality can leave nothing out from what it is. Real practice instead puts a far more subtle and demanding proposition to us: the possibility of intimately and minutely observing the self, just as we are, as an act of letting go of all of our concepts, contrivances, grievances, and judgments. For what we haven't fully recognized and accepted will certainly never let go of us.

The small and often vulnerable sense of self insists on occupying the foreground of our consciousness—and largely succeeds. But we find we are not completely at its mercy whenever we sit and grow still into any real depth of awareness, because the alert, persisting, non-judgmental, non-interfering awareness that we practice in meditation gradually gets to be very familiar with the self we continually construct. That awareness remains intimately related to that small self, and steadily curious about it, but under the calm, open scrutiny of meditation, the true self turns out to be far wider and more spacious than we ever could have dreamed. It's a great relief when that fact becomes plain. So meditation and the enquiry it conducts into the nature of the self is not becoming lost in self-interest; it is a properly alive and dynamic interest in deeply resolving the riddle of the nature of the self far beyond its original frame and preconceptions; it is dedicated to really meeting the koan that life presents to consciousness as "the self."

When that koan breaks open, the universe breaks open as us, and the self that sees then is amazed beyond all recognition. Finding and recognizing our true nature in some unrepeatable gesture or particular of this extraordinary world is indeed a forgetting of great magnitude, a breaking free, at least for one deeply instructive and timeless moment, from all the besieged and limited notions of "my self" we have ever subscribed to. Forgetting the self is letting go the self so that we might meet the true self, at last.

Uncontrived

As the practice of sitting deepens we generally find ourselves growing much more tender toward other beings. To sit deeply is an act of becoming less defended and strategic, and more vulnerable, embodied, impermanent—more here. Then, like tiny children at roll call, we may hear our true name called by some sight or sound or touch of the world and all of our being shouts out, "Here!" We have been taken up by the Way.

One sign that this is happening may be that it becomes more difficult to fudge things. Even to tell a non-harming but self-protective white lie just feels less acceptable, even when you assure yourself it is purely to protect the feelings of the other. When you really look closely, any lie offers some measure of injustice to the other and is a breach in connectedness; and a withdrawal of trust, for you are unilaterally deciding that the other is not wholly to be trusted with what you know is really so. A lie of any color sidesteps the present moment and what is actually happening by substituting a greater or smaller contrivance of reality that we secretly hope will ease our way, or help us get what we want. Could what is true to experience, presented in the way of least harm, actually be simpler, more interesting, and eminently worth risking?

Intimacy with the other

It just doesn't seem possible to touch the essential matter, which so radically changes our angle of view, without growing more acutely interested in how we find ourselves in the field of relationships with other people. All of the ten grave precepts, beginning with "I take up the way of not killing," "I take up the way of not stealing," "I take up the way of not speaking falsely," are designed to sharpen this interest; each one addresses how we negotiate the no-gap between ourselves and others, and while they offer a guide to walking the Way well in the most practical sense, each has its actual source in emptiness. Compassion alerts us to the beauty of the precepts, but insight opens their Dharma eye. Practice maintains an ongoing, practical relationship with the impact of our lives on others that each precept points to in a different way. Sometimes the ceremony of formally taking the precepts is compared to a marriage to the Way. In a marriage, we undertake a conscious relationship to something, to someone. But in this case it is a conscious relationship to our own essential nature—who we are really—in all the most ordinary, everyday circumstances of interaction with others.

Obviously, to depart from the precepts by killing, stealing, or consistently lying would be a gross betrayal of the experience of insight—an abrogation and loss of relationship with our own essential nature. More subtly, to indulge laziness, self-deception, anger, grievances, prejudice, projections, the endless minute and petty details that construct and protect the self, is to resign and accustom ourselves to a sly, pervasive unease of being separate from this—rather like being trapped in a barely conscious and rarely alive marriage, and being too lazy to attend to it, until you find yourself a stranger both to yourself and to the other with whom you share your life. But in this case, the other is your life.

However, being present to how we are with others is not a matter of legislating the self into being a good or better citizen of the human order, or being corralled into it by others. This is a matter beyond the reach of all legislation. Goodness is already abundant as what we really are—the self we literally realize in the unconfined awareness called "realization." The gold standard is the gold itself. Every precept encourages us to remain accountable to our inner sense of how we stand with that.

We only have to be fully and finely aware that we are not separate from reality and from each other, for goodness to be not even good, and not even attained—for indeed there is nothing to attain. The *Tao Te Ching* speaks of "people of old" (or people closer to our own original simplicity) as being good without knowing that they were good, and being just without knowing that they were just. When we stop supposing this or that and freely become what we actually are, we leave generous room for the other to be free to be exactly what they are. What a gift!

Character

The *Concise Oxford Dictionary* meaning of the word *character* offers a kind of medicine bundle of interestingly varied things that all seem oddly to fit. In the bundle we find a distinctive mark; an inscribed letter or figure; mental or moral nature and idiosyncrasies; moral strength and backbone; a known person; a created imaginary person (a character in a drama or story); an eccentric person ("a real character").

This strange array feels exactly right. As we practice, we lose our boundaries and find we contain multitudes, which is an understanding that grows its own new coherence about what our grandmothers might have called "backbone." The same old stories and dramas, starring that imaginary character who answers to our name, start to feel tired and effortful to maintain. As we shake loose of what's not really true, we become more our idiosyncratic selves than we could ever have imagined—our own true eccentrics, shaped and scarred and made beautiful by the distinctive and indelible marks of life experience, but at the same time, smoothed and polished, rolled by the action of awareness like river stones under the ceaseless action of water.

There is a way in which the whole of character cannot easily be hidden and declares itself clearly even in the smallest gesture, like an indelibly inscribed figure that is recognized faster than thought by the soul of another. So *character* is seen like a tree or bush against the bright sky, each branch clearly growing according to its length and shape, each twig and twist a revelation of how a fate unfolded in the actions of a human being. To be in the presence of a person of character is to feel your own bones take on more mineral, your own soul stir with life and nameless gratitude.

Karma

Karma is another interesting medicine bundle. Its assortment of meanings seem to include the wheel of birth and death; doings and actions producing resultant states of being; forces of habit; the reverberant meaning and effect of deeds; ceremony and its performance; a knot; affinity, or mysterious affinity. Sometimes it is imagined as if it were like money, as when we speak of "karmic debt"; and in old usage, karma made and paid off each day was referred to as "ready-money" karma. Other times, it seems to be imagined in terms of a ripening: we speak of the "fruits" of karma. Interestingly, the packet of karma we are born with is called "ripe karma"—always ready for harvest it seems, even at birth.

It's easy enough to see that "forces of habit"—consistent ways of doing and being—embody or enact karmic patterns in our lives, sometimes again and again and again. How often we seem to go around the same block unawares until we reach the same old brick wall. There it is again! But how interesting that we call it a force of habit. Do we almost hope that it may be a little like a force of nature, not completely of our doing?

There's so little conscious perspective around these blocks or ruts or patterns of character that it can easily feel that someone else did whatever feels wrong. And it's wonderful how there are always suspects at hand—usually the people dearest to our heart are required to be our fall guys. A habit becomes a force of habit, in time, replacing direct meeting with reality, cutting its own deep rut that gradually seems inescapable. Seems inescapable, except that every moment when you are fully present and awake is actually a wide open one, completely free of all supposing of any kind, if you dare to notice.

And here at every juncture opens the creative and daring leap of agreeing to practice, which means choosing your fate. That's establishing a whole new custom of awareness in the place of unexamined habits of action and reaction.

The ongoing ceremony of awareness

Ceremony is a slightly stranger association at first—yet births, deaths, graduations, marriages, and divorces are so plainly karmic ceremonies, marking the moments that shape the course of our lives. At each of these a "knot of karma," a knot of change that links birth to death, and links becoming to letting go, is tied forever. Then there are the "lesser" ceremonies of karma—of welcoming somebody into your house and sharing a meal or a cup of coffee with them, or going for a walk, or chopping the carrots, or kissing your child goodnight. Any action is lifted to ceremony by mindfulness. And ceremony, from the old Greek goddess Ceres, evokes reaping the entire rich harvest of the earth.

Perhaps the most common sense of karma is the one that lines up with the "reverberant meaning of deeds." And so we talk of "good" and "bad" karma, as if actions leave a turbulence that shapes future possibility, and indeed it seems they do. Great novels and plays often follow the trajectory of a character trying to outrun or harmonize with the wake of their own karmic churn. Even if karma can be understood as the kindly reoffering by the universe to us of teachings we have misunderstood again and again in the limitless past, still heaven is merciless. Cultivation of good karma may have its place, but the idea of good karma carefully "stockpiled" and enumerated can grow very dubious indeed. I prefer the more modest enterprise of avoiding bad karma, guided by feeling in the dark to rediscover what my sense of integrity intuitively knows.

But karma finally refers to neither good nor bad. From this side of life, who can say anything final about good or bad? Karma most simply is what is, and realization most simply is agreeing with this—a profound gesture of radical acceptance. This is where the most beautiful sense of all opens to us, concerning karma—that of "mysterious affinity," where we find and recognize ourselves in each other and in each detail of the amazing world.

Forbearing

Integrity is like a late-developing sensory organ in the process of human maturation. The clue to its presence is not pride but shame that arises from within, which can gradually be distinguished from the sensation of being shamed by others. This is the *Te* of the *Tao Te Ching*. *Te* is how we express the Tao in actual living—how the Tao walks about, soothes a fever, chops vegetables, writes a book, makes love—and so we might say it is a kind of refinement of character in response to awareness of Tao, a sensitivity that may be cultivated to become a sensibility. The form of its cultivation is the enduring work of detecting and going with the flow of Tao, which depends upon maintaining close and subtle attention from the center of your being: noticing even tiny ways in which we may violate the boundaries of the other; checking for the sense of inner wholeness and well-being and, more importantly, its loss or disturbance.

Te, which responds to our sense of the Tao or what it wants, is never still but, like the Tao, always alive and moving. It is a kind of tracking awareness responsive to what lies always just before direct knowing. Cultivating *Te* and allowing it into how we respond to others is a little like alchemy—a patient, slow transformation, one thing growing or decaying into another, suffering change. Sometimes *Te* is translated as "virtue," and I think of this partly as holding power, the ability to accept difficulty and not react.

This grace in living develops as an ability to hold steady and listen keenly to the informing sense of shame, allowing its due process and slow composting. It matures as the ability to stay seated at the center and let the psyche of the other work upon you, waiting on the slow emergence of inner truth, suffering its gradual revelation.

What sustains this quiet, fearless holding power is *prajna*, the penetrating energy of realization that we awaken in ourselves with a strong practice of meditation—the intuitive realization of being one with what is, one with the Tao, affinity with emptiness. So the Way of wisdom is the watercourse Way—perceiving, accepting, moving wisely with what is.

Nobody said it was easy, to stay in the fire, stay alert, and forbear. But the alternative is to suffer what is anyway, but with no true or reliable relationship with it. Perhaps this is what Hamlet meant when he spoke of enduring "the slings and arrows of outrageous fortune"; whereas the *Tao Te Ching* says, "If one recognizes the eternal, one becomes forbearing…All one's life long one is not in danger."

Integrity

John Beebe, who has made a lifetime's study of the psychological depths of integrity, says that we learn about integrity when someone brings us their genuine outrage and we have it in us to see what they are talking about and why it was felt as a violation. Letting in that sense of the other's violation might bring a hot scorch of shame, but in the wake of the bushfire appear the truly amazing green shoots of recovery. This kind of opening to the psyche of the other, and its renewal of awareness, can only take place in exchanges of mutual honesty and care, where what is disclosed respects and fits the actual nature and boundaries of the relationship. It is not about maintaining indiscriminate porousness, or making unsolicited or misplaced self-disclosures. When you are seated at the center, a natural sense of checking boundaries and taking care of the boundaries of the other is always in play.

Nor does this openness mean a bland acceptance of every projection that might come your way. For just as integrity starts to nudge us inwardly with shame at our lack of wholeness as we deepen into practice, so too intuition begins to develop in the dark. Intuition sharpens the emotional eye that sees character. And as it develops, so does a more acute sense of the difference between integrity's shame that arises within, and the projection imposed on us by another person to attempt to make us feel bad.

The seeing of the heart

Coupled with compassion, which can be an early fruit of practice, this intuition is a seeing of the heart, a knowing of the gut. Interestingly, the character for *Te* brings together three elements: an eye, looking straight ahead or within; *shin*, or heart-mind; and the sign for movement, or change. *Te* is the weight and depth of how we sense the Tao and bring it forth in actions, gestures, and words. It is our karmic, characteristic response to the eternal Tao. Our sense of *Te* is our sense of integrity, which can intuit the movement of the Tao and the action most aligned with that.

So *Te* is Right Action, which is not a set of prescriptions but a mystery contemplating and responding to a mystery. Exploring it is a lifelong work of bringing awareness as much as possible to that cliff-edge of birth and death, and making a home there. The grace such work bestows is hard won; there are no tourists in that place.

Our own death is the light that shines back on our lives, our stories, our character, making them vivid. Work in the field of character is the development of our ability to see into emotional and moral experience and to bear dark emotions, to move from evading pain to accepting suffering, and to acting in accord with the touchstone question, "What does this mean in terms of my own mortality?" That question has the power of paint-stripper—it all comes away, all but life itself.

And such work unfolds in relationship, intimacy with what is, intimacy with the other. Zen practice is the practice of intimacy with the other, including all of the moods and formations and parts of the self. Our insight and values, which are hallmarks of character, are lines of flow between the self and the other, carving channels in which emotional and moral experience can move, shaping and being shaped by the topography of our soul, deeply marking our every gesture with unmistakeable character.

Accountability

If we were not beings who pass quickly away like all other things, none of this would matter. Rumi says this dream we call life must be interpreted; we are accountable:

> *This place is a dream.*
> *Only a sleeper considers it real.*
>
> *Then death comes like dawn,*
> *and you wake up laughing*
> *at what you thought was your grief.*
>
> *But there's a difference with this dream.*
> *Everything's cruel and unconscious*
> *done in the illusion of the present world,*
> *all that does not fade away at the death-waking.*
>
> *It stays,*
> *and it must be interpreted.*

"The death-waking," of course, is not just waking to the powerful fact of death itself, although that may help prompt it. It is waking to the full and formidable light of life, which includes death and so is not haunted or obsessed by it. That waking is a kind of dying to the fear of life that had boxed us in to such a small and fiercely guarded dream of self. "You wake up laughing at what you thought was your grief."

But, says Rumi, our cruel and unconscious actions are not melted away by the death-waking. Our seeing is transformed, but something stays—like karma—and it must be met, accepted, worked with. That dream stays, and it must be interpreted. It is hard work, and its deepest interpretation is called wisdom. And this is why we bend to the gritty, gruelling, galling work, present in some form in every day, of bringing grace to our life of marvelous mistakes, of paying our karmic dues, saving all beings.

Why were you not who you really are?

When the old Hasidic master called Zusya—a most playful, humble, and genuine human being—was on his deathbed, very close to the end, all who loved him were crowded about, weeping and straining to hear his last words. At a certain point he said, "You know, when I get there, they will not ask me, 'Why were you not one of the great ones?' They will ask me, 'Why were you not Zusya?'"

"Why were you not Zusya?" That old teacher's great question strips all pretence and complication from the matter, and pierces the heart. It is not far removed from "What does this mean in the light of my own mortality?" Zusya touches the secret, elusive sorrow that may well haunt every last human being. What if we were given a life and never lived it? What if we lived instead a little way off from our lives, and never dared real intimacy, never gave ourselves completely, never risked living the providence of this life all the way down to the ash?

What if self-importance and skepticism and calculation of advantage and disadvantage—the whole sly iniquity by which we cheat ourselves of truly being here, and truly being us—turned out to be the final seal upon our life, the telling form and evident character of our every gesture?

The habit that ends all habit

Practice is the great chance to come to life in every moment and gesture to which you can manage to bring mindful awareness. It is the dropping of every habit in favor of just one, inhabiting it completely, living and dying right there—the habit of being true to what you really are. Not being good, or great; not being aware of being good or great; and certainly not "acting compassionately." Always just becoming what it wants.

That is force of habit transformed to force of character. It grows from freely choosing forbearance, which means accepting all the amazing offers of life; and it finally has nothing to fear, for it cannot harm another. Its business is just completely manifesting a being never to be repeated anywhere on the Earth. The true human being is utterly ordinary, and that is its own clear light.

So let your choices be guided and provoked every day by Zusya's question, which grows sharper when your days are clearly numbered; and in which you can already hear the pointed shortness of your days, if you are even half awake.

Why were you not Zusya? While you had the chance, why were you not who you really are?

CHAPTER 13

A thousand mistakes, ten thousand mistakes

T HE KOAN KNOWN AS "BAIZHANG'S FOX," Case Two of Wumen's *The Gateless Barrier*, takes up the problem of reconciling the one continuous mistake we sometimes call "life" with buddha nature, which is complete grace from the beginning. It asks, How does a life in karma reconcile with eternity? How does eternity meet intimately with karma? And what can grace possibly be, if not the complete realization and concordance of these two? But how is such grace realized? Baizhang's story of a man who becomes a fox and then a man again visits these great questions, and asks us to find ourselves within them. Here is the story.

Once when Baizhang gave a series of talks, a certain old man was always there listening, together with the monks. When they left, he would leave too. One day, however, the old man remained behind. Baizhang asked him, "Who are you standing here before me?" The old man replied, "I am not a human being. In the far distant past in the time of Kashyapa Buddha, I was head priest at this mountain. One day a monk asked me, 'Does an enlightened person fall under the law of cause and effect or not?' I replied, 'Such a person does not fall under the law of cause and effect.' With this I was reborn five hundred times as a fox. Please say a turning word for me and release me from the body of a fox."

He then asked Baizhang, "Does an enlightened person fall under the law of cause and effect or not?" Baizhang said, "Such a person does not evade the law of cause and effect."

Hearing this, the old man was immediately enlightened. Making his bows he said, "I am released from the body of a fox. The body is on the other side of this mountain. I wish to make a request of you. Please, Abbot, perform my funeral as for a priest."

Baizhang had the head monk strike the signal board and inform the assembly that after the noon meal there would be a funeral service for a priest. The monks talked about this in wonder. "All of us are well. There is no one in the morgue. What does the teacher mean?" After the meal, Baizhang led the monks to the foot of a rock on the far side of the mountain. And there, with his staff, he poked out the body of a dead fox. He then performed the ceremony of cremation.

That evening he took the high seat before his assembly and told the monks the whole story. Baizhang's great student, Huangbo, stepped forward and said to Baizhang, "As you say, the old man missed the turning word and was reborn as a fox five hundred times. What if he had given the right answer each time he was asked a question—what would have happened then?" Baizhang said, "Just step up closer and I'll tell you." Huangbo went up to Baizhang and slapped him in the face. Baizhang clapped his hands and laughed, saying, "I thought the barbarian had a red beard, but here is a red-bearded barbarian!"

No time, no near and far

Baizhang weaves a fascinating shape-changing story in which time seems to telescope: if you look through the lens of a telescope one way, the distant comes close; if you look the other way, the close is strangely far off. But when you immerse in all-at-once time in the deeps of zazen, it is not so hard to feel into the way that this story actually presents how all time and space meet in us when we are truly here, as well as how we are when we are not completely ourselves, and how we find our way back to grace. Not all consciousness is bound to the sense of time that ticks away, and of space that keeps things apart. If you are uncertain about this, have a look at your dreams, which, like certain stories, are free in their sense of near and far, this time and that one. Sometimes, stories that lie close to dream, like this one does, are the only simple way to hold the true nature and fullness of awareness.

When we look at it this way, we may see the old man condemned to life as a fox in an interesting new light. In ancient days he too was head priest at this mountain called Baizhang, and so would also have been known by the name Baizhang. Are there really two Baizhangs in this story, or only one? How many forms of ourselves, how many lifetimes, do we encompass in a single lifetime? What we do and how we act—especially if it leaves us uneasy—can seem to recede very fast indeed into the ancient past, remote from self-scrutiny. It can appear as far distant in time as Kasyapa Buddha, one of the mythical ancient seven Buddhas of the world age preceding the one that brought forth the Buddha! This subtle, slippery move of the mind away from some action and its long chain of consequences is what sets in motion the many oblivious lifetimes we can lead as a kind of fox-spirit, too quick to be held accountable—and it leaves us both not quite fully human, and never quite fully at rest.

And this continues until the day we do not slip away but stay behind. We stop, needing to know the answer to a question that is hard to ask, and the intense, secret suffering of our condition at last begins to make itself known to us. Whatever badly needs to come to our attention we seem to do again and again until at last we notice and agree to meet it with our whole attention.

If we really stop and attend more deeply, a thousand lifetimes with their ten thousand mistakes can truly come to rest in a single moment.

A life and death question

Baizhang is a great figure in our lineage; he is an ancestor of Linji, who is the progenitor of the Rinzai or koan-based training tradition of Zen study. He was a student of Mazu, who was, together with Shitou, the source of the real flowering of Chan Buddhism from the sixth to the tenth century in Tang dynasty China. Baizhang, founder of the Zen monastic schedule of work and zazen, was famous for saying, "A day without work is a day without food." Even when he was, as in this story, immensely old and gnarled, he worked tirelessly every day, and they had to take the hoe from him and try to drag him from the garden. (They didn't succeed.)

In Baizhang's story, an old man begins to appear in the assembly each day. He doesn't say or do anything but turn up and listen to the Dharma talks. This not quite worldly being comes, and then he goes away. He always comes back. But one day he doesn't go away again. Baizhang immediately goes up to him, very interested. The old man explains the fox curse that has burdened him for a kind of eternity. Someone once asked him an earnest question, a question of life and death: "Does an enlightened person fall under the law of cause and effect, or not?" And Baizhang, so many moons ago, answered in the negative: "No, they don't." Because of his response to the question, it seems the long-ago head priest Baizhang had to live five hundred lives as a fox. He now begs the present-day head of this temple, Baizhang, "Please say a turning word for me and release me from the body of a fox."

What got the old man into this predicament? What is it about saying, "No, an enlightened person does not fall under the law of cause and effect" that is so harsh in its consequences?

From one side, his answer to the question seems simply incorrect—cause and effect appear to be implacable laws of our embodied state of being. Let go of an apple and it will fall to the ground. Cut yourself and you will bleed. Get born, and you will surely die. And yet, from the other side, are there not profound moments in this life when being has no limit, no confines of time or space, no up or down, no inside or out? You notice something perfectly simple and all that you "know" falls away from it, leaving you suddenly in contact with what you have always been—a mystery falling through mystery, a song inside a roaring, a night of turning stars walking around in an ordinary human body. When you see like this and realize like this, do you fall under the law of cause and effect or not?

So why did such a response condemn old Baizhang for lifetime after lifetime to a condition that was less than fully human, deeply haunted by his choice of answer to this question?

The traditional Buddhist view of karma and enlightenment is that we practice moment after moment, lifetime after lifetime, to reach a point where we may at last step off the wheel of birth and death, cause and effect, and permanently enter nirvana. This is a view of personally attaining something beyond all reach of time, transcending karmic existence and the realm of cause and effect: a perfect equanimity that brings us to complete rest.

The Mahayana account of this matter has a different emphasis: the bodhisattva is dedicated—by the very nature of the awakening experience—to serving the awakening and liberation of all beings by penetrating to a complete realization of the greater self, which leaves nothing out and wipes away all thought of attainment. From this point of view, no one can know true happiness and peace unless everyone shares in the bounty. This understanding offers a roundly human and humane sense of what enlightened activity may be: giving yourself away more and more thoroughly; finding a place of accord with the wonderful shambles of ordinary life by closely attending to what it really is; and then helping it be the best it can. But the old Baizhang, in his green years as a teacher, responded with confidence and purity from the ground of Buddhist doctrine with the very words of the Buddha and was reborn for his troubles as a fox. Very interesting! What did he miss seeing?

Fox lives

Old Baizhang's condition of being stranded between fox spirit and human being seems to point to a position that is at once straining for a kind of immortality and yet condemned to a condition that is less than fully human. Any stance of spiritual transcendence strands us a little outside our real lives as human beings in a realm that can feel quite suspect to others and estranged even to ourselves. (We are usually the last to notice the bushy red tail so obvious to others.) So, too, does the powerful human urge to evade consequences with a dream of a trouble-free existence, the forgivable yearning for things to go "better."

Our deep human resistance to difficulty is figured here in the dream image of inheriting a curse of life after life as a fox. Chinese and Japanese folklore see foxes as tricky creatures that shift and shade disconcertingly across the barriers between the human, animal, and spirit realms. Japanese folklore warns of women who walk down the street in their kimonos but betray a fox's tail in the shadow they cast behind them. Akira Kurosawa's film *Dreams* portrays a fox wedding—a very dangerous thing to see. It seems that foxes always hold their weddings on a day of sunshine during rain. If you go into the woods at such a time you are in serious danger of glimpsing a fox wedding. And if you do, the foxes will rarely forgive you.

So there's something secret and powerful and a little bit unlucky in getting too involved with foxes, and old Baizhang gets very involved with them indeed—five hundred lives as a fox! It seems you can be a long time lost in the rank foxiness of the dream of evading the seamless net of actions—a net that includes the definitive knot of your own mortality—and to be saved from the body of a fox, you must come back by the long hard road of facing difficulties, yourself, and things, just as they are.

Les Murray's poem "The Young Fox" touches on the uneasy human enchantment with foxes that casts its spell despite the natural enmity of two species that share common prey. Is it because there is a tricky part of ourselves that foxes reflect back with uncomfortable clarity? They seem to share with us a keen mind that can be its own undoing in the end— the ability, or at least the deft attempt, to slip out of all our own consequences. Isn't it our own self-preserving cunning, our reflex skill at immediately supposing something instead of meeting what is, that so deftly takes us out of connectedness and undoes us?

> I drove up to a young fox
> on the disused highway.
> It didn't scare, but watched me
> roll up to it along the asphalt.
> I got out. Any poultry it would kill
> wouldn't now be mine, no feud between us.
>
> It watched quizzically then bounded
> away with an unmistakable headshake
> that said "Play with me!"
> and stopped, waiting. I remember
> how sharply perfumed the leaves were
> that lay on the pavement in that world.

To be invited by any wild animal a little way into its world is to begin to lose your usual boundaries—and that's a kind of grace, fragrant with possibility. But when we are falling on the side of "No, an enlightened person does not fall under the law of cause and effect," which world are we in then? Are we really in this world? Can we be fully here, pierced by sharply perfumed leaves on a hot road?

Every life is fraught with difficult choices—doesn't the grace, the fragrance, the sting of life itself originate right here in the very effort of living within both the limitation and immense complexity of cause and effect? Just by being living beings, briefly here by extraordinary chance, are we not profoundly graced by cause and effect itself from the very beginning?

Our human shiftiness

Old Baizhang did fall out of such a rich web of connectedness through his answer to the question, into five hundred lifetimes alone as a fox. So it seems we are foxes when we're either too transcendent or shifty to be mortal and vulnerable, attentive and accountable—which is to say, connected. And we thereby lose our gift to be pierced by the other in whatever form it appears. We lose our gift of openness, of compassion.

But then in the story there is a shift, and this can happen as suddenly in practice as one breath becoming another: one moment heavy with weariness, the next moment clear and light; one moment a fox alone and lonely, the next moment an old man stepping free and bowing in gratitude. If you remember, Baizhang now responds to the question quite differently. He says, "Such a person does not evade the law of cause and effect." And just hearing these words releases the old man from the fox body. Baizhang speaks, and his very words pierce far beyond where words and meanings can reach. One moment we are sure we're never, ever going to see beyond the platitudes of our own minds, and the next moment we're just staring in wonder, lost in the roar of it. So when he asks the question again and gets a different answer, why does this save him? Is the answer to the question right this time where the other one was wrong?

By now you possibly smell the fox that lurks in such a question.

Precarious

When you live life at peace with every circumstance of your life, favorable or terrible, you situate yourself at the still point of the turning universe. Then you are the world of cause and effect itself, you become this. You become, with nothing between you and it, this precarious world. You are precariousness itself and so you are no longer subject to precariousness. When you live like this you are the master of precariousness, master of cause and effect, and then everything is blessed, just as it is.

Interestingly, the root of the word *precarious* is "prayer," or "imprecation." When you fully enter precariousness, our ordinary human world of one mistake after another, you are "full of prayer," open to connectedness. Then you can see how a life of human limitation is also a life of grace.

At the heart of this koan is the news that freedom comes when we do not seek to evade cause and effect, when we are not blind to it but free within it. Only when we face it completely can we locate that subtle point of freedom, and it is exactly there in the very teeth of events. Freedom is not found in either evading or not falling under the law of cause and effect. It is realized in a deeper reconciliation of these two that are less than two, and it completely releases the old man from his fox thrall.

The moral fact

This moment of stepping free leaves in its wake a distinctly mortal fact, bare and humble: The old man says, "Now that I am an old man reborn as a human being, there is a fox body on the other side of the mountain in a cave." He seems oddly confident that this makes complete sense, and that Baizhang will know exactly where to look. He asks that Baizhang honor these five hundred fox lives as lives of grace, to give the fox the cremation rites for a Zen priest.

And so Baizhang enacts a beautiful life and death drama for his monks, a wonderful Zen *upaya,* or an act of skillful means, to draw his monks onto new ground of realization. There can be a lot of drama sometimes in Zen—a lot of apparent play and joking—but there's always a serious matter at the heart of a joke, and a playful matter at the heart of real seriousness. Baizhang has someone strike the signal board for a funeral and leads them all around the mountain, without explaining a single thing. They're all abuzz with "Who can it be?" It turns out to be just an old fox body that he pokes out with his staff from a cave. Who knows—perhaps he saw the fox on a walk the evening before. And very surprisingly he announces, "Now this fox will have the funeral of a priest." Sacrilege! The body of an old fox will be treated no differently from the body of a priest! This turning upside-down of ordinary sense is entirely resonant with the core of this koan. Indeed, it accords with the core of every koan.

Which is which?

In the old funeral ceremonies for a nun or a priest, somebody waved a flaming torch over the body from one side to the other. On one side they would say, "Saṃsara!" and on the other, "Nirvana!"; "Nirvana!," "Samsara!," the torch creating one unbroken arch of flame in the darkness: not falling under the law of cause and effect; not evading the law of cause and effect. We see that they are inseparable, finally even indistinguishable, one from the other. The clear categorical distinction that condemned an old man to so many lives as a fox cannot survive the singularity of eye that opens in the dark when knowing falls away.

In the darkness of unknowing we begin at last to discern the face of karma in eternity, and of eternity in karma, whereas the narrow beam of discriminating mind can make out only one opposed to the other. Nicholas of Cusa said, "How needful it is to enter into the darkness and admit the coincidence of opposites, to seek the truth where impossibility meets us." Old Baizhang is driven into that darkness by the acute need to lift his curse of five hundred lifetimes as a fox, and impossibility meets him squarely to release him.

At the end of this day of mysterious doings, Huangbo, Baizhang's great student who became his Dharma heir, steps forward with another upaya. Just as the old man stepped forward from the assembly, now someone else steps forward and has another question of life and death importance to present to Baizhang. Huangbo asks, "What if he had given the right answer each time he was asked the question, what would have happened then?" Like the fox on the sharply scented pavement, Baizhang beckons him forward for a little bit of play. But before he can show Huangbo what would have happened then, Huangbo jumps in first and drives right through the barrier of right and wrong with a single clap of the universe. Slap! Here it is! Nothing but this! His instantaneous slap leaves no room for conjecture and snatches us free of any lingering temptation to find in terms of "right" and "wrong."

Huangbo and Baizhang are not even remotely arguing right and wrong. As Wumen says elsewhere in *The Gateless Barrier*, "If you argue right and wrong, you are a person of right and wrong." Do you want to be stuck with that? And Baizhang thoroughly approves Huangbo's play with a great rolling laugh, saying, "I thought the barbarian had a red beard but here is a red-bearded barbarian!" Bodhidharma is the "barbarian," the astonishing foreigner who came from India to China with his fox-red beard, bearer of the Dharma, one who could say to the diligent Emperor Wu that the highest merit of the practice is "vast emptiness, nothing holy." So the epithet *barbarian* is a mark of glad respect, resonant with an immensity free of the slightest taint of holiness. (Fortunately, there are no Zen saints at all.) There is not a speck of difference between these two, Baizhang and Huangbo.

There is no self to impede them. And somehow I also catch a fleeting glimpse of a lone fox that will never scare—ready for play, ready for anything in the sharp fragrance of reality.

Wumen leaves us with a comment that reverberates right through every ordinary, falling-down human life: "If you have the single eye of realization," he says, "you will appreciate how old Baizhang lived five hundred lives as a fox as lives of grace." Can this be so? Can this ordinary life of one egregious mistake after another be seen for what it truly is—a life of grace?

Return to fate means eternity

Here's how the *Tao Te Ching* pokes that old fox body out from under the mountain and lays the matter bare:

> *Things in all their multitude:*
> *each one returns to its root.*
> *Return to the root means stillness.*
> *Stillness means return to fate.*
> *Return to fate means eternity.*
> *Cognition of eternity means clarity...*
> *If one recognizes the eternal*
> *One becomes forbearing...*
> *All one's life long one is not in danger.*

Things in all their multitude: each one returns to its root. That's a little like Wumen's "single eye of realization," the way things look when we settle deeply and grow still, coming down to one.

But right there, that very *stillness means return to fate.* Fate is another way of saying five hundred lives as a fox, or ten thousand mistakes, or an ordinary human life in karma. Even if you try exceptionally hard not to step on an ant, might you not tread on one you never saw? If you strain to hurt not a single feeling, can you ever really presume to truly know the feelings felt by another? Can you live without consuming or hurting other lives? Can you even breathe without doing so? So this very settling into our bones and sinews, this very growing still, will return us ever more keenly to "fate," to the dream that must be interpreted.

But next we learn, *return to fate means eternity.* Karma—fate—and eternity are like two faces of one leaf, turning bright, dark, bright, dark as it twirls falling through sunlight. Every single mistake is a miracle of a kind, a door that opens to emptiness. *Cognition of eternity means clarity*...Seeing into emptiness, being seen right through by emptiness, sweeps away ten thousand concerns and clears the single eye of realization that can more steadily recognize the eternal in each fleeting thing, each pulse of emotion, each clouded thought, each sharp jab of error.

And so, *if one recognizes the eternal, one becomes forbearing.* Practice brings us face-to-face with the eternal. Then the task is to become still in the face of commotion and at rest even on the point of each sharp needle of circumstance. To be forbearing is to be able to tolerate and not react to the flow of "one insult after another" that the self is so ready to perceive.

This forbearing is how the true brilliance of *mistake* can begin to shine. What we do well is already of less interest than what is still mistake-ridden and difficult. Each mistake defines an interesting edge for us, and that "edge" is a place of lively, intense learning that we can only access through failure or risking failure. This is to seek the truth where impossibility meets us. Forbearance in this light is not dull but sharp and full of life. The brilliance of a mistake can be accepted as a kind of curious gift when we drop expectations and accept responsibility—that step into real freedom.

So when we see with the single eye of realization, we realize an extraordinary refuge right at the heart of precariousness: *all one's life long one is not in danger.* That single eye is the eye of life-and-death, and when we see with that eye we can see beyond the frame—and the name of the frame is "mistake."

A life of grace

Can you look at your vulnerable, unrepeatable life and recognize it as a life of grace? Antonio Machado's great poem, "Last Night," proposes that while we sleep so deeply into our hundreds of fox lives of canny oblivion, we also dream a great dream—a "marvelous error!"—that inside our own heart there is a beehive alive with transformation. We recoil in shame and try to hide our mistakes, and all the while, Machado tells us, "the golden bees / are making white combs and sweet honey" from our old failures. If we can dare to live completely into our failures and allow them into full reality, and agree to suffer appropriate shame rather than neurotically deflect it toward fear and anger, then great sweetness can grow where all was bitter.

It's like the all-but-indefinable quality of "bittahness" defined in Saul Bellow's novel, *Henderson the Rain King*, that I read years ago. Bittahness, as I recall it, is what grows inside a person when they have the depth of character, the holding power, to agree to live face-on to their own portion of bitter experience, and to do this without blaming anybody else or requiring others to pay the psychic bill for them. Bitterness held with integrity and humor turns out in the fullness of time to have a quality of ineffable sweetness that nourishes everyone who comes in contact with it; the bitter is transformed into life-bestowing bittahness. White combs of sweetest honey, formed entirely in the dark.

No error

So we can see that eternity dwells in cause and effect at every point in the universe. Time is the narrow footpath in eternity that we walk in our magical, momentary bodies. The "Nyokyokan Treatise" says, quite reasonably, "The innumerable eons of the past firmly establish the future and present." So in this embodied consciousness we are answerable to our fate, responsible for the karma of our actions, utterly graced by cause and effect! There is no evading the law of cause and effect. But then it goes on to say, with no contradiction at all, "The innumerable eons of the future transfer their merit to the ages of the past"! Ah, so in the fullness and roundness of eternity there is no time, no small self, no error at all!

When we practice, we face directly into the sharp fact of our world of cause and effect, in which even the best planned lives will gradually unravel and come to pieces. When we bear with our shame, discord, sorrow, regret, or anger and don't move off, it can be acutely painful, like sitting on the point of a needle. When we make our home in that fact and stop fighting the impossible, in this very allowing the entire matter shifts. We come into more complete agreement with what is, with a clearer mind and a more magnanimous heart. The point of the needle becomes, in time, the only comfortable place to be.

This ordinary, mistake-strewn life is one complete life of grace when we are fully open to it. And it joins with every other life seamlessly. A friend of mine joined a circle dance, singing the words exactly as he had misheard them when they were given at the beginning: so while everybody else was singing, "And we all share our sweet harmonies," my friend loudly and gladly sang, "And we all share our sweet unease." That's it! *Our sweet unease.* Whenever we really know how we share that throughout time and space, a man or a woman steps free, released at last from the body of a fox-spirit, reborn as a human being.

Realization is not distinct in the slightest detail from the whole marvelous error of our life just as it is. Inside the eye of the acute needle of our circumstance is where we find the vast night of turning stars. The single eye of realization opens through any one of the ten thousand "mistakes" of embodied consciousness, to immensity itself.

Right there! And nowhere else.

CHAPTER 14

Mysterious affinity

THE TRADITIONAL KOAN PATH has among its treasures another koan deeply nestled in a story, this time a traditional Chinese ghost story that is also a love story. It's very much in the spirit of "once upon a time," a story that sits right upon time, untroubled as all such stories are by anxiety concerning what we ordinarily take to be the fierce, decisive and irreversible nature of time. This is not unlike the mind of meditation in deep samadhi.

A really good story is like a seed inside a burr, and the burr can stick to your clothing and then you take it with you, like it or not; you remember it, even if you don't yet quite get its deep, encoded seed meaning. And so it can travel with you for days and months and years and lifetimes, until one day it is ready to germinate and greenly unfurl, and you finally get it.

"Chien Separated from Her Soul" is a story like that. It is about a woman, which already marks it as unusual among traditional koans. It touches upon great themes of splitting, loss, reintegration, and forgiveness, although that is not the central concern of the koan, which reaches beyond all time and story to open the great matter. An old teacher called

Wuzu took this traditional story, widely known in eleventh-century China, and used it to pose a great question about the true eros of the Way. Here is the story.

Chien separated from her soul

Once upon a time, there was a beautiful girl called Chien. She lived beside one of the great rivers of ancient China, with just her father, Kien. Her sister had died young, and her father, Kien, cherished her even more deeply after that. Nothing is known about her mother (which is often the way with stories of this kind).

As a young girl, Chien was inseparable from her cousin, Chau, a boy slightly older than her, a playmate, gradually a soulmate. One day, watching Chien and Chau together, Kien said in play, "You're such a well-matched couple. When you grow up we should marry you to each other, for you seem to belong together." And so they childishly thought of themselves as engaged, and in the course of time they found themselves in love with each other. But when Chien finally reached marriageable age, an important official approached her father for her as a wife, and Kien, who had long forgotten his lightly spoken words, gladly consented.

Chau was devastated, and vowed at once to go and live in a distant province, far from the heartbreak of losing Chien. And Chien was likewise lost in grief, for she was a dutiful and loving daughter. But on the night that Chau was pushing off in his boat from the river, heading toward forgetfulness, he was startled to hear Chien's voice as she came running down the river path, saying, "Wait, it's me—I cannot bear to lose you. Let me run away with you!" Shaking with joy and fear, the two travelled up the river to a remote province, far enough away for the wrath of Kien to be forgotten, for a time, and were married.

They lived there in all the usual ways of considerable happiness and, in the course of time, had two children together. Life grew thick, and busy, but as the seventh year approached, Chien grew sad and sorrowful.

Finally she came and told Chau that she had to go back to ask forgiveness and to honor her father before he grew old and died—that she could not remain forever an outcast from her home. Chau was full of anxiety about this but he assented to her wish, and they planned to make this difficult journey together as soon as possible. And so they set out to travel back down the river.

When they arrived back in her father's province, as was the custom in old China, Chau went first to see her father and receive the brunt of his anger, while Chien remained in the boat. And so he was astonished when Kien received him with obvious pleasure, saying, "Where have you been all these years? I've missed you!" Chau bowed his head and asked his forgiveness, reassuring him that his daughter Chien was well and had been very happy as his wife, and that she was now the mother of two fine children. But what Kien said in reply nearly stopped his heart.

"Which Chien is that?" asked Kien. "For more than six years—ever since you departed so suddenly for a distant place—Chien has been ill in bed, hardly moving and unable to speak. Come with me, and see for yourself." Fearfully, Chau went with him and saw that, indeed, Chien was lying in her old room barely conscious, but seeming to register his presence as he came into the room.

"This is very strange," he told Kien, "but stranger still is what I have to show you. Please, come with me." Together, they walked out of the house and down the river path toward the boat where Chien had been waiting. But Chien had grown tired of waiting in the boat, and she was walking toward them. And behind them, coming from the other direction, the other Chien had risen from her bed and was also walking along the river path.

The two men stepped back and watched in astonishment as the two Chiens met on the path and took each other in. And then each Chien stepped forward into the arms of the other to embrace her completely, becoming in that moment a single Chien more astonishing than ever before.

Chien made a deep bow to her father. "If indeed you are my daughter," he said, lost in wonder, "I have nothing but love for you."

And Chien turned to Chau. "I couldn't bear to lose you," she told him, "and I was happy with you, except for my deep shame. But all the time, I did not know that I was sick at home in my father's house, devastated by a sorrow beyond dreams.

"I myself am not sure which was the real Chien, the one as if dead, at home in my father's house, or the one who has lived with you, wife and mother to your children."

So, Wuzu asks, which is the true Chien?

A ghost story

How beautifully this near-ghost story resolves as a love story. Our lives can be like that—more like ghost stories than we may dream, for whole seasons of life. We can also grow abstracted and a little ghostly to some of the people we love, and make ghosts of them as well through prejudice, neglect, self-absorption, and distractedness. It is good from time to time to search patiently and gently through your dearest relationships for the ghostly aspects of yourself and others close to you, and to befriend the ghosts you've created. How do you do that? Open yourself imaginatively, meet them with empathy, get to know intimately the exact nature of their complaint. Soften your heart to the suffering that they are carrying and let their cries resound through you as if they are your cries—the sorrow of being starved, abandoned, misinterpreted, or ignored. When separation dissolves like the dream it is, a ghost is saved.

And this listening and resounding and reunion is how ghost stories can resolve as love stories.

At a psychological level, much of the story is about the splitting that can happen to us when we are torn in life by strong conflicting feelings and loyalties. Chien loves and honors her father. That remains so strong that her soul is torn away and left behind when she follows her lover into a new life, breaking with filial duty. Her shame bars her way back.

It would probably be difficult to find a man or woman who could not hear this story and identify some sense of "splitness" in themselves—a forced sacrifice of some important propensity or gift or inclination of the self, often brought about by the wish to please another, or by pressure of life circumstances that bore down too hard at the critical time. What parts of yourself feel shamefully, sorrowfully lost from reach? Chien found her lost soul "as if dead"—and yet strangely safe—in her family house. What did your childhood self know about you and your original spirit that you believed you had forgotten, surrendered, "lost"? Is it perhaps not lost; in fact, never irretrievable, but in strangely safe keeping in the very place it seemed stolen from you?

Even a hostile family home is still a repository for the soul's treasury, in that it housed the earliest self. *Integrity* carries the meaning of both "one," or "singular," and "untouched." Chien "as if dead" in her family house is partly an image of the powerfully untouchable quality of the very core of ourselves. That is unassailable, and perhaps never beyond recovery, though the estrangement can be profound.

Yet the story of Chien separated from her soul is finally a story of a powerful urge toward reunion. Another name for this is *bodhichitta*—the urge to wake up in this life. Its fruit is insight—the act of seeing all the opposites reconciled in every gesture of this universe. Its energy is an objectless gratitude. The Heart Sutra tells us, "Form is no other than emptiness, emptiness no other than form. Form is exactly emptiness, emptiness exactly form." Can you sense a hint of that perfect fit—like Chien longing for Chien, Chien embracing Chien.

And can you hear the love song in this, and the urgency? William Blake said that "eternity is in love with the productions of time." What are the productions of time? Everything and every being in form—us, for example! We appear, and then we disappear. The people we love recede into a photograph; our deaths separate us from our lives in time and return us to the remoteness of rock, glacier, the origin of the planet, origin itself. We leave our socks behind, folded in our drawers, and our unfinished projects, and yet there is no hole to be found where we were.

There is a place where it makes sense to say, "Yes is exactly no, no exactly yes," where eternity is reconciled with all the productions of time. It is where the two Chiens so utterly meet on the riverbank.

A love story

So this koan springs from a love story—a story about the longing for reunion, the yearning for wholeness. And equally it is a story about how each thing in the universe is yearning and longing for your recognition, which completes it, which wakes it up. To save the many beings is to awaken yourself. Each thing in this universe is like this. The Earth yearns for the sun. We may call it gravity, but that's just a way to speak of the yearning; the universe is created with it, held together with yearning. And there's a poignantly elusive quality about this matter, for us humans. Now you see it, now you don't. Now you hear it, now you can't.

The universe is extravagant in its efforts to have you wake up. An old Chinese song tells of a woman secluded in her house at night. Somewhere out in the dark is her lover, hoping for some sign of her. Repeatedly she calls out to her maid, "Little Jade! Little Jade!" Little Jade runs in each time and says, "Yes, mistress. What do you want?" But, she has no reason to call her maid, she just wants to find another excuse to let her lover hear her voice. Just that reason.

Have you heard her voice? The magpies are carolling across the valley. A low plane drones in the distance. The soft sunlight pools and quivers through the leaves onto my desk.

The eros of the Way

Zen is traditionally quiet, even silent, about the eros of the Way, and the huge refinement of the senses that zazen brings to our emotional lives, growing new senses, regrowing early and prematurely abandoned ones. It is a rich kind of silence—a generous spaciousness that invites our courage and poetry. It seems to trust that quietly being with the actual nature of things will teach us all about joy, and that joy is not narrow but includes every emotion in the human spectrum. Zazen cultivates an embodied awareness, and can open us in a deeper way to the knowings of the body. It is learning to be present with the whole body rather than just that pinpoint of the intellect and the customary buzz of thought, which deafens the world even more than all of our mechanical contrivances.

Eros is the heart's leaning toward relating and including, toward communion. Eros expresses itself in play, a young kind of energy, even in the very old; it is a savoring of life, voluptuous and delicious. In Hildegard von Bingen's words, it is good to keep the heart "green, wet, moist"—in sympathy with this moist, blue-green planet of ours. As an old Chinese saying tells us, if you keep a green branch in your heart, the singing bird will come. And if you have learned from stillness, you will feel it arrive.

Reunion

The Buddhist principle of the fundamental interdependence and co-arising of all beings is in this sense an erotic and deeply playful seeing of the reality of the universe we're in. Play creates curved instead of linear time. Zazen is pure play, in that it inhabits and draws you into that curved and edgeless time. Practice, just like play, brings people eye to eye, with feeling and vulnerability; and in bodies, rather than with bodies dimly in attendance.

I remember once watching a dog asleep in the middle of a party. At the feet of all the tensely talking and drinking adults, she lay in deep self-abandon, her paws in the air, a beatific smile on her face, fully at home in the world. We were edgily being at a party; she was a full member of the celebration, of being alive in a body.

Eros is not a holding on to joy—it opens also to pain, impermanence, imperfection, all of the hard and only guarantees we're offered in this life. The point is, it opens to them, just as Chien opens her arms to Chien. The practice of zazen is the practice of eros, a gradual opening to connectedness. It makes us near and alert, not distant and secondhand, and nearness is another way of talking about being at home in this world.

So this reunion, this great meeting on the river path, is the act of deeply befriending reality, extending a kind of unlimited friendliness toward it. Meditation is an intentional act of kindliness toward reality, a poised and calm kindliness, equanimity. In this poise of the mind, you don't move toward it, and you don't flinch away from it. That very commitment to stillness in the face of each thing that arises is already reunion—the opportunity, the possibility of that. And anything can ignite it, anything can set you ablaze. "Oh, how I have yearned for you," says Chien to Chien.

What happens at that most intimate moment when the two Chiens walk along the river path and meet each other, step into each other? Which is the true Chien? asks the koan. There is reintegration of soul, restitution of karma, and the death of the small self, all melting one into the other, as Chien steps alone into the embrace of the brilliant darkness. At that moment, Chien is unhindered by supposing anything at all. She has no hindrance, and therefore no fear. Everything leading to this moment—her perseverance with suffering, her willingness to endure and to keep faith with both of her split selves, her courage in turning back to face her karma, her intuitive ability to find her way in the dark, her ability to love, finally even to love herself—is the river path of forbearance that she has walked to meet herself more truly.

Grace

The story of Chien tells us that, in a fundamental and final sense, nothing is lost. Like our own lives, it seems at first to be a story about forced choice, about splitting at the point of the really sharp choices that just cannot be avoided. And yet, clearly there is more to see here. Wumen's verse to this case points the way:

The moon and the clouds are the same,
Mountains and valleys are different.
All are blessed. All are blessed.
Is this one? Is this two?

"The moon and the clouds are the same. Mountains and valleys are different." The second part is probably slightly less mysterious to us than the first. All the refinements of education and language, of naming and of calling, of responding by name, create in us a powerful refinement of the ability to name the parts, to identify the parts, to see the parts of things, to differentiate. Our practical survival depends upon it. If you can't distinguish the path from a cliff, you fall off it; if you can't differentiate a red light from a green light, you may not survive the next intersection. This highly trained ability to analyze and name the parts has brought about all the ever more rapid change that spins around us: the industrial, technological, electronic eras are all born of this ruthless power to split one thing from another, to split even atoms. But it is also merciless toward us, for it adapts us to being part, not whole.

Practice restores and trains the eye of wholeness; and it opens in the dark sky of emptiness. What does it see? That "the moon and clouds are the same," and equally in the same moment, "mountains and valleys are different." How is it so? Exactly because it is so, "All are blessed, all are blessed," and all that is left is staring in wonder: "Is this one? Is this two?" Knowing nothing, knowing emptiness, losing your knowing. Wumen's words dissolve words. They point beyond "one" and "two," to not two, not even one.

So we become more able to tolerate both the dissolving of our boundaries and also being free and unencumbered in minute, amazing differentiation. We rejoin the original ground of our own being, which can bless everything just as it is, with acceptance. Resistance itself becomes a kind of path that teaches us; it trains us in not-resisting, just as Chien's torn state inducts her into her journey of reconciliation. Working closely with resistance teaches us how to yield, to step free, and to not know.

The whole marvelous error of your life perfects your longing and is the exact provocation that you need to catch sight of grace. And grace is the angle of view of the whole-adapted eye that can genuinely ask, deep in wonder, "Is this one? Is this two?" It is the moment when Chien, apparently split, finds herself whole from the beginning. And time, so apparently lost to us when we are split from ourselves, turns back upon itself. And that's just an ordinary miracle in zazen; it happens all the time.

A member of the feast

The 1987 Danish film *Babette's Feast*, based on Isak Dinesen's great short story, touched upon the same miracle. This is also a story about choices made in the early part of life which lead to a lifelong sense of apparent "not-quite-rightness" for several people—a feeling that is endured, beautifully held and managed, and lived with well enough. But gradually toward the end of the film many threads are pulled together at a feast. An extraordinary meal, a true work of art and love, is prepared by the French cook, Babette, for an anniversary celebration of a religious sect of very old people who have stuck rigorously to their narrow path. For religious reasons, they have resolved not to taste the food. For them, it is a kind of a sin to taste this succulent and artful food that is being so lovingly prepared.

And so they carefully don't know that they are at the feast—and even less, that they are the feast itself. But of course the feast works its magic upon them anyway, and gradually they begin to spontaneously release each other from ancient twisted karma of grudges and betrayals. Toward the end of the feast, the old general gets up and makes a toast, and in his way he is acknowledging that he was in love with one of the now-elderly ladies who was at one time a beautiful young girl. She was in love with him but they didn't marry. Dutiful love for her father split her from taking the path that went with him. He raises his glass, full of the best champagne to be had in Europe in the early nineteenth century, and although the old folk are carefully not tasting this wonderful wine as they drink it, nevertheless they do drink the toast—a kind of grace after the meal.

His words, reconstructed here, could as well be used to mark the reunion of Chien with her soul:

We have all of us been told that grace is to be found in the universe, but in our human foolishness and short-sightedness we imagine grace to be finite. For this reason, we tremble. We tremble before making our choice in life, and after having made it we tremble in fear of having chosen wrong. But the moment comes when our eyes are opened, and we see and realize that grace is infinite. Grace, my friends, demands nothing from us but that we shall await it with confidence and acknowledge it in gratitude. Grace, brothers, makes no conditions and singles out none in particular. Grace takes us all to its bosom and proclaims general amnesty. See, that which we have chosen is given us. And that which we have refused is also and at the same time granted us. Aye, that which we have rejected is poured upon us abundantly. For mercy and truth have met together, and righteousness and bliss [and the two Chiens, I might add!] have kissed one another.

So there it is, when we finally stop and meet ourselves. "That which we have chosen is given us. And that which we have refused is also and at the same time granted us." All are blessed, all are blessed. When you reunite with your own self-nature, you will see that it is so.

And what is the blessing, the grace? "Is this one? Is this two?" It is the marvel; the not-knowing; the plenitude of that.

CHAPTER 15

Every day
is a good day

YUNMEN SAID TO HIS ASSEMBLY, "I do not ask you about the fifteenth of the month. Come, give me a phrase about after the fifteenth!" And he himself responded, "Every day is a good day."

This is an old koan about the matter of what happens after we touch some experience of enlightenment, which in the old Chinese literature was sometimes rendered in a kind of shorthand speech as "the fifteenth of the month." This was the date that signified the day of enlightenment, because in the old Chinese calendar the full moon always rose on this date. We are truly born on that moon. After we have been born, we are faced with the great koan that Yunmen bequeaths us for every difficult and welcome day of our ordinary, sacred lives: "Every day is a good day." How do we live with this daily koan?

And then what happens?

"After the fifteenth" is rather like that dread phrase in a fairy story, "And so they all lived happily ever after." We know there's something wrong with this. Even as a very small child we know. Cinderella, we may be sure, got married on the fifteenth of the month. It wasn't all that long after the fifteenth that she "accidentally" dropped her almost unwearable glass slippers on the stone flagging, shattering them into ten thousand pieces. The day comes, a good day, when we demand to know, "Well, after they got married, then what happened?" Like the small boy who asked, brightly, "What's next?" after being roused from his bed to watch a full eclipse of the moon. "That's great, Dad, but what comes next? What about at 10 A.M. the next day?"

We fall into a story about enlightenment—about life, in fact—and we can get trapped there for many lifetimes. I wonder more and more how well any life really fits a story. What if our life is not this, then that, in a flat and sensible way, but is equally round like a globe, like the Earth itself? Maybe our life never did lie flat on the page and read from left to right, from the fifteenth to the sixteenth of the month.

Maybe, too, life is far wider than that. "Life is short, but it's wide!" was a graffito I read on a restroom door in the mid-1980s and have never forgotten.

And it is not only wide but it is braided too. I discovered a wall-hanging in the Quaker's Meeting House in Christchurch, New Zealand, woven from indigo-stained Maori flax. It was called "Life Is a Long Braided River." Like the great, wide, gravel-strewn rivers threaded across the Canterbury Plain of the South Island, life is many river beds in one, finally unmappable, ever criss-crossing and rechannelling and shining so intricately all the way to the sea.

A curse and a gift

In the middle of many enlightenment stories in Zen comes the arresting phrase "sudden enlightenment." What if this matter of being struck by grace like lightning is not, at its heart, a story about this leads to that, or rather, that leads to this! What if it is an image instead of the completeness and fullness of even the most fragmentary fragment, a way of saying that glimpsing the toenails of God is glimpsing all of God, complete? Just this toenail, a little horny and untrimmed, and the whole world comes along, passes right through!

The Heart Sutra, chanted by Buddhists in many traditions, given in full in the appendix, tells us there is "No old age and death and also no ending of old age and death." This is the space of our practice: the great, reverberant space between these two profound truths. One day, probably the fifteenth of the month if we cared to check, we stand as the anxious, hopeless suitor in the street craning our neck up at the balcony, and the flowers we have offered at last are not tossed out into the street; and when we rush up the stairs the door opens, and we hear the music, at last—and we are, after all, beloved on this Earth! "What's next?" we ask, like a sleepy child roused in the night to curious wakefulness. And a lifelong commitment opens up, a unending practice to live with the curse and the gift that Yunmen offers his tongue-tied assembly: Every day is a good day.

The quiet, bright reed song

The true meaning of "conversion" is not a sudden swerve in your life that utterly changes its direction forever, thank God, but a lifelong turning and attuning of your life to the glimpses through that door, the music from that room.

Rumi says:

All day and night, music,
a quiet, bright
reed song. If it
fades, we fade.

Tuning our lives to that most quiet and bright, most dark and passion-ately roaring ground note of our being, demands a very acute listening. A listening that can catch the reed song even in the midst of the most noisy, messy assaults of the ordinary world.

It's one thing to catch the quiet, bright reed song there in the depths of silence in peaceful countryside or in the depths of a long retreat; it's quite another to keep turned toward it when we come back from such deep resting in what is. The harshness and strangeness of that return from great silence can be very instructive. I remember a seven-day retreat that I took at a very hard time of my life when I was questioning every-thing in my upturned universe. In the depths of that retreat, the door opened a little, I caught one or two notes of the music, I was very, very happy…And then it was coming-home time. So I drove home along the tiny, green, barely rutted track from our retreat site in the wilderness, which then became a more definite dirt road, which became wider, and tarred in places, and then it turned into a highway, and then I was back in the roaring, whizzing "Sydneyness" of things. And I came into the house, and my half-estranged husband and my two young children had ordered and eaten pizza for dinner, and the kitchen was strewn with yawning cardboard boxes, full of crusts and blobs of pizza, and they were all watching a video, and it was *Terminator.*

For a while, after touching the depths of zazen, the wrong-way-roundness of most things is starkly apparent. When you come from rigor to ordinary messiness, you see how rigor sets the deep play of just being at the heart of all work and leisure, and how all work then grows leisurely. There is the leisurely one, beyond philosophy, reclining in royal ease, by the charcoal fire, right there in the midst of all the Cinderella-ish demands of life, all the unending demands of the ten thousand Ugly Stepsisters. How do we realize this? Every day, a good day.

The full moon of everyday life

Coming back again and again is not just the work of breaking through. Breaking through again and again is not just the work of before the fifteenth. After the fifteenth, the work is the deepest play of all; the play is the deepest work of all. Practice is not a kind of good prelude to the day, to help make it go a little better, be a little more "good" in some way; practice is the day, the work and point of the day, and that is the deep leisure of the Way.

So, "Every day is a good day." To realize this deeply is a profound move into dailiness, that ordinary miracle that will recur for each of us only a finite few more times. And it is a profound move beyond "good" and "bad." It initiates the lifelong work of abiding here, which is resting completely in what is, not avoiding, not moving off, not needing it to be something else.

No resistance

The word *suffering* is intimately related to the word "allowing." Allowing our suffering is the first softening of the very category, the first melting of its iron grip on us. Kafka said, in *The Great Wall of China*, that you can hold back from the suffering of the world and you have free permission to do so, but perhaps this very holding back is the one suffering you could have avoided. I would say you can also rigidly resist with great effort your own sufferings, whether huge or grittingly and abrasively tiny and daily; but this also turns out to be the greatest suffering of all, and the one suffering you could have avoided.

Zen doesn't ask us to look beyond suffering to our glory elsewhere and hereafter, beyond life, beyond death. It says, "This is our glory. Every day is a good day. We are all going to fail. It is guaranteed."

The gloss a dear friend offered on this phrase, with his beautiful smile, when he was deep in his dying of AIDS, was "Every day is Good Friday." This is a powerful and illuminating turning phrase. The mystery and the passion of Good Friday — and the astonishing fact that such a day is called "Good" — is enacted every day in every life upon the Earth, in some measure. This is where we live. Yunmen was offering no blandishments at all, but the hardest of all possible challenges. We notice, with gratitude, that he didn't say "Every day is a nice day."

The abiding one

When my son turned twenty-one a few years ago, I took him to lunch with my much younger daughter, who happily skipped school. We had a good time. We began to wonder, How important is this turning point these days? My son realized he felt it was important, that it did feel like the beginning of something new, that his life would probably start to shift in its current, to move more swiftly perhaps, to be a markedly different phase from the one of adolescence. And suddenly my daughter realized that it was a year in which she, too, would cross a threshold and turn thirteen, entering adolescence. We all registered a slight sense of awe about all this — and then we went on with our sushi.

But that night, she went through a curious and intense kind of mental anguish. She lay on the floor in tears and unnameable pain. She couldn't articulate the problem for some time, but said things like, "Everything is horrible." But I helped her stay with it and not move off until she could make out some of the shapes of what she was so repelled by, and it slowly dawned that she was in grief — that she didn't want to leave the simple, sure things of childhood, and the deep close bond with me, and that turning thirteen and agreeing to change was also agreeing to old age and death—her death, my death—everything not just opening and flowering but also ripening and rotting and passing away.

Gradually the agony shifted into tears of huge release and even something like gratitude. We were very close and sat up late watching an emotionally satisfying and adult kind of movie together, our feet entwined. The next day she was light as a child again, and also walking forward with considerable interest into her own definite coming of age. So in the staying steady and bearing down on the feeling, she brushed that place in which everything is deeply okay: the abiding one; the reed song that sings us forever.

The providence of each moment

There is a marvelous Russian film from the early 1990s called *Burnt by the Sun*. It is an immersion in the last thirty-six hours of happiness in the life of a former military hero of the Revolution, right at the time in the early 1930s when Stalin began his paranoid purges of the most ardent and proven allies and patriots. Comrade Kotov is spending his summer with his wild, wide extended family of eccentrics and his young, pretty wife and exquisite small daughter in the family *dacha* by a lake.

Into the middle of this good day of laughter, tears, play, and ordinary small disasters, a man arrives who will betray Kotov. The man is admitted into the heart of things because he was once almost a member of this tribe, and almost married Kotov's wife. Now he comes with the whispered, life-destroying message that at 10 A.M. the next day, a car will come for Kotov. And Kotov knows exactly what that means.

So what does Kotov do? He doesn't try to run and hide, which is probably quite useless and would certainly bring terrible harm upon his family. He doesn't mourn and bewail his fate. What he does is live his ordinary, miraculous life exactly as if it will last forever, while knowing it will end at 10 A.M. the next day. He accepts and meets the complete providence of each remaining moment of his good life, and we live that with him. It grows more acutely heartbreaking by the moment, seeing his terrible fate finally arrive outside, and his bright, playful little girl running to ride in the big black car and even drive in it to the top of the rise; and when he kisses his family goodbye and turns his calm eyes to his fate, it is nearly too much to bear. Kotov breaks only when his betrayer begins to whistle through his teeth the popular tango that has been sung, hummed, danced, and skipped to throughout the long days of summer: "Burnt by the Sun." He sobs like a child, his face all broken from blows, one eye collapsed. And we learn the terrible fates that followed, his death five days later, his wife's death six years later in a Siberian labor camp, his daughter's "rehabilitation" only several years after Stalin's death, decades later.

But the miracle this film offers is a man who can hear, and continues to listen for, the reed song not just in his happiness, but even in the agonizing moment of all severance from deep happiness—and we can hear it with him.

You can catch this mind of "Every day is a good day," too, in Thornton Wilder's play, *Our Town*, in which a young girl who has died is given permission to come back to her world for a day. No one will know she is there, but she will be completely present with all of her senses, just as if she had the miraculous gift of a body all over again.

She can choose any kind of day at all to return; but she doesn't choose a great day or a terrible day—she chooses a very ordinary day. And when she is back inside her ordinary life, it is exquisitely, unbearably painful. She can smell the aroma of morning coffee in the kitchen. She can hear each note of the birds outside the window, and make out the tiny swish of one leaf upon another when the breeze stirs. She can see the faces of her family, every beloved line, crease, and meaning of all their faces. And she weeps for them; she cannot bear it, because they don't know. They don't know what is being endlessly offered and poured out upon every single thing. So the dead choose an ordinary day to return; and they weep for us, because we are here inside it now, and we don't know.

When we wake on that night of the full moon, we die to an earlier self and gain a glimpse of life with the eyes that truly see death. "After the fifteenth of the month" offers no reprieve at all from the rest of your life. Things only grow keener; the blade of awareness that you must now walk is sharp. All things will always pass quickly away. But we have more chance of actually being here, present to the overwhelming fact of life.

And when we touch change, death, decay, and impermanence in that light, the long braided river of our time here flows freely, all the way to the sea of all shining.

CHAPTER 16

Accept all offers

WHAT IS THE NATURE OF LONG maturation in the Way? How does realization season into life? A monk asked Master Zhimen, "What is Buddha?" and Zhimen simply responded, "When the straw sandals wear out, you just walk on." The matter is as uncomplicated as the way the incense smoke rises straight up until it twists in the breeze.

Perhaps at that moment Zhimen noticed a pair of worn straw sandals such as monks used to make for themselves—his own, or the monk's. He is not really offering advice, but a vivid response to the great question, "What is Buddha?" How can we arrive at a degree of ease equal to Zhimen's beautiful presentation of Buddha, such that we can say—free of all self-concern, simply intent upon walking the Way—"When the straw sandals wear out, you just walk on"?

I have spoken of accepting all offers as the Way itself—like two actors in an improvisation throwing swift possibilities to each other on the spot. Remember, if one player in any way says "No," the play collapses: it's dead. So finding the alive "Yes" is the origin of the phrase, "accept all offers." Accept all offers the other can toss to you. Simply walking on when the straw sandals wear out is a matter of being present to the immediate offer of your life, without self-pity, and without self-admiration either.

That "yes" is the secret hinge of every "no" our lives may seem to present. Find it, and the world swings wide open like a gate.

The sharpest fact

What is the sharpest fact in your life right now? Take a moment to consider your most haunting terror, your most persistent aggravation or relentless criticism of yourself, or a deep shame you have taken upon yourself. Feel it in your body. That terror, aggravation, shame, or sadness is your dearest enemy. Never trust a teacher who would devise ways for you to avoid meeting with such potential, for all of your creative power for the Way is to be found right there. It is tied up in that, usually tied up in defending the self against that. So turning that way is turning toward your true freedom, and your most fertile condition at every moment. Such is the blessing to be found in a curse.

That painful and difficult matter can be a Dharma gate into a richer maturity. Practice is not just a matter of breaking through the fact of suffering, but of realizing suffering as a Dharma gate. And when a Dharma gate opens to you, it opens to great freedom, nothing holy. There's nothing pious here.

Torei Zenji, successor to the great Hakuin we met in Chapter 10, said that after the great matter has been fully realized, there is, for some ten or twenty years more, only the one Way of long maturation. And he notes that it is uncommonly hard to continue on this path with the fierceness required to attain "unshakable faith"—a deep habit of being awake.

Unshakable faith. Unshakability is great equanimity, a truly thorough realization of emptiness. This is sometimes spoken of as receiving the impress of the Buddha heart seal or mind seal—receiving the impress of realization right into your bone marrow. Each realization experience is an initiation, the taking of a direct imprint of original mind. It's never the right moment to be satisfied with how deeply it has reached in you. It is not enough to be lightly touched by it: it must sink deep and become indelible.

Only for your benefit

Once Dongshan was down at the creek washing his bowls. He saw two birds contending over a frog, tearing it apart right in front of him. A monk who was with him saw it too, and asked, "Why does it come to this?" The master replied, "It is only for your benefit, Acharya." Only for your benefit. (*Acharya* is an honorific implying "Great One.") When you can truly receive that benefit Dongshan is speaking of, you will be great with the universe, and share the equanimity of the rocks and stars and galaxies.

It is a mysterious moment, when something sharply terrible is turned upon itself as pure bonus. "Only for your benefit." How can that be?

It is a very harsh world; heaven and earth are ruthless, as the old Chinese sages would say. What gives us this amazing life also takes it away. Joy will always come and go, and blessings will sometimes come as a curse. At times there is a very strange sense of contortion in world events, and in some moments it can feel like an elevator in free fall, with the floor numbers ticking over out of any sequence. And there are terrible things to read in the newspaper. We have to witness and endure things being torn apart in front of us, as we do the washing up, almost every day. If we're watching the news it's almost impossible to bring our comfortable-enough-world together with what we can see through the merciless eye of the television.

So right in front of the monk two birds tear a frog apart. There are no spin-doctors in the animal or insect world: it's all quite plain, right in front of you on full display. A terrifying thing is simply revealed as what it is, a frog torn apart. Families torn apart. A woman stoned to death when her baby is weaned because the baby is born out of wedlock. Bombs raining down on defenseless civilian populations.

How do you go about releasing the blessing from the curse? How do you get off the wheel of reactiveness that we all seem to be chained to and convert a cursed condition or situation into a fiercely simple blessing? How do you enter the middle of the middle, that open door? Only by resting completely, right here in the heart of chaos.

Royal ease

A reclining Buddha is a kind of invitation to look into this deeply-at-rest condition. Reclining at royal ease in the midst of every condition, every circumstance, even the sharpest and most uncomfortable. There is something to look into in the word *lazy*. After all, what are we doing in meditation but lazing about with great concentration. Like a tiger, apparently doing nothing. We are looking into the secret of not doing.

Mindfulness is the ability to recognize and accept the offer, standing on the ground of your most fundamental being, as far as you have touched it to this point, which is already the action of not-doing.

The key to not-doing is staying in the center, staying true to your deepest intimation of reality. And on that ground you will know how to accept the offer. Every mindful breath in zazen and as you walk down the street is a return to the center. Then, when the sharp moment arises, right there in the very teeth of conflict you have a chance to maintain access to your deepest intimation of who you really are. This is where hours upon hours of practice pay off, of staying with something as difficult as a niggling or nagging pain in the back or in the knees, and not getting up and reacting in some way, perhaps not even moving unduly, and discovering how conditions, when you go with them, change endlessly.

When you go with them, they have already changed by that very fact. When you take away the resistance, the condition has been altered immediately. It is simply and utterly immediate. So the practice here is a kind of bedrock practice that you can then draw on in the moments when you're prone to reactiveness. We all know how stupid reactiveness is, how foolish. It is never something about which you will later proudly say, "God, I reacted well! That was a great reaction!"

Then you open your psyche to the "other," as the hexagram "Inner Truth" in the *I Ching* asks us to do. To open your psyche to the one who is attacking you, to the one or the thing that is the trouble, is a most daring move.

This steady, grounded opening up of your psyche to the other without reserve is not at all like being enmeshed with the other, or unconsciously colluding in a way secret even to yourself. If you're on the ground of connectedness, aware of who and what you really are, there is far too much freedom here for anything abusive to slip in.

There is a way to stay steady inside a state of acute difficulty and to open to the other when a relationship is under extreme strain. It is far from easy. Getting into the place of self-relinquishment is a task you can never stop undertaking; even after it becomes relatively practiced, the reactive habits of ego remain fiercely persistent. There can never be enough practice in bringing the self toward simplicity. But when you can stand there, even for a moment, a complete freedom of choice that was always there at every point becomes almost shockingly obvious, scandalously available. Becoming more attuned to such freedom is worthy of a lifetime's practice.

The not-doing of the self

The first step is to become completely clear that everything you do is your decision and responsibility, including the decision of who you choose to love and what consequences flow from that. Accordingly, when harm has been done, you have to accept some responsibility. This is the work of character, the "dream" of our own actions and reactions that must be "interpreted"—meaning openly acknowledged, resolutely faced, meticulously met.

Taking responsibility is, curiously, a gift from death itself. That might sound strange, but taking responsibility is intimately related to the fact that we die. In a world where we die there is no large or small action or decision: everything matters. There is complete equality, in the end, in such a world.

What seems to come with returning to the ground of your own self-nature, and coming forth from there, is a discovery that when you are open, you cannot be lonely. You cannot really be lonely. Like the lone nun in the hut in Chapter 10 who spoke of "all my followers—the trees, the earth, the rocks, the birds, the stones . . ." All my relations, all my followers, accord.

The accord is so simple; and when it is reached, your heart knows it for itself, and then you can be lonely with equanimity. It is just as it is, neither good nor bad. And if you are not lonely in an anxious way, then you are not reacting out of fear of abandonment. That part is already clearer and cleaner than it might have been.

The important thing that we do in each other's company is discover more profoundly who we really are. Now, that is obviously easier to do when you feel loved, but even feeling rejected, even feeling extreme pain, is just an opportunity of equal value. It is an equal opportunity! And, of course, when you are discovering who you really are, by that very fact you open up the same possibility for the one whose company you share. You ensure that same great opportunity for the other.

We are here to learn to shine our spirit. Like every sentient being, we're star stuff—so why not live up to that? The only way to do so is to give freedom of equal magnitude to the others in our lives, the intimate important others—freedom to love as they wish to love, to be as they wish to be.

The one I enclose with my name

We have no choice but to let go of *shoulds* and *have to's*. That can be very hard to do. So much of the inner conversation, if it is not about guilt and inadequacy, is about injustices, insults, hurts, and grievances supposedly coming from the other who does not meet our expectation. This person does not necessarily even know what it is we expect of them, what we have supposed about them, what we "know" to be true about their less than perfect ways, and their less than perfect compassion for us. That detail hardly matters in the face of a flurry of self-righteousness. Despite the actual nature of reality, our case about self and other is perfectly formed, airtight.

Who is actually caught inside that airless space? Remember Tagore in Chapter 1: "The one whom I enclose with my name is weeping in that dungeon." The first chink of air inside the tomb is the act of becoming conscious of *shoulds* and *have to's*; and whenever you notice them, let them go, like dogs yearning to be free of the leash. Let them go, and feel the release in your neck, shoulders, heart, hands, and legs.

And when you wean yourself of *shoulds* and *have to's*, and the way that reality really should be arranged, then you find that the only things that can truly hurt you are those expectations, hopes, and ideas about the way it's supposed to be. Everything else, and in fact, even that, is "only for your benefit—only for our benefit—Acharya."

Deep, deep laziness

When a baby that you are not at all sure is yours is angrily thrust into your arms, can you hold that mind of "Is that so?," of not foreclosing in angry self-defense, but maintaining curious wonder and interest in what is presented? The task is to not foreclose on that but hold it open, supposing nothing. The task is just to look into how far such a belief can really be true, with a radically open mind. How can I really know that to be true? What is hidden in it about my own resistance and clinging? How am I making use of it to resist and cling and reduce and imprison myself? And most fundamentally, what would I be like without this proposition about reality? What would it be like if I withdrew the costly subscription to my belief that so-and-so is always doing this to me? That so-and-so!

This is the not-doing of the self; a deep, deep laziness, approved of by all the leaves hanging out there in the summer heat, lazy as you can get.

The promise inside suffering

It can feel like a death, going in to the heart of emotional chaos with openness, going in to anything painful with, "I offer no resistance to what you need to say to me. I offer no resistance. I simply listen to it." Standing on that ground of your own being and just opening there can feel like a death. And that's true of any great suffering (and its secret promise): it feels like a death, but to recover even a small part of your own unshakability is to begin to realize that you have unshakability right in the middle of turmoil and storm. The waves are raging, but the floor of the sea is quiet and at rest.

It turns out that the death is, in fact, more like an open door, and the open door is so near in every moment. All the great and little deaths of a half-life—the life tied up in hoping, resenting, supposing, fearing—are the birth-process of a tender, wider, more fearless and resilient kind of being, one that can be practiced again and again, becoming more and more what you really are.

Sometimes it's just a matter of coming to the point of finally feeling sufficient disgust for the "I, I, I . . ." It just wears itself out; suddenly, it's enough. There is a great koan in which a teacher says at one point, "I came here fishing for a great whale, but all I find is a nasty little frog wriggling in the mud." That's the "I" that cannot ever stop wriggling and squirming. Let it go.

When we let it go, we find that we do not die. We do not lose anything at all, by letting go the little self or any one of its ten thousand niggardly yet expensive concerns. An open space appears. A fresh wind, smelling like freedom, is blowing in our faces. We choose our lives, not in the grand karmic tide of events, but moment by moment in how we live that. What do you choose? Clinging to "I"? Or walking freely as the intimate, nameless, beginningless, unimpeded one.

If you are a person of gain and loss, you've already lost. It's a matter of remembering that our business here is to learn to love all the way through to letting go. There's nothing much else we can actually do with the overwhelming opportunity of a human life, which is shaped exactly like completely accepting the offer of a lifetime, and shaped exactly like finally letting go.

Buddhahood is passion

The second of the bodhisattva vows says, "Greed, hatred, and ignorance rise endlessly." These are often referred to as the blind passions; when we look closely, we see that hatred and anger rise from ignorance itself. And ignorance is fundamentally, simply, this immaculate delusion: I am separate from you. I am separate from everything I see with my eyes. I am separate. There's a "me" that must at all costs be protected from anything that might impinge on it harshly. That's the root of ignorance, and anger and hatred can arise only from that pre-existing condition.

The old teacher Zhaozhou once said, "Buddhahood is passion and passion is buddhahood." This is not at first glance a very Buddhist thing to say. And yet, how can you carve anything at all out of the universe and say, "Everything is buddhahood—except this thing, which is problematical for humans who wish to accord with buddhahood"? A monk then asked him, "In whom does Buddha cause passion?" and Zhaozhou replied, "Buddha causes passion in all of us." Is any human being exempt from being human? Is anyone ruled out from the strange offer of strong or difficult emotion? "How should we get rid of it?" asked the monk. Zhaozhou replied, "Why should we get rid of it?"

His reply seems implicitly to accord with the monk and agree—how indeed could we possibly get rid of it! Where can it go? But he takes it to even greater depth: Why should we get rid of it? Inside that "why" is a refusal to be moved an inch from what life really is, and from including every part of it as himself. The "why" disappears into the great fact itself.

So to abandon the passions by finding the no-self right there in the very middle of the wave is to begin to arrive finally at being someone who can love. Like a bodysurfer, placing his or her no-self exactly in the middle of the turbulence of the wave, and becoming wave, effortlessly free of turbulence. Someone who is not concerned with being loved, so much as dedicated to being able to love freely. Someone who can love, who can lend themselves unrestrictedly to the unfolding of the universe. Baizhang spoke of this condition as "one who lets the world be as it is, always acting in countless situations with clear being." This is the not-doing of the self; the self not-doing itself. And so the practice of no resistance, the practice of accepting all offers, lets you arrive at last at who you really are.

There is nothing I dislike

These are the extraordinary words of the great teacher Linji; they are a lifetime koan for anyone who dares to take it on. Lifetime koans like this one never give up on you, luckily. "There is nothing I dislike" is daring and fragrant and alive, and it is like this because it's like *this*. "There is nothing I dislike" rearranges us profoundly, when we offer ourselves to its energy, its scrutiny, its disturbance in us.

Sometimes turning the words around is a way of catching sight of your own original face in a koan. So you may also try it from this angle: "There is nothing that is not like me." This opens another way to endure the curse and blessing of the provocation that Linji offers: another way to flourish.

Of course, it's not hard to hold to this in the face of joy, in the face of someone you love, in the face of a tree suddenly releasing all its blossoms, or birdsong piercing you from the treetops. We can accord with happiness, with joy; we can align with that with some ease, although sometimes joy can be a jump our hearts refuse. But it's much harder to hold to this while you try to look at less lovely parts of yourself or of the human world, and truly take on the truth that "there is nothing that is not like me." To be able to find the part of yourself that can recognize and connect with the difficult and unlovely part of any being in a difficult moment: that takes practice.

To take on "There is nothing I dislike," or to let it take you on, perhaps in the form of "There is nothing that is not like me," is to allow the koan to darken you. It will take you into dark places, and you'll have to find yourself and recognize yourself there. This practice is not about tidying up the world and making it clean and bright; it's about recognizing the world as it is and finding right there the radical freedom of being. (Have you noticed? There is nowhere else to look!)

With a koan like "There is nothing I dislike," you're free to look into every word that is there, including the word "I." It's not so much forming a case against the word "I" as seeing clearly through the word "I," looking steadily with great doubt and great aspiration until its emptiness is you. This is hard practice that changes you forever—until, in the deepest sense, there is no thing, there is no dislike, there is no "I," and truly there is nothing I dislike.

The alternative is a kind of carefully scaled-down life. One that is still extravagantly rich in detail and variety and shot through with beauty despite all our efforts, since we live on the blue-green planet, but a scaled-down view of what it was we really wanted while we were here, so very briefly.

A scaled-down life

What do you want while you're here in this life's body? It may be that you want to get through with reasonable comfort and least alarm, with good friends, enough to eat, a dry place to live and sleep, and maybe a good bookshop nearby; and trees are good, and a reasonable sprinkling of flowers—that is nice. A few great sunsets. Probably at least one truly great lover somewhere along the line. And hopefully an easy death, with not too much foreknowledge required of us. So no undue suffering. A kind of minimal path of suffering, squeezing by as best we can.

Well—good luck! And, of course, we are already overflowing with luck, just being here. But what about scarcity, and cancer? What about the loss of people you love, and the suffering of strangers—abject misery, starvation, war, disease? How painful is it to see that happening, or even more painful to see that happening and become inured to it? What about loss of species? How do you bear with that, and with the sorrow about what's happening to the planet? And what about the chronic discomfort of never really being completely sure that you are quite here, like the James Joyce character, Mr. Duffy, in *Finnegans Wake*, who always lived "a short distance" from his body?

It leaves out a lot, that comfortable but fearfully small view, and it leaves out the wind and the roaring in things; and in a sense it leaves out most of what's in poetry, and it leaves that out of you. Do you want to live like that, an unlit fire?

Freely living within limitation

"He is me, but I am now not him." Dongshan's words almost suggest that there are two of us. Of course there's not even one, but in another sense there is myself and I. There is one who sees, who deeply sees, and the other one who resolutely cannot afford to see. This is the human condition. There's one of me who can actually open even to the approach of my own death, who can recognize that it is unreserved and unlimited and wide open, that it intersects with all time at once at every point, that I intersect with all time at once at every point. And when it truly strikes me open, that's the very source of great gratitude and just freely being.

But of course, there's another one less prepared to burn up in that fashion, like the old folk present at *Babette's Feast* who got through that entire extraordinary meal and did their best not to notice it at all. And yet all of us at the end walk out under the sky to find that the snow has cleared and the stars are there, and we do hold hands around the well in the darkness and sing, and then we disperse.

At its keenest and best, the human condition is a form of living freely within limitation; the old Chan teachers like Linji reconciled that in every gesture, in every word they spoke. "There is nothing I dislike" are true words that reconcile this fifty-fifty human condition with rigorous attention, awareness, and kindness. Our practice demands that we bring whatever we do here back into the thick of life to live here, and live here well. It asks us to live this marvelous error of our lives with Linji's mind of full participation, in the inexhaustible act of agreeing to stay open and pay attention to the fact of life, moment by moment. This is a kind of ritual of living and dying completely alive, and being refined by difficulty and becoming being, until you can accord in every way with Neruda: "I have never seen a wave I did not admire."

Becoming like this

"There is nothing I dislike" taxes us deeply. Like "Every day is a good day," it asks us to embrace every offer of our lives and deaths with a kind of sublime generosity. Practice is friendly toward suffering, even including old age, sickness, and death, but is not limited by them. It treats each state as a guest—hospitable but not indulgent toward the whims of anger, malice, fear, or shame, the energies born of separation from the other. Life is the constant undoing of what we believe we want. It will continually separate you from this daily delusion, whatever you may do. Why not join it, instead of bitterly opposing it (a process we call "suffering")? When we accept these subtle and demanding offers, we lend our selves to the deep nature of the universe; we become, ourselves, the movement of the Tao.

There can be no intimacy unless we make room for the other. And then? This practice of hospitality is a true asceticism, like St. Benedict's foundation rule: "Receive all guests as Christ." Hospitality is always offered to the stranger. Why? Because the stranger is an opening to Christ, to the profoundly unknown, to our own unknown.

Not supposing something

The famous poem called "Shodoka" says, wonderfully simply, "Not supposing something is the Tathagata." When we are free of supposing something, of interposing what we think we know between ourselves and the actual moment of our life, then the inexhaustible radiance of each particle of matter, each moment, is immediately and abundantly clear.

The path of no-self, of not supposing something runs right through the middle of the most difficult realities of our lives: conflict, disappointment, betrayal, fury, bitter grievance, grudge, sickness, old age, death. When we meet these realities with stillness and quietness instead of an uproar of self-concern, then out of great fear is born very simple courage, a kind of praise. Dogen Zenji points to this transmutation when he asks, "Until the cold pierces our bones at least once, how can we be there when apricot blossoms are perfuming the whole world?"

The wink of dew in the grass, the single banana frond nodding slow assent to the breeze, a cricket bravely singing, the ache in your early morning bones, the approach of old age and death—each thing sounds the word "freedom" like a bell. The bell that accepts all offers is empty and resounding, with not a single supposition blurring the tone.

When the straw sandals wear out

A friend once spoke of her mother, who is extremely crippled by arthritis. She could manage only fifteen or twenty steps each day because of the pain of her condition. One time she was getting up from her chair very slowly and starting to inch forward to fetch something from a table, when her daughter said, "No, no. Sit down, I'll get it for you, don't bother yourself, sit down." And her mother said, gently, "No, don't stop me. I love every step I take."

When you become what you really are in every condition, when you can be what you are in every condition, then it comes back as a blessing. This is the true secret of the gift cycle. Completely natural and close at hand, without even a hint of self-pity.

So, when the straw sandals wear out, things get interesting. When the straw sandals wear out, we just walk on. And every step—painful, joyful—is beyond praise.

CHAPTER 17

Walking alone
in the red sky

GREAT MASTER MAZU WAS UNWELL. The accountant-monk asked him, "How is Your Reverence feeling these days?" The great master said, "Sun-Face Buddha, Moon-Face Buddha." This tiny record of an encounter forms Case 3 of *The Blue Cliff Record*, the great eleventh-century collection of one hundred Chan encounters between teachers and students of the Way.

What has been the sharpest thing in the world for you, up to this point of your life? The sharpest thing in the world for me has been the loss of my sister, Gael, some years ago. We were very close, and very different; yet not so different that we could ever lose the mysterious overlap of our souls that sisterhood, shared childhood, creates.

An Australian writer, Gillian Mears, has written about her sisters in a piece she called "The Childhood Gland." The title proposes that there is a little-known extra "gland" that especially sisters, but undoubtedly also brothers, can seem to grow if the childhood is intensely lived and shared. It stores childhood memory in the form of tiny, potent, unpredictable moments and images and stories, and these little jets of shared child-hood memory, released at times of being with your sister at many moments throughout your life, keep your childhood unusually open and alive, woven right through your adult life. You can enter it freely at any time you are together; and even when you are not, the access to that country grows practiced and easy, a great shared dreaming. This works its own effect on your life, and on your relationship with that sibling soul, I think. You are joined, like Siamese twins, at the childhood gland. Not two, not one.

And our childhoods were very entwined, conjoined. Shared room, shared baths, same clothes made up for us in two sizes (different color rickrack braid), overlapping dreams at night; and in the intensely co-creative space we formed between us we had a rich shared make-believe with a dozen different stories running in as many different locations. The Open Sesame was very simple: we would say the words "Just say…" or "Let's say…," and we would be in England in the Fourth Form of an exclusive girls boarding school; we would become various girls called Angela, Imogen, or Frangipani, who conducted ruthless internal gang warfare and savage external persecution of a large and noisy girl called Strauk, the worst possible name we could think up.

Or at night, when the light was finally turned out because we had read so long (shared books) that our mother determined we were risking permanent eye damage, we would settle down into the dark and enter there. In the darkened stables waited two horses, Lightning and Mid-night. We would swing onto them bareback and easy, and gallop and gallop up through the sky to many ports of call, which included a mys-terious place called "The Toyshop" where anything you wanted was available, and given to you; and then on to see God in heaven, to show off to him how incredibly well we could shoot bows and arrows, and after a satisfactory level of approval from God we could stream down, down through the stars and the planets back to the tired stables and the onset of dream itself.

Sun-face Buddha, Moon-face Buddha

What is this mysterious koan about? The Buddha Name Sutra tells us that the Sun-face Buddha lives in the world for eighteen hundred years, but the Moon-face Buddha enters extinction after only a day and a night. What is it, to live in the world for eighteen hundred years? What is it, to enter extinction after only a day and a night? I think that children know a lot about both of these aspects of buddha nature, and can transmit their Dharma effortlessly. You only need to get down at rug level to play with a baby or gaze into his or her ancient shining eyes for a little while to begin living in the world for eighteen hundred years and to be dawning and growing dark, entering extinction tiny moment by tiny moment. Down there you can realize that now is the only time there is. And that there is no time at all.

Deep meditation can be not unlike playing with a baby on the rug, when we are luminous, open, radiant, and living every breath and heartbeat of our lives in such minutely slowed spaciousness that there is no time at all. But what about when we are tender and touchy, unable to settle deeply in a period of meditation, keenly aware of the merciless clock that won't release us for thirteen more minutes, hating the shabby quality of our practice (while everyone else is clearly a soul in bliss), knowing that our lives will run out and we won't become enlightened. Are we any less precious when we are lost in a haze of love, fear, and doubt than when we are boundless and free in the sky of samadhi? Sun-face Buddha—truly marvelous. Moon-face Buddha—beyond compare.

Great Master Mazu lived long and taught with huge energy in eighth-century China, and vivid legends collected around him. It has been said that he glared like a tiger, ambled like an ox, and had a shout that deafened his student Baizhang for three days. He bore important marks of buddhahood that many of us are still working on: he could cover his nose with his tongue and had significant wheel-shaped marks on his feet. There are no such signs on my feet yet—not yet, but later, surely!

He trained monks vigorously and in huge number, producing some-where between eighty-four and a hundred and thirty-nine successors, among them Nanquan and Baizhang. But the dialogue between Mazu and his accountant-monk took place late in Mazu's life, who was proba-bly on his deathbed at the age of eighty, but still pointing directly at the matter with the resources at hand.

I like it that it is the accountant-monk who asks him a question at such a time. Accountants, I think, are obliged to work at the coalface of Moon-face Buddha, in the realm of death and taxes, mortgages, dead-lines, bottom lines. And so, or and yet, his question is simple, heartfelt. "How is Your Reverence feeling these days?" I know you are sick unto death. Can you say something from that borderland? What is your teach-ing at this moment?

Robert Aitken tells a story of Yasutani Roshi's last days. In the after-noon before Yasutani conducted the last precepts ceremony of his life, Yamada Roshi came home and found him sitting in the living room. "How is your health these days?" he asked him. "When I am sitting down it is all right, but when I stand I am very short of breath," was the reply. After the *jukai* ceremony for, among others, both Ann and Robert Aitken, Yasutani stayed with his daughter. A few days later, he was dead. That night, at the first memorial service for him, Yamada gave *teisho* on this case: "How is your health these days?" "When I stand I am very short of breath, but when I am sitting down it is all right." Sun-face Buddha, Moon-face Buddha.

Golden wind

I began driving regularly south from Sydney to the mountain-ringed country of my sister beyond Canberra at the start of the year in mid-summer when it became abruptly plain and unmistakable that the breast cancer had come back with a vengeance, into her bones and liver, and that there was only some limited, and fearsome, time left. Different to those of us who are not sick, of course, who still have eighteen hundred golden years to go. As I drove those roads again and again on that four-hour journey, I came to know every rise and fall, lean and tilt of the land; many trees and rocks became familiar beacons and friends. Gradually, the leaves of some avenues of trees began to change color, fretting my heart.

One time a flock of tiny yellow birds rose from the trees at exactly the moment the wind swooped and flung thousands of golden leaves up into the air like confetti. But the change of season wasn't bringing a wedding, or not the way we usually think of weddings. My own heart was shaken loose by that wind of golden leaves. Each visit, my sister's hold on life was visibly lighter, looser; she was moving closer to that moment of wedding with the air, the wind, the earth, the rain, the stars. And I could not bear it.

In another old Zen koan, a monk asked Yunmen, "When the tree withers, and the leaves fall, what is that?" When the sedge has withered from the lake, everything is completely dark and empty, and no bird sings; when I am totally destitute with nowhere left to turn, what is that? Yunmen replied, "Golden wind is manifesting itself." That's it, exactly, he says! The finest wine is poured out for you. Your self-nature is no other than this grief, this laughter, this turmoil, this very breath of your life. Golden wind is manifesting itself. Golden wind is the traditional deity of autumn, and brings the brilliant death fire of the leaves, yet there is nothing symbolic here at all. Golden wind is always manifesting itself. Just that—nothing sticking to it. And yet the scent of death is there. We die. This spreads gold all over the earth.

One face

Several years before, I had come in early summer, when it was still cool up in the high country, to see my sister after the operation. When I looked into her face for the first time since her life had turned I could see that she was now more consciously holding Sun-face Buddha, Moon-face

Buddha, together in one face. Her eyes looked out at me with all her life and love and vulnerability. We both woke extremely early and found each other in the dark corridor at the center of her house, and in silent accord we made our way to take two chairs and a cup of tea to the big windows that face east. A slender moon in company with the morning star was slowly, slowly losing itself into a sky that was lightening by infinitesimal degrees. Gradually, gradually, the soft heads of the trees stepped out from the dark sky and announced themselves in some quality of the air that you couldn't yet call light. We talked, and we sat in deep, companionable silence. We didn't have a single trivial thing to say. We were so laid bare to each other, there was not a veil left between us. Or between us and the eternity of a fading moon. How long is a moon setting? How long is a sunrise?

When the day has begun

I remember a tale from the Hasidim that I like very much, one of many that I find can be taken as koans. I remember it a little differently to Martin Buber's original telling; I have to acknowledge that I have begun to let it drift in a Zen direction.

An old rabbi was talking with his assembly. He asked his people, "How do we know when the night has ended and the day has begun?"

After a moment someone ventured, "Is it that moment when the individual trees begin to step out of the forest?"

The old rabbi shook his head. "No, it is not that moment."

Another one spoke up. "Is it that moment when we can begin to tell a cloud from the morning mist?"

"No," said the old rabbi. "No, it is not that moment."

They all fell deeply silent. Finally someone said, "Please tell us, rabbi, how can we know that moment when the night has ended and the day has begun?"

And then the old rabbi said, "It is that moment when you can look into the face of a stranger, and recognize your own original face. Until then, the night is still with us."

The time of the changing of the light—dark into dawn, afternoon into dusk—has always been my favorite time for sitting. There is something about transitional time, its threshold feeling, that is peculiarly rich. It is the littoral zone, the shore between the dayworld and the depths, water coming in, water going out. I have sat intimately with two deaths, in the vast littoral zone of two dyings, in the past few years—a very dear friend succumbing to AIDS, and then my sister, Gael, relinquishing her life to cancer. Both these people were special, gifted, loving people, a huge and radical loss to their worlds; both had to part from life right in the thick of their lives. Parting with the eighteen hundred years and entering extinction is a searingly painful business, almost impossible for the ones looking on to consent to. And yet where is the eternity of Sun-Face Buddha to be found on this Earth, if not right there in every rasping breath?

Blossom

There is something about looking out of windows to the trees. Trees bear such silent and complete witness to our lives, our lives of muddled grace. Czeslaw Milosz wrote a poem about it from one angle of view. He looked out at dawn to see a young apple tree translucent in brightness. Another dawn, and mysteriously, an apple tree laden with fruit stood in its place. Many years had probably passed, he says, "but I remember nothing of what happened in my sleep."

And from the other angle of view, Dennis Potter, the great English television dramatist, managed to give an interview to the BBC in the last fortnight of his life, before his death from pancreatic cancer. He sat there, gaunt and burning with life, with death, and the interviewer asked him, well, "How is Your Reverence feeling these days?" Dennis talked about his passionate desire to complete the series he was writing with all his might, by far his greatest work; and the sharp sense that his time was running out so fast that his work might not make it across the final dead-line—and that was so painful. "And yet," he said, "you know that almost does not matter now. Because you see there is a tree outside my window where I am working. Of course the tree has always been outside my window. But now it is in blossom. And now for the first time in my life, I have seen it. I have seen the blossom! It is the blossomest blossom in the world. And everything is worth it, for this! Everything is worth it."

Moon-face Buddha. Sun-face Buddha. Tell me, which one is which?

It never stops flowing

The special gift of a slowly approaching death, as well as its mesmerizing pain, is consciousness of death itself. However hard that inner relinquishing may be, whatever gut-wrenching and impossible grief may lie on the road to it, I think that the gift is always received, always passed across.

I was awed, privileged, and utterly demolished by being present to my sister's vast, agonizing dropping away of body and mind. She was on heavy morphine for the pain, and only half conscious for much of the time, but when she sensed someone's presence she would swim up into a pure and somehow timeless consciousness, full of grace, completely there as long as she could manage for whoever was present. And her presence was as fragrant and open as a newborn baby's at the other end of life, at that equally mysterious moment when the sudden ball of a new life is tossed onto the fast-flowing stream.

My sister's gentleness had always been extraordinary, but now her touch went right through to the core of you, from the core of her. She still worried and fretted at moments; she anxiously kept her watch on, and indeed her glasses to see it by, but as the story drops away, drops away, the mystery at last is laid bare, directly touched.

She and I had a special, secret pastime. We used to walk to a nearby dreaming place—there is always a nearby dreaming place—and the one on the farm where she lived was a semi-wild hillside gully formed by a tiny creek, or thread of pools, making its way down to the sheep paddocks. The tiny birds, the frogs, the dragonflies, the wombats, the lichens and mosses and crumbling rocks and twigs, all loved this place. It was enchanting—it cast a slow spell that eased you into dreaming openness. We would sit and stare and absorb and move on; we would talk a little, and sit again, and just stare; but all the talk was no more than quiet celebration of being, a long slow feast of it. Walking back across the paddocks after having our secret fill brings to mind another case in *The Blue Cliff Record*, "Changsha Goes Picnicking":

> Changsha, one day, went on a picnic in the mountain. When he returned to the gate, the Head Monk asked, "Your Reverence, where have you been wandering?"
>
> "I have come back from strolling in the hills," said Changsha.
>
> "Where did you stray?" asked the Head Monk.
>
> Changsha said, "First I went following the scented grasses, then came back following the fallen flowers."
>
> "That is spring mood itself," said the Head Monk.
>
> Changsha said, "It is better than the autumn dew falling on the lotus flowers."
>
> Later, Xuedou, whose comments are interjected throughout *The Blue Cliff Record*, said, "I am grateful for that answer."

Our life, our practice, is the scented grasses and fallen flowers in the one vast spring mood itself. The words of the traditional verse touched on through this exchange are used in Buddhist funeral services for monks and nuns. First we go out following the scented grasses, and then we come back following the fallen flowers. We live, and we die. We die, and we come forth. We die the great death into emptiness, into such a deeply autumnal and fiery freedom, but we must turn back again and again to come forth and offer ourselves to ordinary and amazing life, to the deep fresh spring of all beings.

Spring mood itself is this hazy state of human weariness, happiness, aching, longing, impatience, frustration, boredom, hopefulness, grief… "Some people want it pure white, but sweep as you will, you cannot empty the mind," said Keizan, concerning the hazy moon of enlightenment. I, too, am grateful for that answer. Can you hear the answer? Deep fog this morning; the angophoras are just breaking through into light.

Autumn is always fragrantly mixed up in spring, and spring in autumn. We are always waking up to life, letting go, letting go even of life itself, in every moment of our great lives. It is Edgar, isn't it, in *King Lear* who says, "Men must endure their going hence, even in their coming hither. Ripeness is all."

Fortunately, there is nothing that can be done about it. Sun-Face Buddha, Moon-Face Buddha see with the same eyes, our own eyes. Truly not two, not one. "When you know what this public case comes down to," says Xuedou, "you walk alone through the red sky." That's where I meet my sister, now.

Alone together in the red sky is a good place to meet. See you there, now.

Appendix

How to begin seated Zen meditation

Counting the breath is often the first practice assigned and mastered on the Zen path toward this point of becoming intimate with breathing. The in-breath is drawn in simple appreciation of the fact of breathing; the out-breath is silently intoned with the number "one," the next out-breath will be "two," the third nothing but "three," drawing mind into breath. After loss of consciousness, the ability to count is often used as a sign of the return of consciousness; similarly, you may be asked to count down into unconsciousness as you enter a state of anesthesia. Counting is like the last and least effortful rung of the conscious mind, and it is also steely and reliable. So when you find yourself drifting away from the count into swarms of thought, you just notice and then come back to one, again and again and again. "One" is always ready to take you back, with no hard feelings.

At a certain point you may find the counting has naturally dropped away altogether into a very still and low-lit consciousness. Sometimes you can just rest there like a feather on a draft, aware, but not making a single move toward thought. But then the thought may come: "Hey, I'm not thinking at all!" And then? Back to one.

These practices of following the breath can be taken up in an ordinary upright chair, with your feet flat on the ground and your spine straight, supported by a strong slight inward curve at the base of your spine, and preferably unsupported by the back of the chair. When you are ready, and if you can physically manage, it is good to begin to sit in the traditional postures of seated meditation, upon a padded futon or flat cushion, called a *zabuton* in Japanese, with a smaller round cushion, or *zafu*, under the buttocks to give you about eight to ten centimeters of lift. The legs are crossed in one of several traditional ways, such as tailor-style or half-lotus, the knees supported with other cushions at first until the ligaments begin to lengthen with practice and allow the knees to rest on the ground. Or you may use a meditation bench—a low stool that allows the legs to bend back underneath. It is good to get an experienced meditator to show you how to find ease and stability in these postures of alert but fluid focused awareness.

In either case, you form a solid connection with the earth: you are sitting like a mountain, the small of the back slightly curved inwards to give the rest of your spine support and ease. The upper spine and neck and shoulders are now erect in an entirely unforced and energizing posture of alertness. (Notice how a small child carries his or her body, with a natural lift and energy visible in the upper body. Notice too how an adult usually slumps in this segment of the body, with the center of gravity dropped much lower and heavier, a posture of tiredness.) You know you have this right when your belly just naturally rounds into a soft outwards curve in reply. It is good to wear loose clothing so that your softened belly can receive the energy of your breath, unrestricted. The area just below the belly-button is called the *hara*, and it is good to maintain awareness of the hara with every mindful breath. Feel for the flow of energy there. As you follow the breath into deeper states of meditation, it is as though mind gradually settles deep into the body, unobstructed by mental activity, and takes up its true seat quite naturally in the hara.

The eyes are not closed as in sleep, but soft-focused and half-closed, and the tongue rests in contact with the palate just above the upper teeth, centered and softened, with the jaw muscles and eye muscles relaxed. The hands are rested in the lap and held in a traditional mudra—the left hand resting in the right, the thumbs making soft contact at the tips. It is good to sit for around twenty-five minutes and then walk in slow walking meditation for five more minutes before sitting again if you wish. This is the time-honored alternating rhythm you will encounter in most Zen places of practice, marked out with signals (not words) that are delivered by bells and clappers.

Walking meditation is a natural extension of seated focus: you simply continue to stay with your breath while rising to your feet, and then slowly begin to walk, left foot with the in-breath, right foot with the out-breath, letting the loveliness of the body in motion explore you entirely. You can afford to let the world pass through you as you look for your next step, and feel the sunlight fall across your face; a bird sings right through the you that walks, the universe walking. In particular, you now include in your focused awareness the way the foot meets and articulates its many tiny bones to the shape and fact of the floor, the intimate return greeting offered by the floor or the earth to every footfall.

Appendix

The Great Prajna Paramita Heart Sutra

Avalokiteshvara Bodhisattva, practicing deep Prajna Paramita, clearly saw that all five skandhas are empty, transforming anguish and distress. Shariputra, form is no other than emptiness, emptiness no other than form; form is exactly emptiness, emptiness exactly form; sensation, perception, formulation, consciousness are also like this.

Shariputra, all things are essentially empty—not born, not destroyed; not stained, not pure; without loss, without gain. Therefore in emptiness there is no form, no sensation, perception, formulation, consciousness; no eye, ear, nose, tongue, body, mind, no color, sound, scent, taste, touch, thought; no seeing and so on to no thinking; no ignorance and also no ending of ignorance, and so on to no old age and death and also no ending of old age and death; no anguish, cause of anguish, cessation, path; no wisdom and no attainment.

Since there is nothing to attain, the Bodhisattva lives by Prajna Paramita, with no hindrance in the mind; no hindrance and therefore no fear; far beyond delusive thinking, right here is nirvana.

All buddhas of past, present, and future live by Prajna Paramita, attaining Anuttara-samyak-sambodhi.

Therefore know that Prajna Paramita is the great sacred mantra, the great vivid mantra, the unsurpassed mantra, the supreme mantra, which completely removes all anguish. This is truth, not mere formality. Therefore set forth the Prajna Paramita mantra, set forth this mantra and proclaim:

TA YA THA OM GATE GATE PARAGATE PARASAMGATE BODHI SVAHA.

Glossary

Acharya (also "Acarya") Sanskrit honorific term meaning master, especially master of the Dharma.

Amida Japanese name (also Amitabha, in Sanskrit) for the Buddha of Boundless Light, ruler of the "western paradise" or Pure Land of enlightened consciousness, in Chinese and Japanese Pure Land Buddhism.

Baizhang (720–814 C.E.) Dharma heir of Mazu, Baizhang Huaihai established the monastic rules of Zen monasteries, which became more self-supporting and less dependent on alms under his influence — "A day without work is a day without eating."

The Blue Cliff Record The magisterial collection of a hundred koans known as *The Blue Cliff Record* or *Hekiganroku*, was compiled in the eleventh century by the Chan teacher Xuedou Chongxian, who added his own verses and commentaries. In the twelfth century, Yuanwu Keqin added introductions and summaries to the cases. The title comes from the place in Hunan province where Yuanwu gave his Dharma talks on the collection.

Bodhi tree A variety of fig that has subsequently been considered sacred, under which Shakyamuni Buddha finally sat for seven days and nights to deeply realize his own self-nature.

Bodhidharma (d. around 530 C.E.) A semi-legendary figure who is taken as the first Chinese Zen ancestor, who brought Zen from India to China, he fiercely insisted on "direct pointing at mind" to reveal buddha nature, cutting off all reliance on words and phrases of explanation and going directly to the source: "Vast emptiness, nothing holy."

bodhimandala (Sanskrit) means "place of awakening." The first *bodhimandala* was the ground beneath the Bodhi tree where the Buddha sat and looked up to see the morning star.

bodhisattva (Sanskrit) literally means "enlightenment being"—one who seeks buddhahood or enlightened being through systematic practice of the eight "perfections," but renounces complete entry into nirvana until all beings are saved or awoken.

buddha nature Your own essential nature, equally shared by every sentient being and every detail of reality, directly realized when conceptual mind and self-concern fall profoundly away, revealing what was always there.

Chuang Tzu (c. 369–286 B.C.E.) A leading thinker in the Taoist stream of Chinese thought and understanding that pre-dated Buddhism in China and, together with Confucianism, constituted a matrix of thought and practice that strongly influenced the character of Chan Buddhism.

Dharmakaya One of the three "bodies of the Buddha" in Mahayana Buddhism, it points to the vast, empty, equal self-nature in which all things rest. See *Nirmanakaya* and *Sambhogakaya*.

Dogen (1200–1253 C.E.) The Japanese master who brought the Soto tradition to vivid life in Japan, Dogen Kigen or Eihei Dogen is the most important Zen master in Japanese history. His extensive writings are not "philosophy" but at every point a direct expression of the immediate inner experience of reality on the ground of realization.

dokusan (Japanese) literally means "going alone before a teacher," the term refers to the regular private encounter of student and teacher that is a special feature of Zen, in which the student presents and tests his or her understanding, or explores problems arising in practice. *Dokusan* can only be offered by one who has been confirmed as a teacher by his or her own confirmed teacher in an authentic Zen lineage.

Dongshan (807–869 C.E.) Dongshan Liangjie, disciple of Yunyan, is recognized as founder of the Caodong or Soto school of Zen, which, with the Linji or Rinzai school, is one of the two surviving Zen schools that began in Tang dynasty China. He formulated the Five Ranks (of enlightenment) that continue to play an important part in koan training in Zen.

Emptiness From *shunyata* (Japanese), *sunyata* (Sanskrit), *sunnata* (Pali). Emptiness is the doctrine of the essential impermanence and emptiness of all forms: the actual nature of the self and of all beings and things which is directly perceived in deep realization. From this a profound sense of the oneness or the unconditioned original nature of all forms arises in the very fact of their complete impermanence, and this direct experience of the true nature of reality *(shunyata)* is a liberation from conditioned mind into vast, open, clear mind that is no different from *shunyata* itself.

The Gateless Barrier Originally compiled with comment and verse by Wumen Huikai in 1228 C.E., this collection of forty-eight koans with verses and commentaries is a masterpiece of Chan literature.

Guishan (771–853 C.E.) Student and Dharma heir of Baizhang, and master of Yangshan, Guishan Lingyu was the foremost teacher of his time in southern China, with a monastic community numbering 1,500 monks, and 41 Dharma descendants.

Hakuin (1689–1769 C.E.) Hakuin Zenji, or Hakuin Ekaku, is acknowledged as one of the most important Japanese Zen masters of the Rinzai (or Linji) school, to which he brought reform and immense, fresh impetus with his life's work of profound practice and vigorous teaching. He is also regarded as a highly significant artist—calligrapher, painter, and sculptor.

hara (Japanese) The "belly," or the area just below the navel, regarded as the body's center of spiritual energy.

Heart Sutra Also known as *The Heart of the Diamond Sutra*, or the *Prajna Paramita* ("Perfection of Wisdom"), this is regarded as a core sutra of Zen liturgy everywhere. Its 270 Chinese characters offer the heart or essence of the Zen wisdom tradition, based in the doctrine of *shunyata*, or emptiness. See also Emptiness.

Huangbo (d. 850 C.E.) Student and Dharma successor of Baizhang, and master of Linji, he is a forefather of the Linji (Rinzai) school of Zen.

I Ching (or *Ijing*) Possibly the oldest book in existence, the "Book of Changes" received high praise from Confucius 2,500 years ago as a wisdom book that conveys and opens to view the pattern of changes in life from a Taoist and even earlier shamanic perspective. The *I Ching* is very congruent with Chan (Zen) Buddhist understanding and highly revered as a text.

Kasyapa Buddha (Sanskrit) One of the mythical Ancient Seven Buddhas preceding the historical Buddha: this one is the Buddha of the World Age preceding this present one.

koan (Japanese) literally means "public case," pointing to a sense that these interactions, exchanges, turning words, or lines of poetry from the records of masters in the tradition point directly to a matter that is present everywhere and in each thing, in the most public manner. To see into the koan is to align your own understanding with the Dharma of these old teachers. There is no other way to "grasp" them.

Linji (d. 866 or 867 C.E.) Linji Yixuan, Chinese master, successor to Huangbo, founder of the vital and influential Linji (Japanese: Rinzai) school of Chan Buddhism, that set much of its tone, spirit, and character. The school declined in the twelfth century in China but had seeded to Japan where it continued and was sharply reinvigorated by Hakuin in the eighteenth century.

Mahakasyapa (Sanskrit) literally means "Great Kasyapa." Not to be confused with Kasyapa Buddha.

Mahayana (Sanskrit) literally means "Great Vehicle." The Mahayana is one of the two great schools of Buddhism (the other being the Hinayana, or "Lesser Vehicle"), arising in the first century C.E. While the Hinayana seeks the enlightenment of the individual, the

Mahayana is "great" for its intention to open the way of liberation to all beings, and to care for their welfare. The Mahayana also emphasizes the *bodhisattva* ideal of compassion and the notion of emptiness, and places less emphasis on monasticism, opening a path for lay people.

makyo (Japanese) refers to visions and other kinds of hallucinatory experiences arising in deep *samadhi* states. From a Zen perspective, little is made of these phenomena.

mara (Sanskrit, Pali) The literal connotation is "murder, death," but the implication is the negative and destructive passions that overwhelm human beings and obstruct or overturn equanimity.

Mazu (709–788 C.E.) Master of many great teachers, including Baizhang and Nanquan, with more than 130 successors, the (literally) giant figure of Mazu Daoyi exerted a huge, shaping influence upon the development of Chan (Zen) in China. His sudden shouts, wordless gesture, and unexpected blows became part of Chan training methods of delivering sudden shocks to shake the student out of habitual ruts of consciousness.

milonga An Argentine dance form, rather like a tango, but sometimes more strict in tone.

Neruda (1904–1973) Pablo Neruda, the Chilean poet, was an outstanding Latin American poet of his generation, awarded the Nobel Prize for Literature in 1971.

Nirmanakaya (Sanskrit) The second body of the Buddha, the "body of transformation" or differentiation of each thing into its particular unrepeatable form and existence in karma. See *Dharmakaya* and *Sambhogakaya*.

samadhi (Sanskrit) literally means "to establish, make firm." A mind of no separation from anything within the reach of consciousness. *Samadhi* is sometimes translated as "one-pointed consciousness," but this might suggest a state of concentration upon an object, which would simply return you to the mind of me in here and you out there.

It may be more helpful to think of it as a mind pointed to one, return-ing to wholeness, coming to rest there.

Sambhogakaya (Sanskrit) The third body of the Buddha, the "bliss body" of realization.

shikantaza (Japanese) literally means "nothing but sitting." A challeng-ingly simple form of *zazen* without breath-counting or koan prac-tice: resting in a state of brightly alert attention, not subject to the tug of thought, directed to no object and attached to no content, vig-ilant toward, but not captured by, thought and feeling impressions as they rise and fall away. Moment by moment, resolving the challenge of "just sitting."

shin (Japanese) literally means "heart-mind," with the sense of heart, spirit, consciousness, soul, mind, outlook, interiority, and thought. In Zen it has the connotation both of the completely alert and open mind, heart, and spirit, and of the absolute reality perceived by such a fully realized and awake mind.

Shunryu Suzuki (1904–1971) Author of the well-known *Zen Mind, Beginner's Mind,* an influential and important Soto Zen teacher in the West who went to the United States in 1959 and founded the San Francisco Zen Center.

shunyata See Emptiness.

Tagore Rabindranath Tagore, well-known Indian poet of the turn of the twentieth century, who popularized several important works in Eng-lish, including the *Bhagavad-Gita.*

Tao Te Ching Believed to be the work of Lao Tzu writing in the time of Confucius, the "Book of the Way" is regarded as the classic text of Taoism and is the most widely translated work in world literature after the Bible. It harmonizes its timeless wisdom with the Tao, the basic principle of the universe. In Zen, "the Tao" is used virtually inter-changeably with "buddha nature."

Tathagata (Sanskrit) literally means "the thus-gone, thus-come, thus-perfected one." It refers to one who has supreme realization, and is one of the ten titles of the Buddha. It equally refers to that which is realized—the absolute nature of reality—since there can be no difference between this and the one who realizes.

teisho (Japanese) The presentation of the Dharma in a Zen talk. It is not a lecture, and nothing is explained; rather, a *teisho* is an immediate presentation of the essential matter, which treats the listener as an equal and can touch the deepest mind when conceptual thought lies quiet. The character includes the senes of "a cry," a shout," "a song."

upaya (Sanskrit) Skillful means or method of expounding the teaching, chosen in subtle accordance with the capability of the student.

the Way The path of bringing all of the parts of your life into full concordance with your realization of the true nature of yourself and of all beings.

Wumen (1183–1260 C.E.) Considered the most outstanding Rinzai master of his time, Wumen Huikai is composer of the great *Wumenkuan*, or *Mumonkan*, a collection of forty-eight koans, with commentary and verse attached, that form a vital part of all koan training.

yume (Japanese) "Dream."

Yunmen (864–949 C.E.) Successor to Xuefeng, and master of more than sixty successors, the great teacher Yunmen Wenyan is often regarded as the last of the Chan "giants," with his fierce eye and powerfully pared expression of the Way that offers no foothold for thought.

zazen (Japanese) Meditative practice taught in Zen to free the mind from bondage of every kind. It is an alert, awake, upright, fluid act of sitting still, with the mind not directed toward any object and not clinging to any subject; this state of content-less wakefulness does not enact or reinforce the self in any way but can allow the self to suddenly drop away completely to reveal buddha nature, original mind.

Zhaozhou (778–897 C.E.) One of the most important Chan teachers, Zhaozhou Congshen had matchless depth of realization; Dogen called him "Joshu, the old buddha." He is responsible for what has become the first gate of realization for many students since then—the koan *Mu*.

Notes

SOMETIMES THE REFERENCES MADE in the course of Dharma talks drop unexpectedly into the mind and in the moment of delivery from long-term memory, rather than being assembled and attributable in a scholarly way. In some cases it has proved impossible to trace and check the original source. For any unintentional inaccuracies in this realm, I apologize to my readers, and undertake that any corrections that come to light shall be made in future editions. Where I have creatively misremembered the lost original, I stand guilty as charged and apologize to the author concerned for the process that, in any case, all works undergo: that of becoming the inner experience of their readers, no longer a completely objective business.

Zen koans, most of them more than a thousand years old, exist in numerous translations, each one subtly different. I am generally reliant upon the koan translations used in private circulation in Diamond Sangha circles, originating from Robert Aitken and Yamada Koun, which are always held open to subsequent revision. Where no alternative published source is given, those unpublished translations can be taken as my source. However, all of the major collections of koans are available in published form in other translations.

Robert Aitken's landmark commentaries on the *Mumonkan*, *The Gateless Barrier: The Wu-Men Kuan (Mumonkan)*, published by North Point Press, San Francisco, 1990, is a key source throughout this book, as cited in these notes. Shambhala Press, Boston, has recently republished Zenkei Shibayama's brilliant commentaries, *The Gateless Barrier: Zen Comments on the Mumonkan* (2000); it also publishes Thomas Cleary's translations of the *Hekigan Roku, The Blue Cliff Record* (1992), and the *Shoyu Roku, The Book of Serenity: One Hundred Zen Dialogues* (1988), which has since been republished by Lindisfarne Press, Hudson, New York. North Point Press published Thomas Cleary's 1990 translation of the *Denko Roku, Transmission of the Light: Zen in the Art of Enlightenment by Zen Master Keizan*, but I recommend Francis H. Cook's 1991 translation, *The Record of Transmitting the Light: Zen Master Keizan's Denko-roku*, published by Center Publications, Los Angeles, recently republished by Wisdom Publications, Boston.

Chapter 1
Breath, like mind, like water

"Being blind" and "a satisfaction too deep for words"
>   Jacques Lusseyrans, *And There Was Light*, Parabola Books, 2nd edition, New York, 1998: 27.

"The camellia"
>   My own translation of Yosa Buson's haiku. See also Robert Hass (ed. and trans.), *The Essential Haiku — Versions of Basho, Buson and Issa*, The Ecco Press, New Jersey, 1994: 115, and in general for brilliant translations of these three Zen-inflected poets.

"Better than knowing the body"
>   Wumen's verse is from *Wumenkuan* Case 9, "Qingrang's Non-Attained Buddha." See Robert Aitken, *The Gateless Barrier*, North Point Press, San Francisco, 1990: 64.

"Even in rain"
>   Haiku by the author.

Chapter 2
One world at a time

"This word 'practice'"
>   Gail Sher's fine book on writing, *One Continuous Mistake: The Four Noble Truths of Writing*, Arkana Penguin, New York, 1998, gave fresh stimulus to my thinking about the nature of a practice.

"Heart Sutra"
>   See glossary.

"The most important thing in the world"
>   Retold from Martin Buber, "Most Important," *Tales of the Hasidim*, Vol.
>   2, trans. Olga Marx, Schocken Books edition, New York, 1991: 173.

"One world at a time"
>   Quoted, uncited, in Gail Sher, op. cit.

"an orange that found its way onto his meal tray one day"
>   Brian Keenan, *An Evil Cradling*, Random House, London, 1994.

"I have already become like this"
>   *Denkoroku*, Case 41, "The Forty-First Ancestor, Tongan Guanzhi."

"Connectedness is reality"
>   Attributed to Auntie Beryl Carmichael of the Nyaanpia nation by Rose-
>   mary Beaumont, in her unpublished Master's Thesis, "Circle of Women (an
>   indepth study of the spirituality and ceremony of a group of white Australian
>   women)."

"What is the Mysterious?"
>   Cited in Isshu Miyura and Ruth Fuller Sasaki, *Zen Dust: The History of
>   the Koan and Koan Study in Rinzai (Lin-chi) Zen*, Harcourt Brace & World
>   Inc., New York, 1966: 259 (Endnote 50).

Chapter 3
Intimacy with the Other

"the bodhisattva vows"
>   I quote here Robert Aitken's translations of the four bodhisattva vows,
>   widely used throughout the worldwide Diamond Sangha. Other transla-
>   tions exist—for example, those produced by John Tarrant and Joan Suther-
>   land for Pacific Zen Institute, California: "I vow to wake the beings of the
>   world; I vow to set endless heartache to rest; I vow to walk through every wis-
>   dom gate; I vow to live the great Buddha way."

"We asked the captain"

>Herman Melville, *Moby Dick*, as cited by poet Robert Hass in *Praise*, The Ecco Press, New York, 1994.

"Greed, hatred, and ignorance"

>My thinking about the second bodhisattva vow was stimulated by commentary in Manfred B. Steger and Perle Besserman, *Grassroots Zen*, Tuttle, Boston, 2002.

"Don't let your throat tighten with fear"

>*The Essential Rumi*, trans. Coleman Barks, HarperCollins, San Francisco, 1996: 52.

"The world of dew"

>Kobayashi Issa, translation given by John Tarrant in a *teisho* given in Sydney, 1989.

Chapter 4
The great Way of play

"Little Helen's Sunday Afternoon"

>See Helen Garner, *Postcards from Surfers*, Penguin Books, Sydney, 1981.

"each point must flow out from your own breast"

>Xuefeng's beautiful enlightenment story is told in Yuanwu's commentary on Case 22 of *The Blue Cliff Record*. Yantou was holed up in a snowbound hut on Tortoise Mountain with his fellow student, Xuefeng, while traveling to visit a teacher. Xuefeng was tormented, his heart not yet at rest. Yantou helped him explore his condition, and with these words something fell away and Xuefeng was released: "In the future, if you want to propagate the great teaching let each point flow out from your own breast to cover heaven and earth for me." He bowed and cried out repeatedly, "Today, Tortoise Mountain is enlightened!"

"if it pleases the eye, it is not yet dangerous enough"

    See Kazuaki Tanahashi, *Brush Mind*, Parallax Press, Berkeley, California, 1998.

"Once in ancient times"

    Wumenkuan, Case 6, "The World-Honored One Twirls a Flower." See Robert Aitken, *The Gateless Barrier: The Wu-men Kuan (Mumonkan)*, North Point Press, San Francisco, 1990: 46.

"a man who believed he had a fish in his jaw"

    Keith Johnstone, *Impro: Improvisation and the Theatre*, Routledge, New York: 83–4.

"Rabbi Levi Yitzhak of Berditchev"

    Retold from Martin Buber, "The Dance," *Tales of the Hasidim*, Vol. 1, trans. Olga Marx, Schocken Books edition, New York, 1991: 231.

Chapter 5
The whole world is medicine

"the whole world is medicine"

    The Blue Cliff Record, Case 87, "Yunmen's Medicine and Sickness."

"Knowing is delusion; not knowing is blankness"

    Wumenkuan, Case 18, "Tungshan's Three Pounds of Flax" (the verse).

"The Cloud of Unknowing"

    See Anonymous, *The Cloud of Unknowing and Other Works*, ed. Clifton Wolters, trans. Thomas Wyatt, Penguin Classics, London, 1978.

"Mu"

    Wumenkuan, Case 1, "Zhaozhou's Dog." See Robert Aitken, *The Gateless Barrier: The Wu-men Kuan (Mumonkan)*, North Point Press, San Francisco, 1990: 7–18.

"The Meaning of the Universe"

    In Les Murray, *Poems the Size of Photographs*, Duffy and Snellgrove, Sydney, 2002: 101.

Chapter 6
"He is me"

"Dongshan had worked with the great Guishan for some time"
>See William Powell (trans.), *The Record of Tung-shan*, University of Hawaii Press, Honolulu, 1986: 27–8.

"It will be hard *not* to meet"
>Ibid: 27.

Chapter 7
The tiger's kindness

"The tiger fears the human heart"
>I do not know the origin of this Korean Son (Zen) koan, which I heard in a talk given by Chi Kwung in Sydney, 1990.

"the shoulder of the lion"
>See Coleman Barks (trans.), Jelalludin Rumi, "The lion's shoulder," in *Feeling the Shoulder of the Lion: Poetry and Teaching Stories*, Threshold Books, Vermont, 1991: 13.

"a white tiger"
>See Barry Lopez, "Flight," in *About This Life: Journeys on the Threshold of Memory*, Harvill Press, London, 1998: 95.

"For ye shall go out with joy"
>Hebrew Scriptures (Old Testament), Isaiah 55:12.

"the softest thing on earth"
>Verse 43 (Te), Lao Tzu, trans. Richard Willhelm, *Tao Te Ching*, Arkana Penguin, London, 1989: 47.

"the wild reality at the heart of the universe"
>I cannot locate the exact quote from Wendell Berry's writings, but acknowledge his strong influence on my thinking here.

"the hawkness of the hawk"

> This parable is developed in Brian Swimme's video series of lectures, *A Canticle for the Cosmos*, especially "Destruction and Loss," where he mounts a powerful argument about the relationship between loss and creativity.

"A Prayer That Will Be Answered"

> See Anna Kamienska, "A Prayer That Will Be Answered," in *A Book of Luminous Things*, ed. Czeslaw Milosz, Harcourt Brace and Company, New York, 1996: 290.

"one small hand"

> Retold from Martin Buber, *Tales of the Hasidim*, Vol. 1: 74.

"electricity was restored"

> See Raymond Carver, "The Window," *All of Us: The Collected Poems*, Harvill, London, 1996: 211.

"the love that moves the stars"

> Dante's words, as they are commonly translated, spoken to Virgil as he emerges back up under the sky from his visit to the Inferno, in *The Divine Comedy*.

Chapter 8
Songlines of the Way

"on a night of heavy snow"

> See Shih Tao-yuan and Chung-yuan Chang, *Early Teachings of Ch'an Buddhism Selected from Transmission of the Lamp*, 1971.

"when you know the place where you are, practice begins"

> See Zen Master Dogen, "*Genjo Koan*: Actualizing the Fundamental Point," in Kazuaki Tanahashi (ed.), *Moon in a Dewdrop*, North Point Press, San Francisco, 1985: 72.

"as a branch is grafted onto mature stock"

      See Eugene Stockton, *The Aboriginal Gift: Spirituality for a Nation*, Millennium Books, Sydney, 1995: 131.

"everywhen"

      W. E. H. Stanner, "The Dreaming," in *White Man Got No Dreaming*, ANU Press, Canberra, 1979: 23–4.

"If we were to locate ourselves, hypothetically, in Dreaming"

      Deborah Bird Rose, "Ned Kelly Died for Our Sins," *Oceania*, 65(2): 175–86.

"Groote Eylandt clan song for the West Wind"

      Quoted in full in Deborah Bird Rose, *Nourishing Terrains*, Australian Heritage Commission, Commonwealth of Australia, 1996: 11–12. Originally in J. Stokes & Aboriginal Advisers, *Groote Eylandt Song Words*, Angurugu, Groote Eylandt, 1981.

"nothing in this system invites people to assume"

      Ibid: 10.

"just the wild"

      Ibid: 19.

"When we took what we called 'land'"

      W. E. H. Stanner, *The 1968 Boyer Lectures*, Australian Broadcasting Commission: 44–5.

"wilu, killing us"

      Quoted in J. Roberts, *Massacres to Mining: The Colonisation of Aboriginal Australia*, Dove Communications, Melbourne, 1981: 148.

"Morning gives you the flow of a new day"

      David Mowaljarlai and Jutta Malnic, *Yorro Yorro: Aboriginal Creation and the Renewal of Nature*, Inner Traditions, Vermont, 1993: 53–4.

"dadirri"

      Ibid, Miriam-Rose Ungunmerr, "Dadirri": 179–84.

"Zen places at its threshold a ceremony of atonement"

I am grateful to Tasmanian Zen student Ross Coward for his insightful comments on this matter in a private letter in response to the talk I gave on this subject in Melbourne, 1999, in which I first explored these matters.

"When Odysseus was cast out"

See Homer, *The Odyssey*, trans. Robert Fagles, Penguin Putnam, New York, 1996: 165–7.

"being in on the intimate gossip"

Gary Snyder explores this as an aspect of bioregional awareness in "The Place, the Region and the Commons," *The Practice of the Wild*, North Point Press, Berkeley, California, 1990: 28ff.

"Waking up itself is not unlike singing ourselves awake"

I acknowledge Ross Coward's thoughtful comments on their point.

"the song of the frogs"

Martin Buber, "At the Pond," *Tales of the Hasidim*, Vol. 1: 111.

"Wake up, I have a song to teach you"

Alan Marett, an ethnomusicologist and Zen student, first offered this story in an article in *Mind Moon Circle*, the journal of the Sydney Zen Centre, in 1989. John Tarrant took it up as a koan in a koan seminar in Occidental, California, in 2000, in a slightly different form to the one I offer here.

Chapter 9
The hermitage in the street

"cities are old fallen tree trunks"

See Gary Snyder, "Blue Mountains Are Constantly Walking," *The Practice of the Wild*, North Point Press, Berkeley, California, 1990: 110.

"a hatted Jewish New York real-estate photographer"

See Ben Katchor, *Cheap Novelties: The Pleasures of Urban Decay*, Viking Penguin, New York, 1991.

"It's a knipl"

See Lawrence Weschler, "A Wanderer in the Perfect City," interview with Ben Katchor, *New Yorker*, 9 August 1993: 58–67.

"Everyone has his own light"

Case 86, "Yunmen's Bright Light," *The Blue Cliff Record*.

"botanizing on the pavement"

Walter Benjamin reportedly used this phrase in notes toward his never-published "Paris Arcades" project. See Susan Bucks-Morss, *The Dialectics of Seeing*, MIT Press, Cambridge, Massachusetts, 1989.

"they passed eons living alone in the mountains and forests"

Dogen Kigen. I regret that I can no longer locate the original source for this translation.

Chapter 10
Can the Buddha be a mother?

"where has there ever been any mix-up?"

The Kahawaii Koans, collection of women's koans privately circulated in typed form within the Diamond Sangha.

"love that moves the stars and the other planets"

See note for Chapter 7.

"Like gazing into the jewel mirror"

See Dongshan (Tungshan), "Jewel Mirror Samadhi," in Powell (trans.), *The Record of Tungshan*, University of Hawaii Press, Honolulu, 1986: 63.

"the Dharma of a child"

Piero Ferrucci, *The Gifts of Parenting: Learning and Growing with Our Children*, trans. Vivien Ferrucci, Macmillan, Sydney, 1999, is full of penetrating insights that have inspired my thinking in this part of the chapter.

Chapter 11
The koan of dream

"the dream is the entire great earth"

See Dogen, "Within a Dream, Expressing the Dream," *Enlightenment Unfolds: The Essential Teachings of Zen Master Dogen*, ed. Kazuaki Tanahashi, Shambhala, Boston and London, 2000: 165–73.

"Thus, a tree with no roots"

Ibid: 167.

"the great twelfth-century Shingon monk Myoe Koben"

See Hayao Kawai, *The Buddhist Priest Myoe: A Life of Dreams*, The Lapis Press, Venice, California, 1992.

"In a well that has not been dug"

Miscellaneous Koans, a collection of introductory koans used in koan training, privately circulated in the Diamond Sangha. Likewise, "Each branch of the coral holds up the moon," "Snow in a silver bowl," and "Someone comes to you in a dream and asks 'What is Zen?'"

"When I pick it up, this great earth"

Case 5, "Xuefeng's Grain of Rice," *The Blue Cliff Record*.

"Not always so"

See David Chadwick, *Crooked Cucumber: The Life and Teachings of Shunryu Suzuki*, HarperCollins, London, 1999.

"lying in a ditch"

Charles Simic, quoted in a special edition of *Antaeus: Literature as Pleasure*, ed. Daniel Halpern, Collins Harvill, London, 1990.

"it doesn't matter"

Dream recounted by permission of the dreamer.

"What does this mean in the light of my death?"

See James Hillman, *Dream and the Underworld*, Harper & Row, New York, 1979, a marvelous initiation to the realm of dreams.

"The Dalai Lama has aligned the three bodies of the Buddha"

> See Francisco Varela (ed.), *Sleeping, Dreaming and Dying: An Exploration of Consciousness with the Dalai Lama*, Wisdom Publications, Boston, 1999: 126ff.

Chapter 12
The Way of character

"to study the self is to forget the self"

> Dogen, *Genjo Koan*, op. cit.

"we learn about integrity"

> See John Beebe, *Integrity in Depth*, Texas University Press, 1992. I am indebted to his wise thinking on integrity.

"this dream we call life must be interpreted"

> Coleman Barks, trans. *The Essential Rumi*, HarperCollins, San Francisco, 1995: 112.

"Why were you not Zusya?"

> Retold from "The Query of Queries," in Martin Buber, *Tales of the Hasidim*, Vol. 1: 251.

Chapter 13
A thousand mistakes, ten thousand mistakes

"Once when Baizhang gave a series of talks"

> Case 2, "Baizhang's Fox," *Wumenkuan*. See Robert Aitken, *The Gateless Barrier*, op. cit.: 19–21.

"a very dangerous thing to see"

> I wish to acknowledge the influence, here and elsewhere in this chapter, of John Tarrant's *teisho* on this case given in Sydney in Spring 1996.

"I drove up to a young fox"

> Les Murray, "The young fox," in *Poems the Size of Photographs*, Duffy and Snellgrove, Sydney, 2002: 94.

"How needful it is"
> Nicholas of Cusa, quoted uncited by Ad Reinhardt, in Barbara Rose (ed.), *Art-As-Art: The Selected Writings of Ad Reinhardt*, Viking Press, New York, 1975: 10.

"Things in all their multitude"
> Richard Willhelm (trans.), *Tao Te Ching*, "Tao," verse 16: 33.

"marvelous error"
> See Antonio Machado's poem "Last Night as I Was Sleeping," in *Times Alone: Selected Poems of Antonio Machado*, trans. Robert Bly, Wesleyan University Press, Connecticut, 1983.

"Nyokyokan Treatise"
> See Hayao Kawai, *The Buddhist Priest Myoe: A Life of Dreams*, op. cit.: 197.

Chapter 14
Mysterious affinity

"Chien Separated from Her Soul"
> This telling of the story is based loosely on Lafcadio Hearn's telling, which in turn is the basis for Robert Aitken's retelling, in Case 35, "Wu-tsu: 'Which is the True Ch'ien?,'" *The Gateless Barrier*: 215–17. Hearn's version is given in "A Question in Zen Texts," in *Exotics and Retrospectives*, Vol. 9 of *The Writings of Lafcadio Hearn*, Houghton Mifflin, Boston, 1923: 64–9.

"Is this one? Is this two?"
> Wumen's verse, Case 35, "The True Chien," *Wumenkuan*. See Robert Aitken, ibid: 213.

"We have all of us been told that grace is to be found in the universe"
> This version of the General's toast is reconstructed from the film, *Babette's Feast*, which was based on Isak Dinesen's original short story by the same name.

Chapter 15
Every day is a good day

"Every day is a good day"
>Case 6, "Every day is a Good Day," *The Blue Cliff Record*.

"All day and night, music"
>*The Essential Rumi*, op. cit.: 46.

"you can hold back from the suffering of the world"
>See Franz Kafka, *The Great Wall of China: Stories and Reflections*, Schocken Books, New York, 1970.

"*Our Town*"
>Thornton Wilder's classic play can be found in *Penguin Plays: Our Town, The Skin of Our Teeth, and The Matchmaker*, Penguin Books, Middlesex, England, 1962.

Chapter 16
Accept all offers

"When the straw sandals wear out"
>Zhimen Guangzuo (d. 1031). Also translated as "When the straw sandals wear out, continue barefoot." See Andy Ferguson, *Zen's Chinese Heritage: The Masters and Their Teachings*, Wisdom Publications, Boston, 2000: 313–14.

"unshakable faith"
>See Torei Zenji, *The Discourse on The Inexhaustible Lamp of the Zen School*, trans. Yoko Okuda, Charles E. Tuttle, Boston and Tokyo, 1989: 469.

"Only for your benefit"
>See William Powell, *The Record of Tung-shan*, op. cit.: 56.

"How can I really know that to be true?"
>See Katie Byron's Buddhist-inflected approach to radical questioning, which can be found in *What to Do When Nothing Works: The Manual for the Work*, The Work Foundation, Barstow, California, 1996.

"Buddhahood is passion and passion is buddhahood."

> See James Green (trans.), *The Recorded Sayings of Zen Master Joshu*, Shambhala, Boston, 1998.

Chapter 17
Walking alone in the red sky

I wish to acknowledge the influence upon parts of this chapter of Ross Bolleter's *teisho* on this case given in Perth, Winter 1997.

"The Childhood Gland"

> Gillian Mears, in *Sisters*, ed. Drusilla Modjeska, Angus & Robertson, Sydney, 1993.

"Golden Wind is manifesting"

> Case 27, "Yunmen's Manifestation," *The Blue Cliff Record*.

"How can we know that moment when the night has ended?"

> Retold from Martin Buber, *Tales of the Hasidim*, op. cit.

"He looked out of the window at dawn"

> See Czeslaw Milosz, "The Window," *The Collected Poems 1931–1987*, Ecco Press, New Jersey, 1978.

"Changsha Goes Picnicking"

> Case 36, "Changsha Goes Picnicking," *The Blue Cliff Record*.

"Ripeness is all"

> William Shakespeare, *King Lear*, Act V, Scene 2.

Acknowledgments

EVERY EFFORT HAS BEEN MADE to trace the holders of copyright material in this book; if any omissions have occurred, the author and publisher would be glad to be informed. We acknowledge the kind permissions granted by the following copyright holders: Robert Aitken, for permission to quote his translations (with Yamada Koun) of koans that circulate privately in Diamond Sangha circles. Coleman Barks for translations of Jellaludin Rumi in *The Essential Rumi*, Harper-Collins, San Francisco, 1996. Les Murray for "The Meaning of the Universe" and "The Young Fox," from *Poems the Size of Photographs*, Duffy and Snellgrove, Sydney, 2002. University of Hawaii Press, for quotations from William Powell (trans.), *The Record of Tung-shan*, University of Hawaii Press, Honolulu, 1986. Arkana Penguin, London, for quotations from Lao Tzu, *Tao Te Ching*, Richard Willhelm (trans.), Arkana Penguin, London, 1989. Oceania, for quotations from Deborah Bird Rose, "Ned Kelly Died for Our Sins," *Oceania*, 65(2). The Australian Broadcasting Commission, for quotations from W. E. H. Stanner, *The 1968 Boyer Lectures*. The family of the Late David Mowaljarlai, for quotations from David Mowaljarlai and Jutta Malnic, *Yorro Yorro: Aboriginal Creation and the Renewal of Nature*, Inner Traditions, Vermont, 1993.

Index

About the Author

SUSAN MURPHY IS A ZEN TEACHER in the lineage that comes through Robert Aitken and Ross Bolleter in the Diamond Sangha branch of the Harada-Yasutani line, and John Tarrant, who has established an independent Zen school, the Pacific Zen Institute. She lives in Sydney where she regularly conducts sesshin (Zen retreats) with the Zen Open Circle (www.zenopencircle.org.au). She also travels to Melbourne and the US to teach. Susan is a writer and feature film director, with a special interest in place, dream, and the affinity of Dharma with aboriginal spirituality. She is a widely published author on subjects as varied as cinema and Zen.

About Wisdom Publications

WISDOM PUBLICATIONS, a nonprofit publisher, is dedicated to making available authentic works relating to Buddhism for the benefit of all. We publish books by ancient and modern masters in all traditions of Buddhism, translations of important texts, and original scholarship. Additionally, we offer books that explore East-West themes unfolding as traditional Buddhism encounters our modern culture in all its aspects. Our titles are published with the appreciation of Buddhism as a living philosophy, and with the special commitment to preserve and transmit important works from Buddhism's many traditions.

To learn more about Wisdom, or to browse books online, visit our website at www.wisdompubs.org.

You may request a copy of our catalog online or by writing to this address:

Wisdom Publications
199 Elm Street
Somerville, Massachusetts 02144 USA
Telephone: 617-776-7416
Fax: 617-776-7841
Email: info@wisdompubs.org
www.wisdompubs.org

The Wisdom Trust

As a nonprofit publisher, Wisdom is dedicated to the publication of Dharma books for the benefit of all sentient beings and dependent upon the kindness and generosity of sponsors in order to do so. If you would like to make a donation to Wisdom, you may do so through our website or our Somerville office. If you would like to help sponsor the publication of a book, please write or email us at the address above.

Thank you.

Wisdom is a nonprofit, charitable 501(c)(3) organization affiliated with the Foundation for the Preservation of the Mahayana Tradition (FPMT).

On Zen Practice
Body, Breath, and Mind
Edited by Taizan Maezumi and Bernie Glassman | Foreword by Robert Aitken
208 pages, ISBN 0-86171-315-x, $16.95

"This book offers a vital service to us all: it clears away our fantasies about Zen and redirects us to the harmony and clarity in the very life we are living, right now. This is an intimate manual for contemporary Zen practice. I recommend it to beginners and advanced Zen practitioners."—Sensei Pat Enkyo O'Hara, founding teacher of the Zen Peacemaker Order

Bad Dog!
A Memoir of Love, Beauty, and Redemption in Dark Places
Lin Jensen
288 pages, ISBN 0-86171-486-5, $15.95

"Lin Jensen writes with a deep understanding of life, the land, and the human spirit. This memoir reads like something Steinbeck might have written had he been a Buddhist, and I can pay an author no higher compliment."—Christopher Moore, best-selling author of *A Dirty Job*

Zen Master Who?
A Guide to the People and Stories of Zen
James Ishmael Ford
244 pages, ISBN 0-86171-509-8, $15.95

"This might well be subtitled 'Everything you ever wanted to know about Zen but were afraid to ask.' Ford doesn't presume to demystify the mysterious, only to clarify the obscure."—Forrest Church, author of *Freedom from Fear*

Saying Yes to Life (Even the Hard Parts)
Ezra Bayda with Josh Bartok
Foreword by Thomas Moore
272 pages, ISBN 0-86171-274-9, $15.00

"Ezra Bayda is one of our favorite Buddhist teachers. In this astonishing collection of sayings and short meditations, Bayda delivers profound Buddhist wisdom laced with simplicity, practicality, depth, and inspirational vitality."—*Spirituality and Health*